Jordan

Loomes
7/96   15 —

15⁹⁹
T..

D1555124

FATHER
COUGHLIN
AND THE
NEW DEAL

A *Men and Movements* book

Men and Movements

FATHER
COUGHLIN
AND THE
NEW DEAL

CHARLES J. TULL

SYRACUSE UNIVERSITY PRESS 1965

*Manufactured in the United States of America.
Composition and presswork by The Heffernan
Press of Worcester, Massachusetts; binding by
Vail-Ballou Press of Binghamton, New York.*

For my wife

CONTENTS

PREFACE

One of the most controversial figures to appear on the American political scene in the 1930's was the Rev. Charles E. Coughlin of Royal Oak, Michigan. Endowed with a magnificent radio voice, Father Coughlin employed this rare talent to build a large following of devoted listeners numbering in the millions. The priest originally shunned politics, attempting to win general acceptance of the social reforms outlined in the encyclicals of Leo XIII and Pius XI. In 1932, however, he became an enthusiastic supporter of Franklin Roosevelt. Then, not satisfied with the President's middle-of-the-road program, Father Coughlin dramatically broke with Roosevelt, organized his National Union for Social Justice in November of 1934, and his own political party in 1936.

After a humiliating defeat at the polls in 1936, the radio priest became more extreme in his assaults on Roosevelt and more hysterical in his crusade against communism. In 1938, he openly espoused anti-Semitism and held the Jews conveniently responsible for all the nation's ills, real and imagined. At the same time he advocated an extreme form of isolation which appeared to many to be more pro-German than American. Many contemporary journalists, as well as numerous authors of history textbooks, have denounced Father Coughlin as a demagogue and a would-be fascist.

Despite the severe limitations imposed by the refusal of Father Coughlin and the Detroit Archdiocese to cooperate in any way, the purpose of this study is to probe thoroughly the controversial political career of the most colorful American Catholic priest of twentieth-century America.

There are many people to whom I am indebted for assistance in this project. The late Mrs. Franklin D. Roosevelt, Raymond Moley, and Msgr. Maurice Sheehy all supplied prompt and helpful answers to my questionnaire. I am especially grateful to Professor James P. Shenton of Columbia who so courteously loaned me his notes on the Ryan Papers and Roosevelt Papers. Sincere thanks are due also to Father Thomas McAvoy, former Chairman of the History Department, University of Notre Dame, who supplied me with a complete set of Father Coughlin's weekly newspaper, *Social Justice*. I am deeply appreciative of the assistance of Mr. E. Perrin Schwarz, the former editor of *Social Justice*, who so graciously consented to a personal interview. Mr. Herman Kahn of the Franklin D. Roosevelt Library was extremely cooperative as were the staffs of the Notre Dame and St. Vincent libraries. Thanks are extended to Mrs. Nancy McHugh and my sister, Theresa Tull, who helped with the typing. I am particularly grateful to Dr. Vincent P. DeSantis, Chairman of the History Department, University of Notre Dame, who has always generously given of his time and historical insights. Mere words do not express my appreciation to my wife, who not only patiently endured the author throughout the entire project but typed the great bulk of the manuscript as well.

CHARLES J. TULL

Chicago, Illinois
Summer, 1964

I
FROM SUBURBAN PASTOR TO RADIO PRIEST

On a Sunday afternoon in October, 1931, a dynamic young Catholic priest stepped to the microphones in a Detroit radio station and bitterly denounced the "so-called leaders" who had been assuring the people that prosperity was "just around the corner." Two years had passed since the "great crash" of October, 1929, and hunger and despair stalked the once-prosperous United States. Desperate parents stood in breadlines for hours or pawed through garbage cans for bits of food in a grim battle to feed their offspring. Unemployment steadily mounted, savings dwindled, countless thousands lost their homes, their farms, their businesses, and their confidence in the Hoover administration's ability to solve the most severe economic crisis in the nation's history. In his speech that afternoon, the young priest (known locally for his popular children's radio programs) sternly rebuked Herbert Hoover for his cold indifference to the miserable plight of millions of his fellow Americans. This was his first entry into the mainstream of politics.

Father Charles E. Coughlin, well-known to many Americans in the 1930's as "the radio priest," was born in Hamilton, Ontario, in 1891, of an American father and a Canadian mother. After receiving his early education at St. Mary's School in Hamilton, Coughlin attended St. Michael's College of the University of Toronto, where he received an honors

1

degree in philosophy in 1911 at the age of twenty. Young Coughlin found himself attracted to a career in three different fields: the Church, politics, and sociology. He resolved his doubts in favor of the priesthood and entered the Basilian novitiate at St. Michael's in the fall of 1911.[1] In the normal course of events he should have been ordained in 1915, but illness forced him to interrupt his studies for a year and retire to a warmer climate. This time was spent teaching philosophy at St. Basil's College, Waco, Texas. After his ordination in June of 1916, the young priest assisted at several parishes in the Detroit area: St. Agnes' in Detroit, St. Augustine's in Kalamazoo, St. Leo's in Detroit, and Sts. Peter and Paul's in North Branch, Michigan.[2]

Under the new code of Canon Law of 1918, all pious sodalities of priests such as the Basilians were required to disband. Father Coughlin and his fellow Basilians were presented the choice of joining a religious congregation, such as the Redemptorists, or a religious order, such as the Franciscans or Benedictines. Along with many other Basilians, Father Coughlin decided to remain a secular priest and was formally incardinated into the diocese of Detroit by Bishop Michael James Gallagher on February 26, 1923.[3]

It is interesting to note that by this time Father Coughlin had already obtained a modest reputation as a pulpit orator in the Detroit area. It was a regular occurrence for parishioners to call the rectory of whatever church he was assigned to and inquire at which Mass Father Coughlin was going to preach. His Masses were usually attended by overflow crowds and it was not unnatural that some of his fellow priests resented his popularity with the people, but his relationship with Bishop Gallagher was always cordial. The Bishop seemed delighted to have such an eloquent young preacher in his diocese.[4]

Not until 1926 was Father Coughlin assigned to Royal Oak, a small residential community which his radio fame was to make a household word. The rapidly expanding auto industry brought to Detroit a steady stream of workers who soon overflowed into the suburbs. One of these was Royal Oak, twelve miles north of Detroit's city hall. Bishop Gallagher, having recently returned from Rome where he had witnessed the canonization of St. Therese of the Little Flower of Jesus, eagerly dedicated a church to her in Royal Oak, appointing Father Coughlin the pastor. With only twenty-five Catholic families in the embryo parish, the young priest certainly did not appear to be on the threshold of a national radio career.[5]

There seems to be some confusion as to the exact circumstances which motivated Father Coughlin to embark on a career in radio. His critics assume that it was his egotistical ambition which drove him to seek the limelight. It is just as likely that he was sincerely interested in building up his parish and spreading the word of God to as large an audience as possible. Whatever may have been his original motivation, there can be little doubt that the mellifluous-voiced Father Coughlin and radio were made for each other.

In September of 1926, Father Coughlin was introduced by a mutual friend to Leo Fitzpatrick, station manager of WJR, Detroit. During the course of the conversation, the young pastor explained the problem he faced in raising the necessary finances for his small parish and the hostility he had encountered from the Ku Klux Klan as evidenced by their burning a cross on the lawn of his church. Fitzpatrick proved to be a sympathetic listener and suggested that Coughlin initiate a series of religious broadcasts over WJR to create a more favorable climate and to appeal for financial support. Under the terms of Fitzpatrick's generous offer, station WJR was to provide free time, but Coughlin had to pay the cost of the telephone lines, which came to $58 a week. The first broadcast went out over the airways directly from the Shrine of the Little Flower on October 3, 1926. Entitled the "Golden Hour of the Little Flower," this initial series was aimed primarily at children and only occasional comments on political and economic affairs found their way into these talks.[6]

For 156 broadcasts, WJR remained Father Coughlin's only radio outlet; in the fall of 1929, station WMAQ, Chicago, and station WLW, Cincinnati, were added. By 1930 the program had become so popular that he was successful in procuring the facilities of the Columbia Broadcasting System.[7] Coughlin made use of his expanded facilities to speak out against the menace of communism in the United States. In his radio address of January 12, 1930, he launched an all-out assault against the evils of Bolshevism, placing particular emphasis on the degradation of family life in Russia. Much to his surprise, the priest was deluged with letters criticizing him for his attack on Russian communism. He was particularly alarmed by the large number of college professors and educated people who wrote in defense of communism, and he concluded that far too many Americans were oblivious of the communist menace to America. Never one to shirk what he conceived to be his duty, the Royal Oak pastor immediately followed up his initial attack with a series of hard-hitting anticommunist broadcasts. Coughlin did not confine himself to negative criticism but called upon American capitalists to eliminate the appeal of communism by providing a decent standard of living for American workers.[8] On the basis of his radio reputation as an anticommunist crusader, the Royal Oak priest was a star witness before Hamilton Fish's House Committee to Investigate Communist Activities, which visited Detroit in July of 1930.

In the fall of 1930, as the nation fell deeper into the depths of its most severe depression, the priest began a strenuous effort to sell the social justice encyclical of Pope Leo XIII, *Rerum Novarum*, to the American people. On his first broadcast of the 1930-31 radio season, Father Coughlin rather prophetically mused upon the dangers inherent in a priest's discussing economic problems.

In venturing upon this subject of labor and its relative questions of wages and unemployment I am not forgetful that the path of my pilgrimage is both treacherous and narrow. On the one side there are the quicksands of idealism, of radical socialism, in whose depths there are buried both the dreams of the poet and the ravings of the revolutionist.

On the pathway's other side there are the smiling acres of Lotus Land where it is always afternoon, always springtime, always inactivity. It is peopled by those who are dulled by the opiate of their own contentedness to such a degree that they possess no prospect of what the future years hold in store for our nation. . . . It is not a political question in the sense that it is partisan, that is Democratic or Republican. It is an American question, God's question which transcends the platforms of all political parties.[9]

Having thrown caution to the winds, the "radio priest" boldly attacked the abuses plaguing the American economic scene, always stressing the need for a return to the old-fashioned principles of Christian charity. As radical as many of his ideas must have sounded to an American public conditioned to glory in the somewhat elusive benefits of rugged individualism, there was nothing that should have alarmed or shocked a well-informed Catholic layman, for everything Father Coughlin espoused in the name of social justice at this early period could be clearly traced to *Rerum Novarum.* With the increasingly severe depression seemingly verifying his theories on the evils of unregulated capitalism, the Detroit priest attracted a vast audience of mixed religious affiliations, many of whom were induced to pay a dollar a year for membership in the Radio League of the Little Flower. This organization ostensibly existed to provide funds for Coughlin's broadcasts and also to meet the heavy expenses incurred in maintaining a large office staff and publishing and distributing copies of his talks, papal encyclicals, and other leaflets. Later the Radio League became an important source of funds for the National Union for Social Justice.

It is important to emphasize that Coughlin never advocated the overthrow of capitalism; but he very strongly urged, begged, and pleaded for its reform, while at the same time defending the right of private ownership. On this vital point of the right of the state to place restrictions upon the use of private property, Coughlin, as one would expect of a Catholic priest, drew his inspiration from St. Thomas Aquinas. He openly acknowledged this in one of his first broadcasts on economic problems when he quoted the great Dominican philosopher as follows: "The temporal goods which God permits to a man are his in regard to property. But in regard to use they are not his alone, but others' also who can be sustained by what is superfluous for him. If the individual owner neglects his social responsibilities, it is the duty of the state to enforce them."[10]

Fully accepting this Thomistic interpretation of property rights as he did, it was only logical that Coughlin should advocate some form of government intervention to protect the workers from capitalistic exploitation. The priest was understandably vague about the exact details, but one gathers that he envisioned an agency similar to the National Recovery Administration, except that it would operate primarily for the benefit of the laboring class. There is so much confusion over what Father Coughlin really meant that it is best to quote him directly on this question:

> There is no one who dares assert that any factory or mill or mine may run as it please without just supervision by the state officials, whose first care is the lives and the continuance of the lives of its citizens. This is the logical conclusion if you admit that a government exists of the people, by the people, and for the people.
>
> Now, by no means does this supervision imply that the State shall own either factory or mill or mine. By no means does this logic lead us from the pathway of reason into the quicksands of socialism. It does imply, however, that both human rights and State rights, which latter, after all, are only an amplification of the former, shall take precedence over industrial rights and commercial rights greedily guarded by the few.[11]

According to Louis Ward, his close friend and admiring biographer, the turning point in Coughlin's career came in January of 1931. Congressman Louis McFadden of Pennsylvania, a close friend of Father Coughlin and an outspoken critic of the Treaty of Versailles, supplied the priest with statistics purporting to demonstrate that a drastic revision of the economic provisions of the treaty was necessary if the world was to recover from the economic collapse of the 1920's and 1930's. Father Coughlin planned to use this material on his January 4, 1931, broadcast. Somehow, CBS officials learned of the controversial nature of his material and put pressure on the priest to delete anything which might be construed as objectionable, since the network was already receiving numerous complaints about his inflammatory remarks. This request was made by Edward Klauber, CBS vice president, in a telephone call to Royal Oak on the eve of the proposed broadcast. Coughlin gave his word that he would speak on an entirely different subject.[12] Instead, he devoted his entire talk to exposing the attempt of CBS to censor him. This maneuver brought a wave of pro-Coughlin mail crashing down on radio stations throughout the country. The number of protests has been estimated as high as 1,250,000. Louis Ward described this incident as a decisive moment in Father Coughlin's career since the priest, confident of public support, now felt free to speak out on any issue.[13]

Coughlin defiantly demonstrated his independence from network control by delivering his controversial Versailles speech on the following Sunday, January 11, 1931. He vehemently denounced the international bankers for endangering the world's peace and prosperity to salvage their European investments.[14]

Thwarted in their efforts to muzzle Coughlin, CBS executives devised a clever stratagem to rid themselves of their famous but embarrassing client. A totally new religious program known as the "Church of the Air" was created which called for the granting of free air time to representatives of different faiths on a rotating basis. Thus, under the guise of a new format for religious broadcasts, Father Coughlin was eased off the network in April of 1931.

Coughlin attempted to buy radio time from NBC but was rejected by the network upon the advice of its Religious Advisory Committee. This was revealed three years later in testimony before the House Merchant Marine Radio and Fisheries Committee by Merlin H. Aylesworth, President of NBC. The network executive refused to give the committee any reason for this negative action.[15] Apparently fearful of the reaction of American Catholics to such cavalier treatment of Father Coughlin, Franklin Dunham, NBC program executive in charge of religious broadcasts, hurriedly denied that NBC had barred the priest. Dunham insisted that NBC did not make a practice of selling radio time to any religion and, therefore, could not make an exception in Father Coughlin's case. The network supplied the National Council of Catholic Men a half hour of free air time every week for the Catholic Hour and allowed this group to name the speakers. Dunham maintained that Father Coughlin's name was never presented to NBC by this group, thus creating the impression that the National Council of Catholic Men had pressured NBC to keep Coughlin off the air.[16] The details are obscure but it is significant that President Aylesworth of NBC felt obliged to issue a vigorous denial of this charge in the March 26, 1934, *New York Times*. Aylesworth insisted that the NCCM was responsible only for the Catholic Hour, nothing else.

Failing in his attempts to buy time on NBC, the Royal Oak pastor simply organized his own network. Leo Fitzpatrick, aided by Alfred McCosker, station manager of WOR, New York, handled the project, which involved leasing connecting telephone lines. Beginning with eleven stations, the makeshift network grew to twenty-six from Maine to Colorado; the cost was $14,000 a week.[17]

Never one to evade a lively controversy, Father Coughlin also entered the lists against prohibition. In three speeches on October 25, November 8, and November 15, 1931, he gave the supporters of prohibition the full Coughlin treatment. His sharp Irish wit was never more evident than when he began his discussion of the problem on October 25 as follows:

> Prohibition is identified with a Persian philosopher by
> the name of Manes. This dreamer believed that he was

appointed by Almighty God to become the moral leader of the world. He regarded all things material as essentially bad. He specifically condemned wine and women. I suppose the poor fellow did not know how to sing and consequently left song out of his litany of condemnations.[18]

Father Coughlin deplored the fact that many ministers were more concerned about enforcing prohibition than helping to feed their hungry people. For his part the Royal Oak pastor personally organized a charitable organization known as "God's Poor Society" which distributed food and clothing to thousands in the Detroit area. Outraged by what he considered to be a very unfair attack on American veterans, he engaged in a first-class donnybrook with Dr. Clarence Wilson, Executive Secretary of the Methodist Episcopal Board of Temperance, Prohibition and Public Morals. Coughlin read over the air an excerpt from the *Kansas City Journal Post* which represented Dr. Wilson as charging that "Legion Conventions are planned ahead of time as drunken orgies. . . . The ex-soldier who will do that—and practically all of them did it in Detroit—is a perjured scoundrel who ought not to represent the decency of the flag under which he fought."[19] The priest, always at his best in dealing with emotional issues, seized upon such a golden opportunity to spring to the defense of the American veteran.

A few short weeks ago my ears were shocked with a sacrilegious infamy. These dead soldiers whose lips no longer can themselves defend; their old mothers and broken-hearted wives and little boys and girls whose voices are too inarticulate to shield themselves—these have become the latest target of attack in defense of prohibition.

"Perjured scoundrels" is the epitaph spoken of the dead. "Perjured scoundrels" is the cold consolation which the executive secretary of the Board of Temperance, Prohibition and Public Morals would sneer into the ears of those children and wives and gray-haired mothers when on this Armistice Day they are mindful of their loved ones.[20]

There were probably few dry eyes among his listeners on that December Sunday afternoon.

Father Coughlin did not inject himself even indirectly into the mainstream of American politics until October, 1931, when he denounced Herbert Hoover for failing to take effective action to combat the depression. Coughlin spoke for countless Americans when he stated that the economic crisis could not be cured "by waiting for things to adjust themselves and by eating the airy platitudes of those hundreds of so-called leaders who have been busy assuring us that the bottom has been reached and that prosperity and justice and charity are waiting 'just around the corner.'" Referring directly to Mr. Hoover for the first time, Father Coughlin continued:

I remember that on March 7, 1930, more than one year and a half ago, the former Secretary of Commerce, Mr. Hoover, announced: "All evidences indicate that the worst effect of the crash of unemployment will have passed within the next sixty days." That was in the spring of 1930. I recollect that he and hundreds of others to whom 10,000 facts were well-known were busy preaching to us that prosperity was just around the corner. It appears to have been a circular corner to which they referred; a corner which if we could turn, we would not be willing to negotiate if it foreshadows a repetition of these recent occurrences for the children of generations to come.[21]

In this same broadcast the priest bitterly assailed the international bankers, a group which came to enjoy the dubious distinction of being Coughlin's whipping boy. Every civilized nation, he said, had grown weary of their attempts to "perpetuate their gambling and gold seeking at the expense of a torture more refined than was ever excogitated by the trickery of the Roman or the heartlessness of slave owners."[22] There can be no doubt that Coughlin sincerely believed that the soulless international bankers were responsible for most of the world's economic woes, as he constantly reiterated this all too simple explanation of a vastly complicated economic problem. It proved to be a very effective approach, as a large segment of the American public, unschooled in economics or finance, demanded some unsophisticated explanation for the apparent failure of American capitalism.

An even more scathing attack on Hoover was launched on November 30. Father Coughlin scornfully rejected the President's argument that relief was a local matter in which the federal government should take no part. Using his own county as an example, the priest related that there had been a desperate need to supply the preschool children with milk. His own Shrine of the Little Flower had donated $7,500 of the needed $15,000 and in a year's time the rest of the county had been able to collect only $3,500. Coughlin wondered aloud at the spectacle of a federal government which would lend millions, even billions, to foreigners to build up their industry, which would feed the people of Belgium, and the pigs and cattle of Arkansas, but which refused to aid its own citizens because its leaders did not believe in a dole. Yet this same government thought it proper to lend funds to banks and railroads to aid them in their difficulties. If relief was a purely local matter, Father Coughlin contended that local authorities also had the responsibility of aiding the local banks. He totally rejected the Hoover concept that unemployment in great national industries and mining empires was a local concern. In this same vein, the radio priest charged that by Hoover's standards, God Himself would be condemned for giving manna to the Jews in the desert when it was impossible for them to produce the necessities of life. Coughlin was especially irritated at the peculiarly American folly of want amidst plenty. "And so, my fellow citizens, we are actors upon the stage of life in one of the most unique tragedies which has ever been chronicled. Peerless leaders, abundance of foodstuffs, millions of virgin acres, banks loaded with money alongside of idle factories, long bread lines, millions of jobless and growing discontent."[23]

This vigorous assault on the Hoover administration openly involved Father Coughlin in politics for the first time. The response of his listeners was overwhelming. Over a million letters poured in praising the priest for his stand. If so many Americans took the trouble to write the radio priest a personal letter of approbation, it is reasonable to assume that several million others felt the same way. He would have been less than human if he did not feel himself to be in some measure a spokesman of the distressed masses.[24]

As the weeks passed, Father Coughlin continued to denounce the Hoover administration. He labeled the Reconstruction Finance Corporation a $2,000,000,000 dole to banks, industries, and capital, and declared it was based on the Hamiltonian concept that "salvation comes from the top." Coughlin was greatly concerned that the RFC was giving unlimited power and wealth to a few individuals in an effort to restore the old-style prosperity of 1928 and 1929 under the guise of solving the problems of the depression. Paradoxically, for a man committed to government intervention, the priest criticized the RFC as legislation leading to "financial socialism." He was greatly alarmed that the agency was authorized to accept frozen first mortgages of banks as security for loans. Thus, he envisioned the spectre of the United States Treasury holding thousands of home mortgages. He did not elaborate as to why this was so horrible but assumed that his listeners understood.[25]

Another government agency to incur Coughlin's wrath was the Federal Farm Loan Bank. The priest violently condemned the government for purportedly foreclosing an average of 451 farms daily, labeling the Federal Farm Loan Act "an agent of torture and destruction and confiscation." To complete his criticism of Hoover's program, Father Coughlin attacked the Agricultural Marketing Act as another example of "financial socialism." Once again he was extremely vague as to specific flaws, but charged that the program had wasted $200,000,000 without alleviating farm misery.[26]

In the spring of 1932, Coughlin energetically worked for the immediate passage of the much disputed soldiers' bonus. Appearing before a congressional committee on April 12,

1932, the priest advocated the bonus, not only for the humanitarian reason of aiding the veterans and their families, but also as a feasible way of devaluating the dollar to its 1929 value and taking the United States off the gold standard:

> Thus, we can employ the stepping stone of the so-called Soldiers' Bonus to get down from the dais of the unjustifiable gold standard, upon which a few have enthroned themselves. For almost two years, we have persisted in giving transfusions of financial blood to the sickly system which we are nursing. But we will soon have a corpse on our hands, because the last financial transfusion has certainly been given through the agency of the RFC and in no wise has it removed the major cause of our trouble. The disease known as concentration of wealth in the hands of a few still remains. It seems to me, that if through the payment of the so-called Bonus we can increase the value of the farm products, of the laborers' toil, of the 1932 earned dollar, even at the expense of decreasing the hoarded wealth represented in bonds and hidden gold, a mighty victory will have been won over the massed armies of depression and growing discontent. Let us remove the cause legally lest this growing discontent in the minds of our people shall do it illegally. Remember Russia of 1917; remember the French Revolution, and remember, also, our own Revolution in 1776.[27]

In response to Secretary of the Treasury Andrew Mellon's contention that the bonus would bankrupt the nation, Father Coughlin sarcastically quipped: "Billions to the international bankers who never fought. But none to the soldiers who risked life and limb."[28] He was in complete sympathy with the bonus march of June, 1932, and backed his sentiments with a $5,000 donation to the marchers.[29] Extremely critical of Hoover's handling of this incident, Father Coughlin lauded Police Superintendent Pelham D. Glassford who, it is generally agreed, had the situation under control until President Hoover ordered the army to interfere.[30]

Completely disillusioned with the Hoover administration,

Coughlin became one of the earliest and most enthusiastic supporters of Franklin D. Roosevelt. Unfortunately, all too little is known of the circumstances surrounding the early relationship between the Detroit priest and the popular Governor of New York. As early as May of 1931, however, G. Hall Roosevelt, Comptroller of the city of Detroit, wrote to his New York cousin of Father Coughlin's desire to enlist in the Roosevelt cause:

> Father Coughlin is probably known to you by this time and is famous for being the director of fifty-two secretaries, which he has found necessary to handle his mail which gets as high as 250,000 letters a day. He would like to tender his services. From what I can make out his brethren in the Church tolerate him. He would be difficult to handle and might be full of dynamite, but I think you had better prepare to say "yes" or "no". Of course, he has a following just about equal to that of Mr. Gandhi. We would probably enjoy the leadership of a lot of Indians however.[31]

Franklin Roosevelt apparently took no action on his cousin's letter; a similar letter from G. Hall Roosevelt arrived in the spring of 1932. On this occasion Frank Murphy is identified as the intermediary, and the number of secretaries employed by Father Coughlin has drastically declined:

> In the utmost confidence he [Frank Murphy] has been advised by Father Coughlin who has been following these events very carefully that they are for you 100%, and he is ready to go on the air when the proper occasion presents itself to outline his stand and indicate your position. You probably know that this gentleman has the biggest following of any single person in the United States. His twenty-six secretaries handle 200,000 letters a week, as a result of his Sunday broadcasts. He cannot use these occasions for political purposes and has never previously taken any stand politically but is willing to do so in the present instance.[32]

There is no record of Franklin Roosevelt's reaction to this second offer of Father Coughlin's services, but Frank Freidel, one of the major Roosevelt biographers, states that Coughlin and Frank Murphy visited Roosevelt in New York City in the spring of 1932, presumably to cement the alliance.[33] Nothing is known of their conversations, but they must have gone smoothly; Father Coughlin sent Roosevelt a glowing telegram congratulating him on winning the Democratic nomination at Chicago: "Sincere congratulations on your speech. I am with you to the end. Say the word and I will follow."[34] They met at Albany in August, but there is no record of what was discussed. It is obvious, however, from the tone of their future correspondence, that the famous Roosevelt charm had scored another success.[35]

A matter of much concern to both Roosevelt and Coughlin in the spring and summer of 1932 was the Jimmy Walker case. The colorful Democratic mayor of New York was under investigation for various fraudulent activities, and Roosevelt's political opponents were determined to embarrass the Democratic candidate for president by placing him in the position of antagonizing Tammany Hall by cracking down on Walker or appearing to be soft on corruption by whitewashing the mayor. Father Coughlin, a self-appointed champion of Walker, publicly defended Walker at a Communion breakfast for New York City firemen in April of 1932. The priest insisted the charges against Walker were part of a communist plot to shatter respect for government in the United States and denounced Rabbi Stephen Wise and the Rev. John Haynes, civic leaders in the movement to oust Walker, as parlor pinks. This talk was broadcast over stations WOR and WHN and apparently irritated Cardinal Hayes who felt it was indiscreet for any Catholic priest to associate himself with the Walker case, least of all an outsider.[36]

In August the priest interceded with Roosevelt on the Mayor's behalf, requesting that he be given every possible chance to defend himself. He none too subtly reminded Roosevelt of the great danger of alienating large numbers of Catholic voters if he appeared oversevere in dealing with Walker.

> Of course, your personal welfare and success as well as the success of the Democratic Party in the forthcoming election are both close to my heart. With this thought in mind I lay awake last night while traveling to Detroit greatly disturbed about the outcome of this Walker trial. Whether it is fortunate or unfortunate, religion does play a prominent part in major political campaigns. I was thinking of the twenty odd million Catholics in this country, among whom are 5,000,000 voters. I was thinking of the tremendous influence which Mr. Walker has upon the majority of these voters.

Unwilling to accept the possibility of Walker's guilt, the Detroit priest maintained that the whole episode was a Republican plot to defeat Roosevelt and pointedly compared the Walker case with the Biblical story of Susanna and her unjust accusers.

> If I may repeat what I suggested to you while a guest in your home, it is possible for clever Republicans and others who feel that they have been victims of circumstances to use this Walker case against your best interests.
> In no way am I insinuating that because a man is a Catholic he should be immune in the courts of justice. But I am thinking of the story of Susanna which is found in the book of Daniel, chapter 13. You can read it for yourself and learn how two reputable ancients of the people were willing to destroy themselves before God in order to destroy the reputation of the chaste Susanna before men.

Coughlin also saw the sinister hand of the Ku Klux Klan persecuting a fellow Catholic.

> More than that it is a known fact that Mr. Seabury is a member of the Klan. Thus, while this does not militate against his bringing charges against a Catholic, I am of the

humble opinion that a cross-examination of the chief wit-
nesses would prevent any misinterpretation of his actions
and of yours.

Finally, it would certify to all Catholics that you have
gone to the extreme limit in the matter of this perilous case;
it would rob every critic of his weapon of unjust criticism,
thus making of the Walker Case a boomerang which would
do more to harm those whose main motive is not only to destroy the Mayor of New York but to impale your Excellency
upon the horns of a dilemma.

Aware that the intercession of a priest on behalf of a fellow
Catholic might be misconstrued, Coughlin explained his position as follows: "I would not be loyal either to you or to the
Democratic Party unless I spoke fearlessly and truthfully of
those pertinent things."[37]

Proof of Roosevelt's desire to retain Couglin's support in his
campaign was his cordial reply to the Detroit priest wherein he
promised to give Walker every opportunity to clear his name.

My dear Father Coughlin: It is good to have your letter
and you may have seen that my old Friend, John Curtin, the
mayor's counsel, thought of the book of Daniel. He used the
story and I perforce turned it on him by accepting the application and suggesting that he occupy the place of Daniel
and that I gave him the same right to call the accusers who
had testified against the Mayor. I think he will do so this
coming week. I am, as you know, giving the defense every
latitude and I am being scrupulously careful not to make up
my mind in any way until their case is wholly in.

I do hope I shall have the privilege of seeing you again
soon.[38]

A month later, after the Walker matter had been settled
satisfactorily by the Mayor's resignation, Coughlin wrote to
Roosevelt again to ascertain his views on the soldiers' bonus.
The priest emphasized that he had favored its payment primarily as a means of forcing the United States off the gold

standard, but he was now willing to accept Roosevelt's solution and endorse it over his radio network if the Democratic Presidential Candidate would but inform him of his views:

> In other words, your excellency, I am willing to adopt your views which I know will be just and charitable. But the main point is that we work in harmony.
> Already I have twenty-six of the most powerful stations grouped in our network. The east is thoroughly covered as is the middle west and the west as far as Denver. I will have four Sundays before the Presidential election. Of course you realize that in no manner can I directly take sides. But I certainly can pause to praise principles or condemn them.[39]

In this same letter Coughlin suggested that Roosevelt make some reference to the priest in his Boston speech: "Perhaps it would be wise in your Boston address to refer to 'that priest either from Michigan or from Florida' who spoke for the rights of the common man. A mention of this would certainly do you no harm in that particular spot."[40] Coughlin did not receive a personal reply to this cordial message since Roosevelt was on a campaign train somewhere in the West. Guernsey F. Gross, a Roosevelt aide, acknowledged receipt of Coughlin's letter and suggested that he try to contact Roosevelt when he reached Michigan around the 30th of September.[41] There is no record of Father Coughlin meeting with Roosevelt, but it is entirely possible that the two men conferred informally.

Although, as a Catholic priest, he did not deem it prudent to endorse Roosevelt openly over the air, Coughlin, true to his word, made his own sentiments quite clear. In the fall of 1932 he delivered a series of blistering attacks on the policies of the Hoover administration. In these broadcasts he ridiculed the Hoover administration for not solving the economic problems of the depression and advocated the devaluation of the dollar as an essential step to economic recovery.[42]

As might be expected, Father Coughlin's bitter indictments of organized wealth did not go unnoticed in the ranks of the Catholic hierarchy of America. The first to speak out against him was William Cardinal O'Connell of Boston. Speaking at a Communion breakfast in Boston of the Guild of St. Appollonia (Catholic dentists), the conservative Boston cardinal maintained that the Catholic Church is for everyone: "It deals in human souls. You can't begin speaking about the rich or making sensational accusations against banks and bankers or uttering demagogic stuff to the poor." Although he did not mention the Detroit priest by name, the inference was clear to all, including Father Coughlin.[43] But in marked contrast to the bitterness of later disputes, the priest defended his own position without being particularly critical of the cardinal. Father Coughlin emphasized that all his speeches were approved, prior to delivery, by his religious superior, Bishop Gallagher, and reiterated his belief that the concentration of wealth in the hands of a few individuals was the most serious problem facing the United States. As proof that many agreed with him, Coughlin announced that he had received over two and a half million letters in response to his twenty-seven broadcasts of the 1931-32 season.[44] O'Connell's criticism was not publicly repeated by any other member of the Catholic hierarchy at this time and the Buffalo diocesan newspaper, the *Echo*, reported that no Catholic newspaper agreed with the Boston cardinal's stand on Father Coughlin.[45]

Little-mentioned as an influence on Father Coughlin's career, his Bishop, Michael James Gallagher, did all in his power to encourage the Royal Oak pastor to propagate the social encyclicals. The easygoing Bishop of Detroit was far more than Coughlin's religious superior. He was a dear friend, a trusted confidant and advisor, and a loyal defender against all critics. Gallagher had studied at Innsbruck as a young man and was greatly influenced by the advanced Catholic social doctrines then gaining prominence in Austria. E. Perrin Schwarz, the editor of Father Coughlin's *Social Justice* from 1936 to 1942, has said that the Royal Oak pastor and his Bishop were of one mind on the encyclicals and that if the Bishop had been blessed with a good radio voice there would have been a "radio bishop" instead of a "radio priest." Schwarz also revealed that it was his understanding that Bishop Gallagher was on very close terms with Pope Pius XI, whose *Quadrage-simo Anno,* a modern reiteration of the Church's social doctrine, was issued in May of 1931 to commemorate the fortieth anniversary of *Rerum Novarum.*

Few non-Catholics realized at the time that Bishop Gallagher was Father Coughlin's sole religious superior in the United States. No other American Catholic prelate had any jurisdiction over Coughlin whatsoever. Thus, every other Catholic bishop in the United States could openly censure Coughlin's conduct, but as long as Bishop Gallagher gave his blessing the radio priest was free to continue his controversial public career.

In the years 1926 to 1932, Father Coughlin underwent an amazing transformation from obscure pastor of a small Michigan church to nationally known orator with a radio audience estimated at thirty million. His mail had reached such vast proportions by 1932 that he required the services of 106 clerks and four personal secretaries to keep abreast of it. An incredibly large number of the letter-writers sent dollar bills to support the priest's cause.

The thousands of visitors who began to make their way to Royal Oak were usually quite taken with their genial host. Coughlin was a big man, weighing about two hundred pounds in 1932. He had played a considerable amount of baseball and football as a youth, but now confined himself to an occasional bit of handball. Good humor and charm seemed to radiate from the gray-haired, blue-eyed priest, attracting many who had come prepared to dislike him. Coughlin was a down-to-earth sort of man who lived very simply in a modest bungalow by his church with his devoted parents, his mother serving as the rectory housekeeper. The priest's inseparable companion was Pal, a huge Great Dane, who quickly became a favorite with the tourists.

It is not difficult to account for Coughlin's rapid rise to fame and influence. The nation was in truly desperate straits when he launched his national radio career in 1930. The economy was in a fantastic tailspin and millions of ordinary Americans demanded to know who was responsible. Possessing a magnificent radio voice, Coughlin persuasively supplied convenient scapegoats in the "international bankers" and the communists. The present generation of television-bred Americans can scarcely realize the attraction of radio to the average American in the 1930's. At that time the radio was almost a cherished member of the family. Favorite programs were slavishly followed by millions of avid listeners. Father Coughlin's Sunday talks became a weekly ritual for millions of Americans who would hush their children and attentively hang on the Royal Oak orator's every word. To these people Coughlin was the one man whose views they could trust. After all, he was a priest dedicated to social justice, not a politician seeking votes.

Despite his immense personal popularity, there is no evidence to support any of the charges of political ambition leveled against Father Coughlin; he did enjoy a feeling of power at his ability to influence millions of fellow Americans through his radio broadcasts. Along with many other Americans, Coughlin was deeply affected by the suffering he saw on all sides. Detroit was especially hard-hit by the depression; the priest had but to look about him to observe the desperate plight of thousands of unemployed workers and their families. Ignoring for the moment the economic complexities of the situation, it is not difficult to imagine how aroused a sympathetic observer could become by watching such extreme suffering amidst the abundance of food and consumer goods available in America. Aside from his occasionally bitter personal attacks on financiers, there was little in Father Coughlin's radio talks that could be construed to be out of harmony with his Church's social teachings.

Summarizing Father Coughlin's early years as a radio broadcaster, one sees the high hopes that he must have had of drastic reforms in the American economic structure. Obviously, he felt that Roosevelt was the man of the hour who would "drive the money changers out of the temple." Father Coughlin was convinced that the depression was caused by the greed of international bankers who created an artificial scarcity of money to enrich themselves. There is a wide variety of opinion concerning the real causes of the crash of 1929 and the depression which followed, but few economists feel that the causes were as simple as Father Coughlin depicted them. The Detroit priest was right in step with the times by singling out bankers as the principal villains of the plot, as the highly publicized Senate banking investigation of 1933 and 1934 amply demonstrates.

It is obvious that Father Coughlin expected great things from Franklin Roosevelt; it is also clear that he considered himself at least partly responsible for Roosevelt's victory, an assumption that few political historians are willing to grant. As for Roosevelt, he was happy to have the priest's support, but apparently he did not return Coughlin's warm admiration. One of the most influential braintrusters of the early New Deal, Rexford Guy Tugwell, has written in his biography of Roosevelt that the latter referred to Coughlin as a demagogue in the summer of 1932, at the very time their relationship was to all appearances very cordial. Never is Roosevelt's pragmatic approach to politics more evident than in his comment to Tugwell with respect to Coughlin, Long and their associates: "We must tame these fellows and make them useful to us." Tugwell continued: "And as time passed he did try. He made something of Father Coughlin, and so did others in his behalf."[46] Further illustrating Roosevelt's lack of genuine regard for Father Coughlin is the statement of Mrs. Eleanor Roosevelt that her late husband "disliked and distrusted" Coughlin from the beginning.[47] Blissfully unaware of Roosevelt's true feelings, the radio priest undoubtedly expected to exercise considerable influence on the Roosevelt administration.

II

"PARTNERSHIP" WITH ROOSEVELT

VERY LITTLE is known of the true relationship between Father Coughlin and Franklin Roosevelt in the first weeks and months following the 1932 election. *The New York Times* reported that Father Coughlin visited Roosevelt in New York City on January 17, but nothing was said about the purpose of their meeting.[1] The priest attended Roosevelt's inauguration in March, but there is no evidence of their meeting personally on this occasion. Coughlin was much impressed with Roosevelt's inaugural address and sent a warm congratulatory message: "Together with untold millions I was thrilled beyond words by the expressions of love and courage and of inspired understanding which marked your inaugural address. My constant prayers and my loyalty will continue."[2]

Later in the month, it was reported by *The New York Times* that Father Coughlin called on Roosevelt at the White House and was asked to continue his support of Roosevelt in the farm areas. Coughlin supposedly agreed to do so on the condition that Roosevelt initiate some form of inflation.[3]

E. Perrin Schwarz, the editor of *Social Justice*, maintains that Father Coughlin assisted in some measure with the writing of Roosevelt's inaugural address, but this is categorically denied by Mrs. Eleanor Roosevelt and Raymond Moley.[4] Roosevelt's speech did contain one of the radio priest's favorite phrases, "driving the money changers out of the temple," but this rather common biblical expression certainly does not prove any real connection with Father Coughlin. Schwarz also disclosed that it was his understanding that Frank Murphy's appointment as Governor-General of the Philippines was a political payment to Father Coughlin for his support in the campaign.[5] James A. Farley, Democratic National Chairman, denied this in a telephone conversation with the author, as did Mrs. Roosevelt and Raymond Moley in the letters cited in footnote 4. Whatever the realities of the situation, it is obvious that the priest regarded himself as an unofficial member of the administration. This was never more evident than in the Detroit Banking Crisis of March, 1933. The Union Guardian Trust Company collapsed and threatened to drag the other Detroit banks down with it. Coughlin charged that the Detroit bankers had approved fraudulent loans to themselves in order to cover their own investments during the 1929 stock market debacle. Because of this, the priest bitterly opposed any use of RFC funds to shore up the still solvent Detroit banks. Over the angry protests of the Detroit financial leaders, Secretary of the Treasury William Woodin, taking notice of the many attacks on the Detroit banking community, appointed federal conservators to assume control of the resources of both the Guardian National Bank of Commerce and the First National Bank of Detroit. Apparently on his own initiative, Father Coughlin decided that the administration's policy needed defending, and volunteered his services. The Roosevelt Papers contain the following memorandum for Marvin McIntyre, Presidential appointments secretary, dated March 23, 1933.

Ed. Donovan called up. Said Father Coughlin called up from Detroit and wants to get this to the President; That Police Commissioner denounced the plan in a radio address last night and that there are 2800 telegrams on the way here which Father Coughlin advised President to throw in the waste basket. Wall Street crowd got to this police commissioner in order to get depositors all upset. Murphy is going to let this Commissioner go.[6] If President and Woodin want Father to go on air and explain new plan, (national bank) he will be glad to do so. His telephone number is Royal Oak, Michigan, 4122.[7]

Written on the above memo, presumably in McIntyre's handwriting, was the brief notation: "Phoned and I had him talk with Woodin."[8] Exactly what transpired between Secretary Woodin and Father Coughlin remains a mystery, but the latter assumed after this call that he was authorized to speak for the administration. Acting in his unofficial and self-appointed role as administration spokesman, Coughlin made a special broadcast over a Detroit station in which he unleashed a savage attack upon the Detroit banking community, charging that the bankers had organized special holding companies to escape liability as bank stockholders under the law. Singled out for special abuse was E. D. Stair, a member of the governing board of the Detroit Bankers' Committee and Publisher of the *Detroit Free Press,* a bitter critic of the priest's radio activities. Particularly damaging to the bankers was Father Coughlin's charge that $63,000,000 had been suddenly withdrawn from the First National on the basis of "inside" information shortly before President Roosevelt had declared the now-famous bank holiday of March 9, 1933. Coughlin further asserted that the First National was only 12½ per cent liquid a few days before the Bank Holiday, although it claimed to be 80% liquid. Adding weight to the priest's accusations was a statement by Federal Prosecutor Harry S. Toy that Father Coughlin had supplied him with leads specific enough to warrant further investigation by the government.[9]

Father Coughlin definitely had some official sanction for this broadcast; he was a member of the Detroit Depositor's Committee appointed by Mayor Frank Murphy. Whether or not he really spoke at the request of McIntyre and Secretary Woodin, as he told his audience, is another matter. If Secretary Woodin asked the radio priest to speak out, Roosevelt's own staff was not aware of it. The following memo of Marvin Mc-

Intyre to Louis Howe, dated March 27, 1933, is one of the most interesting documents concerning Father Coughlin in the Roosevelt Papers.

Before we get through this may prove embarrassing and I want to submit the facts in the case.

Father Coughlin called me and said they were getting him to go on the air to answer Commissioner Watkins. He wanted to know whether we wanted him to do this or not and I told him I did not want to advise him in this matter. With reference to the number of telegrams received, I told him that we didn't have any estimate and that Mr. Woodin had told me they were not all favorable to Watkins.

Specifically, in reply to his question, I told him that I didn't know whether 5 or 55% were favorable to Watkins, as there had been no opportunity to even read them, much less segregate them.

I finally told him that I had better refer him to Mr. Woodin, "who is handling the entire situation." Mr. Woodin did talk to him on the telephone but I don't know in detail what he said. Professor Moley can probably throw some more light on this matter.

Confidentially, I think the Reverend Father took considerable liberties with the facts and most certainly misquoted me and misstated the case in saying that the request for him to go on the radio and to answer the Commissioner came from the Administration.

Will take up with you the question of whether we should pass this up or take some action.

I told the President at the time just what was said. I believe that the Father asked to talk with the President but am not absolutely sure about that now.[10]

Another memorandum dated March 29, two days after Father Coughlin's talk, from Stephen Early, Roosevelt's press secretary, to Attorney General Homer Cummings, refers to fulfilling the latter's request for a transcript of Father Cough-

lin's talk and a copy of the *Detroit Free Press* for March 27.
Just what use Cummings intended to make of this material no
one seems to know.

Professor Moley declined to elaborate on Coughlin's role
in the Detroit banking crisis.[11]

The reaction to Coughlin's role as spokesman for the administration, self-appointed or otherwise, was quickly felt.
Most agitated, of course, was E. D. Stair of the *Detroit Free
Press*, who threatened to sue him for slander. An editorial in
Stair's paper denounced the priest as a demagogue and accused
him of destroying the people's confidence in the Detroit banks
through his radio attacks. The editorial writer defended his
publisher, as one might expect, by insisting that Stair only
served on the board of governors of the banks out of a sense of
public duty and received no salary for his services. Furthermore, the editorial pointedly noted that the Catholic Archdiocese of Detroit was the biggest debtor of the First National
Bank and that the Church's inability to meet its payments was
a great part of the bank's trouble. The paper's feelings in regard to the Royal Oak pastor were tartly summarized by a
personal attack on Father Coughlin in which the latter was
labeled an "ecclesiastical Huey Long."[12]

Besides threatening to sue, Stair fired off a telegram to
Roosevelt demanding an official investigation of the whole
business:

Dear Mr. President: A slanderous radio attack has been
made against myself and other citizens of this city in connection with the banking situation here by Fr. C. E. Coughlin who presents himself from time to time as the spokesman
for your administration. To clarify the situation and to save
our city from such inflammatory attacks, to still all false
rumors and to vindicate the decency and the dignity of our
community I urgently request that you direct your Department of Justice to begin an immediate and thorough and
complete investigation. We stand unafraid and eager to co-

operate in every way to save our city from slanderous wreckers.[13]

Somehow Father Coughlin learned of this telegram shortly after it was sent and counterattacked with one of his own to Marvin McIntyre:

> Publisher of *Detroit Free Press* sent telegram to President today. This paper is one that attacked him bitterly during the past three weeks copies of which were sent to Ray Moley. It is also the one which compared the President's visit to Detroit last year to Joe Mende the monkey at the Detroit Zoo. Federal investigators, as you know, are probing the Detroit banks. This same publisher Mr. Stair is also the President of the Detroit Bankers Association. He opposed the organization of the new bank. Yesterday I told the people why he opposed it.[14]

Stair was not alone in his criticism of Coughlin. Typical of other protests received by Roosevelt was that of W. J. Parrish, President of the Detroit Aerocar Company. Mr. Parrish telegraphed the President: "Use of Fr. C. E. Coughlin as Administration Mouthpiece sad mistake as his views nationally broadcast are not those of Detroit's best citizens."[15] In the same vein is a letter from F. L. Lowmaster, President of the Matthews Company of Detroit, to Harold Ickes: "Personally, I expect a certain amount of this sort of thing after any major cataclysm such as happened in Detroit, but for political as well as business reasons I would like to urge as strongly as the urging will be received that a statement . . . come out of Washington that Father Coughlin is talking for Father Coughlin."[16] Ickes referred this letter to McIntyre and received the following memo in return: "This matter has given us some concern and has been pretty difficult to handle. However, I think it has quieted down."[17]

Coughlin was not without his defenders, however, as the following examples of pro-Coughlin mail demonstrate. A citizen of Sleepy Eye, Minnesota, wrote Roosevelt: "While not a Catholic myself, I would like to say that Father Coughlin certainly has a way of expressing the wide open American opinion. It seems that he is part of the New Deal that the common American people are getting. . . . He is a hero to the common people and let's pray that no money powers can snuff out his voice."[18] Another letter in the same vein came from a Philadelphian who told the President that, although he was not a Catholic, "I deeply admire the man in Detroit who has had the courage to tell the people of the United States about the true conditions of the financial structure."[19]

The proprietor of a variety store in Brooklyn wrote: "I heard this particular address and many others and I believe Father Coughlin to be one of the great orators of our time. It was right from the shoulder. . . . The new broom is sweeping clean and we are hoping it will continue. With strong, fearless straws such as yourself and Father Coughlin, it's a great broom that will sweep not only the centre of the room but the corners also."[20]

Desperately exploring every avenue of attack, the *Detroit Free Press* instigated an official probe of Father Coughlin's income tax returns, charging that he had failed to pay a tax on stock profits. After a complete investigation in which the priest proved very cooperative, the Chief Field Deputy of the Bureau of Internal Revenue, Fred N. Cook, submitted a confidential report on the matter to McIntyre:

> The examination disclosed that there was no merit whatever to the statements made by the *Detroit Free Press* and it is my opinion that the *Free Press* having knowledge that the Collector must necessarily investigate any complaint made, entered such complaint with intent to embarrass Father Coughlin, with whom they were in controversy. In fact, their entering a complaint on flimsy evidence amounted to a subsidization of governmental functions to assist them in their private feuds.

The net result of Stair's vendetta was the government's awarding Father Coughlin a refund of $8.61.[21]

The private war between the Detroit bankers and the Royal Oak priest was renewed on a ferocious scale in the late summer of 1933 when Coughlin was the star witness at a one-man Grand Jury investigation of the Detroit financial scene. Testifying before Judge Harry B. Keiden, Father Coughlin charged that both the Union Guardian Trust Company and the First National Bank were "wrecked by the philosophy that money in the hands of the masses is a menace." Mincing few words, the priest seized the opportunity to unleash a scathing denunciation of Herbert Hoover:

> Hoover tried to cure this damnable depression by pouring in gold at the top while the people starved at the bottom . . . He fed grain to the pigs in Arkansas, but he wouldn't give a loaf of bread to the people of Michigan. I'm not criticizing him, but I condemn his philosophy and I cite him as a definite and concrete example of the philosophy that money in the hands of the masses was a menace. I'll show that the Detroit bankers were brought up in that same school.[22]

In vivid contrast was Father Coughlin's warm endorsement of Roosevelt: "I am defending a Protestant President who has more courage than 90% of the Catholic priests in the country . . . a President who thinks right, who lives for the common man, who knows patience and suffering, who knows that men come before bonds and that human rights are more sacred than financial rights."[23]

After Coughlin completed his testimony, E. D. Stair attempted once again to put the priest on the defensive by charging that he had purchased sixty shares of stock in Kelsey-Hayes Wheel, a company involved in unorthodox financial dealings. Nonplussed by this latest development, Father Coughlin accused Stair and the *Detroit Free Press* of forging his name on the stock, although he admitted that the Radio League of the Little Flower had purchased the stock in question. Then, resuming the offensive, the radio priest told reporters there would be federal indictments against E. D. Stair and other Detroit financiers.[24] Special Assistant Attorney General John S. Pratt, who headed a team of special government investigators, denied that any indictments were planned.[25]

Exactly what role Coughlin played in the government's decision to investigate the Detroit bankers is still not clear. In June, 1933, the priest wrote to Jesse Jones, newly appointed Chairman of the Reconstruction Finance Corporation, relaying additional information about the Detroit situation and requesting a federal investigation. Coughlin explained that he was interested in this matter "because I fought the battle for Mr. Roosevelt upon the frontier of Detroit to establish a decent government bank when the two old structures had crumbled to the ground."[26] There is no record of any reply to this letter. On the same day the priest also wrote to William Julian, the Treasurer of the United States, urging an investigation of the Detroit banking situation.[27] Determined to get his information through to Roosevelt, Father Coughlin also wrote to Marvin McIntyre, enclosing copies of his letters to Jones and Julian and reemphasizing his own personal interest in the affair:

> I am sending you copies of letters which I addressed to Jesse Jones and to Bill Julian.
> I am damnably in earnest about this thing. Perhaps I have a clearer incite [sic] into this whole affair because I am on the ground where I enjoy a ringside seat.
> I am asking you as a sincere favor to bring this to our beloved President's attention. One word from him will set Homer Cummings in action.
> For your information I have started building the new church to cooperate with the chief's recovery program.[28]

There is no record of any action taken or reply made to any of these letters. The failure of the administration to acknowledge such specific communications points to a rather obvious conclusion: having been burned once, the administration was cautiously trying to avoid any further embarrassment over who was authorized to speak for it. The following year, however, when Father Coughlin was drifting out of the Roosevelt camp, this shabby treatment was reconsidered. A memo in the Roosevelt Papers from an unidentified figure to Missy LeHand clearly attests to this: "These letters to Jesse Jones and W. A. Julian detailing the Detroit bank situation and those connected with it, might act as a boomerang if information contained therein was not taken into account. Also fact that there was no acknowledgment from this office."[29]

The question still remains: Was Father Coughlin representing the Roosevelt administration in the Detroit bank situation, or was the radio priest assuming unauthorized powers? If he was in no way speaking for the administration, it seems strange that no official denials were forthcoming from the President. It is difficult to escape the conclusion that Coughlin was in some nebulous capacity being used by the administration in Detroit. When events took an awkward turn, it was politically convenient for Roosevelt to deny responsibility for the priest's actions.

This conclusion takes on added weight when one considers the obvious uncertainty among the President's staff as to Coughlin's status. As late as 1942, a Pfc. E. Schubert wrote to Presidential Secretary Stephen Early to ask if Father Coughlin was one of Roosevelt's economic advisors in 1933.[30] At a loss for an answer, Early wrote the following memo to McIntyre: "I suggest . . . that someone do a research job and ascertain definitely whether the alleged statement is true. If it is false, I would reply to attached letter; if the statement is true, I would suggest you file it."[31] There is no record of any research having been performed, nor is there any record of a reply to Pfc. Schubert.

Father Coughlin sincerely believed that the major problem confronting the United States in the early 1930's was a monetary one, and in the fall of 1932 he decided to concentrate upon this highly controversial matter in his radio lectures. The priest had long been interested in monetary matters, but his decision to speak out on the question was greatly influenced by two New York friends, Robert M. Harriss, a cotton broker, and

George LeBlanc, a gold trader, who journeyed to Royal Oak in October of 1932 to persuade Coughlin to champion monetary reform over his radio network. Louis Ward relates that their visit decided the radio priest in favor of such a course.[32]

Never a believer in halfway measures, Father Coughlin devoted a great many of his 1932-33 and 1933-34 broadcasts to the money question.[33] His first series, which was heard from October to December of 1932, was entitled "Eight Discourses on the Gold Standard and Other Kindred Subjects." These talks dwelt upon the evil machinations of the "International Bankers," who, it was charged, had greedily wreaked economic havoc for the sake of personal gain. Coughlin demanded the immediate revaluation of the gold ounce, pointing to the fact that most European nations had already brought their credit money into a reasonable relationship with their gold holdings. To the Detroit priest, the money problem was at the root of the depression: "My friends, the fundamental cause of this depression is the stupidity of trying to retain the 1900 valuation of our gold ounce in a ratio of 12-1 in the face of the fact that this gold, as related to currency money and to outstanding credit money, has been rendered absolutely impractical."[34] The radio priest claimed that the real ratio of credit dollars to gold dollars had been juggled into a wild proportion of 117 to 1 instead of 12 to 1. With his usual forthright simplicity, Father Coughlin asserted that the United States faced two choices: revaluation and Christianity or repudiation and Bolshevism. Naturally, his listeners were told the only correct choice was revaluation and he demanded that the price of gold be raised from $20.67 an ounce to $41.34. This stratagem would not only operate to increase the amount of money in circulation but it would also reduce the national debt by 50 per cent. Coughlin made it clear that he regarded gold only as a medium of exchange, not as real wealth. He devoted an entire radio hour to educating his audience on the evolution of gold as a medium of exchange.[35]

Although the chief emphasis in this series was on the money question, other matters also received consideration. Discussing the use of mass production machinery, Father Coughlin un-hesitatingly acknowledged that machines were a genuine bless-ing to mankind, but charged that greedy employers often abused their ownership by paying inordinately low wages. This practice, of course, ultimately backfired because it decreased the purchasing power of the worker and limited the demand for mass-produced goods. Once again resorting to Aquinas as his authority, the priest emphasized his belief in the institution of private ownership: "The Catholic Church stands foursquare behind the capitalist, although it does condemn the abuses which have grown up around him."[36] This point is extremely important. Coughlin believed in the right to hold private property, but he also insisted that this right carried with it an obligation of equal importance to use this property for the common good.

Father Coughlin followed up his initial venture into the troubled waters of high finance with a second series in the early months of 1933, appropriately called "Driving Out the Money Changers." For the most part the tone of these talks was extremely bitter. The initial broadcast was a blistering attack on the proposed Glass banking bill which authorized the establishment of branch banks of the Federal Reserve System. Asserting that this arrangement would further concen-trate wealth in the hands of the few as well as destroy many independent banks, Coughlin labeled the Glass plan "the most subtly vicious bill that the entire seventy-two Congresses have ever considered."[37] Most of the broadcasts dealt with what the Detroit priest termed "the money famine." He insisted that this money shortage had been deliberately created by the bankers to increase their own profits and demanded some form of controlled inflation to put the dollar back in circulation at its true value. He calculated that the United States, possessing a gold reserve of four and one-half billion dollars, could have as much as eleven billion in circulating currency as well as fifty-four billion in credit money. Instead, Coughlin claimed the United States had only five billion dollars in circulation and a total debt of 235 billion. The only solution the priest saw to this dilemma was the revaluation of gold at a ratio of approximately 2 to 1 of its current value. He assumed that this would automatically end the depression and initiate a new era of prosperity, but he never elaborated on exactly how this was to come about.[38]

Revaluation was only part of the solution Coughlin advocated. He also demanded the nationalization of all gold, with the government paying the holders in paper currency. The priest was extremely critical of all international bankers for using gold as an instrument of private power, but he singled out the Rothschilds for special attack. Not only were they guilty of manipulating the gold market, but he also accused them of reestablishing the "pagan" principle of charging interest on nonproductive debts. The priest acknowledged that money was productive and approved interest on productive bonds but demanded the recall of all nonproductive bonds such as World War I Liberty Bonds which he termed "slavery bonds," and suggested the bearers be paid in paper currency.[39]

It should be noted that only the four March broadcasts were made after Roosevelt was inaugurated. Two of these Sundays Coughlin devoted to the Detroit banking problem. In his final two broadcasts he lavishly praised the New Deal and even had kind words for Jim Farley, a man he later came to despise. Coughlin appeared confident that the new administration would enact his currency reforms and counseled his audience to be patient and give Roosevelt a chance to work things out. The priest even loyally defended Roosevelt's unpopular Economy Bill, which reduced veterans' pensions and federal salaries. Roosevelt, Coughlin maintained, was attempting to get the nation back to work, a task far more important than putting people on doles.[40]

Whatever Franklin D. Roosevelt may have thought about Father Coughlin in 1933, the radio priest was a potent political force in Congress. This was demonstrated in June when six senators and fifty-nine congressmen signed a request that the priest be named an economic adviser to the London Conference. According to the lawmakers, Father Coughlin had "the confidence of millions of Americans." The senators who signed were Edward Thomas of Colorado, "Cotton" Ed Smith of South Carolina, Huey C. Long of Louisiana, Thomas D. Schall of Minnesota, Henrik Shipstead of Minnesota and William Gibbs McAdoo of California. The House petition contained the names of fifty-three Democrats and six Republicans. Twenty-eight were from the midwest, sixteen from the southern or border states, and the other twelve were widely scattered. Most significant was the fact that seventeen had German or Scandinavian names and represented districts with large German populations. Equally noteworthy was the fact that only two eastern congressmen signed, Representatives Emanuel Celler of New York and Arthur Healy of Massachusetts. This may indicate that eastern congressmen did not want to antagonize the Catholic hierarchy of the East who were opposed to the Detroit priest. Professor James Shenton of Columbia, whose incisive article on Father Coughlin and the New Deal appeared in the September 1958 *Political Science Quarterly,* contends that the diverse backgrounds of the signers suggest "how real the possibility was that Coughlin might serve to unite the Bryan democracy, which in 1924 had supported the candidacy of McAdoo, and the Irish Catholic voter." Needless to say, Father Coughlin, with his hopes of genuine monetary reform and his abiding hatred of international bankers, was thrilled by Roosevelt's refusal to bind the United States dollar to foreign currency at London. Although Roosevelt's handling of this conference has been widely criticized, Coughlin sent Roosevelt a congratulatory telegram praising his "bombshell" message. The Royal Oak pastor was rewarded by one of the increasingly rare personal replies from Roosevelt, thanking Coughlin for "your nice telegram about my message to the Conference at London. It was good of you to send it and I am grateful for it."[41]

Pressure was very strong on the Roosevelt administration in 1933 to experiment with some form of inflation. It required all of the famous Roosevelt political dexterity to ward off congressional passage of inflationary legislation. Eventually a compromise was reached by Roosevelt's reluctant acceptance of the Thomas Amendment to the AAA in May of 1933, which authorized the President to take any or all of the following steps: to coin silver at 16 to 1, to issue paper money, or to change the gold content of the dollar. In actuality, the Thomas Amendment was a strategic retreat forced upon the cautious Roosevelt by the apparently irresistible Congressional sentiment for inflation as evidenced by the near success of Senator Wheeler's 16-to-1 silver bill in April. Roosevelt only accepted the Thomas Amendment in a bid to retain as much control as possible over monetary manipulation.[42] But his ultracautious use of this provision was especially galling to the inflationists in and out of Congress who felt that the President's acceptance of the legislation implied an obligation to make use of it. The inflationists, in the true Bryan tradition, insisted that placing more money in circulation was the only way to achieve higher prices with resultant prosperity for farmers, small businesses, and workers.

That the situation was acute in 1933 no informed person will dispute. As to the solution, arguments and theories abound, but Father Coughlin spoke for many Americans when he wired Roosevelt in July of 1933: "May I respectfully submit first that there has been but a psychological revaluation. Our difficulties cannot be solved until there is a real revaluation. In other words, there must be an issue of federal greenbacks. Actually, there are fewer dollars in circulation today than there were a month previous." Coughlin also recommended regulation of the stock market by requiring a higher margin and placing limits on the rise and fall of stocks.[43] Roosevelt's adroit handling of this letter is a good illustration of his mode of operations in dealing with troublesome people whom he did not wish to alienate. He wrote the following memo to McIntyre: "Write nice letter. Delighted to have it and hope to see him sometime very soon." McIntyre dutifully acknowledged Coughlin's letter and added: "Incidentally, he

[Roosevelt] has expressed the hope that he will have an opportunity to see you when you are next in Washington." Ironically, the priest accepted the invitation at face value and asked for a specific appointment, only to be politely refused.[44] Apparently the administration's strategy was to be friendly with Father Coughlin but at a safe distance, and to avoid all comment on his proposals.

Coughlin remained a loyal Roosevelt supporter throughout 1933. He still had high hopes that the administration would swing around to his view on monetary inflation; these were rewarded somewhat by the decision in September to reduce the gold content of the dollar, but he was far from happy with the NRA and the AAA. Writing to Roosevelt in August, he argued that the NRA was not the solution for sagging commodity prices:

> We dare not forget that we are suffering in great part from formerly acquired nonproductive debts. . . . The farmer must work twice as hard to get half as far (shades of Bryan). Conclusion it is inevitable [sic] that prices must be raised so as to permit not only the actual current livelihood but also the ability of the producer to liquidate his debts. . . . NIRA alone cannot break the depression despite the professional advertising of Ayers and Company. It is true that NIRA shares work but in doing it shares prosperity along with poverty.

The priest was also critical of the low wages paid by many companies under the NRA codes:

> It must be remembered that a real unhampered prosperity cannot be constructed upon a $14 farmer and laborer. . . .
> A résumé of many thousands of letters shows that the laborer is not satisfied with a minimum wage which he fears will become the maximum and which at present does not permit him to pay his debts nor to purchase the conveniences of life.[45]

Despite the misgivings contained in this communication to Roosevelt, Father Coughlin paradoxically endorsed the NRA a month later in an interview in *The New York Times*. The NRA was succeeding, he declared, not as rapidly as some would like, but it was not fair to expect perfection overnight; four to five years would be needed before a fair judgment could be made of its success or failure. The radio priest hailed the NRA as the first instance since the thirteenth century of a nation's attempting to control labor's hours and wages to prevent unfair exploitation and competition. "It is an immortal step back to the principle of our being our brother's keeper." At this juncture, Father Coughlin was so enthusiastic about the New Deal that he claimed a place for Roosevelt in the "American Hall of Fame" equal to that of Washington and Lincoln.[46]

Yet, sixteen days later, the priest was telegraphing Roosevelt that immediate inflation was necessary to prevent the NRA from becoming a "colossal failure."[47] Coughlin followed up his telegram with a letter revealing the unpopularity of the NRA with his faithful listeners. "Last week alone I received sixty-six bags of mail equivalent to 198,000 letters. Those were unsolicited letters coming from every quarter and section of the continent and most of them dealing with human misery and human hope. . . . The vast majority . . . have not much faith in the National Recovery Act."[48]

The priest's position on the AAA was also pointedly clear. He was much too concerned about the plight of millions of hungry Americans to appreciate a program of crop reduction and destruction. All of this was done, of course, as part of a concerted effort to raise farm prices, but Father Coughlin had his own, more direct remedy: the government should issue greenbacks and coin silver. Henry Wallace, the Secretary of Agriculture, and Rexford G. Tugwell, his assistant and one of the original "braintrusters," became favorite targets for Coughlin's acid-tongued attacks. The priest's vehement opposition to the AAA was expressed in a letter to McIntyre in August of 1933.

Now there is a proposal of slaughter of approximately 6,000,000 pigs and use their carcasses for fertilizer [*sic*]. The fertilizer which would produce more wheat and more cotton which our present day policy advises to burn and plow under. This is about as logical as pouring water in a sieve. I am truly chagrined at these foolish proposals aimed at starving us into prosperity.[49]

Writing Roosevelt directly in late September, Father Coughlin accused Wallace and Tugwell of defiling the "countryside and the Mississippi River with their malodorous rottenness." If the President would only take action on silver

we would speed up our factories, consume our surplus wheat, cotton and pork and get rid of the assinine [*sic*] philosophy propagated by Henry Wallace. . . . My dear Mr. President there is no superfluity of either cotton or wheat until every naked back has been clothed, until every empty stomach has been filled. There is a superfluity in the minds of these men who with the deflationary policies are opposed to accepting good silver money.[50]

Despite his reservations about the NRA and his outright hostility to the farm program, Coughlin went down the line in defense of Roosevelt's devaluation of the dollar and gold buying program in the fall of 1933. The radio priest was warmly enthusiastic about Roosevelt's "fireside chat" of October 22, wherein the President outlined his monetary policy:

I want you to convey to the President for me my most sincere congratulations.

He is magnificent!

Please tell him that I have hundreds of thousands of letters which have come to my office these last three weeks.

Of course we have not completed reading all of them. However, it is just one long litany of renewal of faith in F.D.R.

While the newspapers severely criticized the President's Sunday, October 22 speech, the newspapers did not know what they were talking about if I am any judge of human nature. That speech made more impression upon the people than any other speech given by the Boss.

The letters are proof of it. . . . By the end of December we will have opened up at least a million letters for the three months' broadcast.

As you know I am securing these letters from the people through their own free will for the purpose of backing up the Boss in his program.

Have you any suggestion as to what I shall do with them after I try to answer them through my large host of secretaries? If you want some of them in Washington—letters from every sector of American life; letters dealing with war bonds and their recall; letters dealing with the restoration of silver; with the nationalization of gold—I will be glad to send you a first truck load whenever you want them.[51]

It does not require the insight of a professional psychologist to see that Father Coughlin was immensely proud of the vast volume of mail he was receiving. He referred to it constantly, and his estimates must be taken seriously, as Roosevelt found when he ordered the Post Office Department to check the accuracy of Father Coughlin's claims. In the twenty months from July, 1933, to February, 1935, the Royal Oak Post Office cashed 65,397 money orders worth $404,145.[52]

Although enthusiastic about Roosevelt's devaluation of the dollar, the radio priest did not feel that the President had done enough to increase the flow of money, and thus, in his radio broadcasts in the fall of 1933, Coughlin became an ardent advocate of the old Populist panacea of silver. Considered in the context of his belief that the nation was suffering from a money famine, the priest's demand for silver coinage was perfectly logical. He added nothing new to the old silver question but simply repeated all the standard arguments for silver as currency: it would place more money in circulation and thus raise prices, and it would also serve to expand American trade with the silver-using nations of the world, especially

China and Japan.[53] Whatever the merits of the silver proposal, it should be stressed that Coughlin was merely echoing, and rather belatedly at that, the demands of a highly vocal band of silver enthusiasts who had been pressuring Roosevelt for action ever since his inauguration. This group revolved around such prominent senators as Thomas of Oklahoma, Pittman of Nevada, and Wheeler of Montana. As it became increasingly obvious that Roosevelt was not going to employ his power to coin silver under the Thomas Amendment to the AAA, the silverites demanded new legislation which would make silver coinage mandatory.[54]

Coughlin's espousal of the silver cause definitely did not mark any noticeable change in his attitude toward the Roosevelt administration. The priest may or may not have been fooled by the President's purposely ambiguous statements on silver, but he unequivocally predicted to his radio audience in early November of 1933 that Roosevelt would remonetize silver in the near future. In the same broadcast, Coughlin glowingly eulogized Roosevelt as America's only hope: "The President is not a miracle man, but he is resolute and courageous. He has not forgotten his public vow which pledged him to a sound and adequate money. He still remembers his sworn promise to drive the money-changers from the temple. It is either Roosevelt or ruin."[55]

An even more vivid indication of Coughlin's loyalty to Roosevelt during this period was his defense of the President's monetary policy at the Hippodrome in New York City on the evening of November 27. An enthusiastic overflow crowd of seven thousand heard Coughlin speak under the auspices of the Committee for the Nation.[56] The Detroit priest shared the platform with Elmer Thomas, the inflationist senator from Oklahoma, and lesser figures, but there was little doubt that Father Coughlin was the main attraction in heavily Catholic New York.

The priest opened his address with a rather self-conscious defense of his right as an American citizen to publicly discuss monetary and political subjects even while wearing the Roman collar of a Catholic priest: "I would be worse than scribes and pharisees, a whited sepulchre if I did not speak out." Having established the propriety of his oratorical efforts, Coughlin launched into a very emotional defense of Roosevelt's policies which included another bitter indictment of J. P. Morgan.

Stoutly maintaining that he himself was not an inflationist, the Detroit priest pointed to Calvin Coolidge as a great president who kept the value of the dollar at 100 cents. Roosevelt, he continued, was now being condemned by many for attempting to do the same. "Inflation is a trick word to scare us. It's a hobgoblin spread on the pages of the *Saturday Evening Post*. No one wants it. All we want is the normalization of the gold dollar, of the American dollar so that it will contain 100 cents and not 165." Then Coughlin made a startling proposal, for a man who was not an inflationist. He suggested that the government simply double the value of the four and one-half billion dollars in gold it then held. This would cut the national debt in half and allow twice as much currency to be issued with gold backing.

In an interview after the speech, Father Coughlin elaborated on his monetary ideas for the reporters. He repeated his contention that it was economically sound to have two and one-half units of credit money for every unit of basic money, and he recommended that gold be priced up to $41.34 an ounce, exactly double its established level of $20.67. This would allow the government to issue twice as much currency without recourse to real inflation. As far as the gold level was concerned, the priest was a reasonably accurate prophet: Roosevelt manipulated the price up to $35 an ounce and fixed it at that point in the Gold Reserve Act of January, 1934.

Hitting hard at the "money changers," whom he blamed for all the nation's ills, Coughlin declared that "Al Capone is not to be compared with those who sold millions of worthless bonds. Need I mention names? They are the ones who deflated our bonds and contracted our currency and they are the ones who call us radicals."[57]

It is interesting to note that Father Coughlin telephoned Presidential Secretary Marvin McIntyre before this meeting to inform Roosevelt that he was "going the limit" for him. The priest asked for Roosevelt's benediction on his efforts— "not in writing or anything like that, but I want him to know that we are with him all the way through."[58] Coughlin's natural craving for some gratitude or acknowledgment apparently was unfulfilled; there is no record of any acknowledgment of this call, much less of the Hippodrome speech. This lends strong support to the supposition that Coughlin's warm regard for Roosevelt was not reciprocated, and that the President by this time felt no need to go through the outward motions of personal friendship.

Coincident with the Hippodrome episode, and a particularly painful incident to American Catholics, was Father Coughlin's surprising assault on Al Smith in his weekly broadcast of November 26, 1933. The four-time governor of New York and unsuccessful Democratic candidate for president in 1928, influenced by his close association with the titans of high finance, his innate conservatism, and his jealousy of Roosevelt's political success, had become one of the administration's most severe critics on monetary policy. In a letter published in the *New Outlook*, Smith bluntly declared "I am for gold dollars as against baloney dollars. I am for experience against experiment."[59] As soon as the letter was released, Coughlin telegraphed Roosevelt that he had certain information that would discredit Smith as a spokesman on monetary policy.

Be not disturbed with the Smith letter which was released this afternoon. I can easily puncture that next Sunday afternoon. In 1929 the good governor sold out to Mr. Morgan. Bishop Gallagher of Detroit and the late Bishop Dunne of New York being seated in the Governor's motor car at the corner of Broad and Wall Street while the sellout took place. The Governor on coming forth from the building boasted to the two bishops that he had received a magnificent loan through the graces of Mr. Morgan and that the Empire State Building could now be saved.[60]

True to his word, Coughlin vehemently denounced Smith on his radio hour, clearly implying that he was a paid stooge of the banking interests. "Are we forgetful that Mr. Smith is a wealthy banker? Naturally he makes at least a part of his living from the County Bank of New York. He [Roosevelt] stands for sound money and will get what he stands for despite the opposition which the bankers and their 'puppets' have organized against him."[61]

Although professing to be grieved at the necessity of attacking so outstanding a Catholic layman as Al Smith, the Detroit priest repeated his charges to the New York press on the occasion of his Hippodrome talk. "I am just as much grieved as if I'd had to say it about my own father. But when any one stands in the way of President Roosevelt, and it's either Roosevelt or ruin, I've got to take a stand. This is war." Smith's reaction to this most unexpected attack was to emphatically deny ever having had dealings with Morgan except for their joint service on the New York City mayor's committee for unemployment relief.[62]

Ironically, Smith had written the foreword to Ruth Mugglebee's hagiographic biography of Coughlin which appeared in 1932 and lavishly praised Coughlin, predicting: "When the history of this period of American life is written Father Coughlin will be known as one who has lifted his voice for his fellow men."

As was to be expected, there were immediate repercussions within the Catholic Church to this embarrassing public feud between the best-known Catholic priest in America and the nation's most noteworthy Catholic layman. Msgr. Thomas G. Carroll, Chancellor of the New York Archdiocese, issued a statement deploring the attack on Smith and criticizing Father Coughlin for not obtaining permission to speak in

New York from his ecclesiastical superior, Cardinal Hayes. The New York monsignor maintained that it was a breach of ecclesiastical courtesy for Coughlin to appear outside his own diocese without clearing his talk in advance with the proper authorities. The *New York Times* article which reported the displeasure of the chancellor also stated that Cardinal Hayes had been irritated with the Detroit priest ever since the latter had praised Jimmy Walker at a Holy Name Communion breakfast in New York City on April 28, 1932. The Cardinal was reportedly so angry about this defense of Walker that he instituted a rule that all future Holy Name speakers had to be cleared through his office.[63] Father Coughlin insisted that he was innocent of any breach of clerical discipline or courtesy, claiming that he was under the impression that Cardinal Hayes had been informed of his plans to speak by James Rand, Vice-Chairman of the Committee for the Nation, or some other member of the Committee, which sponsored his Hippodrome appearance.[64]

Another outspoken clerical critic of Coughlin was Msgr. John L. Belford, pastor of the Church of the Nativity in Brooklyn. Speaking over a New York radio station on November 29, Msgr. Belford denounced Father Coughlin as an "infernal nuisance," a "public enemy" who was "using his church as a soapbox to exploit himself." Referring to the fact that Father Coughlin was born in Canada, Msgr. Belford seemed to imply that Father Coughlin had no right to criticize conditions in America since "he came to this country because he could make a better living here." Not content with assailing merely Coughlin, Msgr. Belford hotly declared that "his bishop is worse than he is."[65]

Coughlin was quick to defend Bishop Gallagher against Msgr. Belford's attack and reiterated his accusation that Smith had "lined up on the side of Morgan consciously or unconsciously."[66] At this point Bishop Gallagher clarified his own position with a public statement which was carried in *The New York Times*.

I think Father Coughlin was justified in concluding from the report he received that Mr. Smith approached Mr. Morgan for financial assistance. I do not believe Mr. Smith is a tool of Mr. Morgan or that his attitude on the money question was influenced by favors received. . . . I have no intention of interfering. No heresy has been preached. Father Coughlin in his addresses is advocating the principles set down by Leo XIII and Pius XI. He is perfectly justified in doing that.[67]

Springing to Smith's defense at this juncture was John Jacob Raskob, Smith's millionaire patron, who served as the governor's campaign manager in 1928. He categorically denied that Smith had obtained a loan for the Empire State Building. According to Raskob, the financing of the building was completed before Smith took over control. Raskob claimed that he had personally arranged the financing with the Metropolitan Life Insurance Company of New York and demanded that Father Coughlin retract his accusation against Smith.[68]

Far from retracting, Coughlin repeated his charges on his broadcast of December 3. After vehemently denouncing Wall Street, the priest defended Roosevelt's policies and reaffirmed his belief that it was "Roosevelt or Ruin." The radio priest also gloried in the public apology he had received from Msgr. Belford over radio station WLWL and in the public press. Coughlin cockily predicted that Smith and Raskob would be next to apologize.[69]

Msgr. John A. Ryan, one of the best-known Catholic priests in the United States because of his long crusade for social justice, both as a scholar at Catholic University and as Director of the Social Action Department of the National Catholic Welfare Conference, enthusiastically rose to Father Coughlin's defense in a speech before the Catholic Conference on Industrial Relations. Maintaining that Father Coughlin "is on the side of the angels," Msgr. Ryan praised the New Deal and asserted that the popes were more radical than Roosevelt.

The NRA, for example, did not go nearly as far as Pius XI suggested in his *Quadragesimo Anno.* At the same time Ryan admitted that he was not in total agreement with Roosevelt and conceded that the President, like other men, made mistakes.[70] In a letter to Msgr. Belford, excerpts of which were published in *The New York Times,* Msgr. Ryan all but canonized the Royal Oak pastor: "I would like to inform you that Father Charles E. Coughlin is a messenger of God, donated to the American people for the purpose of rectifying the outrageous mistakes they have made in the past."[71]

Commonweal, the liberal Catholic weekly, at this period one of Coughlin's most enthusiastic supporters among the national Catholic press, found the Coughlin-Smith imbroglio both embarrassing and unfortunate. The editorial writer stated that he was satisfied with Smith's denial that he had ever sought a loan from J. P. Morgan, and went on to deplore the use of personal abuse by Father Coughlin while at the same time endorsing his crusade for social justice. According to *Commonweal,* such personal attacks as that on Smith weakened Father Coughlin in the public eye at a time when he needed all the support he could muster for his social reforms.[72]

Another Catholic editor, Father James Gillis of *The Catholic World,* defended Al Smith but did not criticize his fellow priest. Father Gillis endorsed Coughlin's preaching of the social encyclicals, but, unlike most omniscient editors, admitted he simply did not have sufficient grasp of the intricacies of monetary management to know whether Father Coughlin was correct on the gold and silver issue.[73]

As a rule the secular press was openly hostile to Father Coughlin, as the following excerpt from a *New York Times* editorial demonstrates: "Father Coughlin would like to suppress or boycott the newspapers that oppose him. They would not think of muzzling him. . . . Let stormy eloquence roll on like thunder. After it will come again the still small voice of reason."[74] A notable exception to the usual journalistic antipathy toward Father Coughlin was a very favorable article in *The New York Times Magazine* by John M. Carlisle; it appeared a few weeks before the Smith-Coughlin vendetta. Carlisle reported that Father Coughlin was besieged by scores of visitors from every state who came to the Royal Oak pastor seeking his advice. The author was visibly impressed at the implicit faith these ordinary Americans had that Father Coughlin would know the solution to their personal problems and concluded from his own personal observations of the Royal Oak scene, as well as conversations with Coughlin, that the priest was completely sincere in his efforts to win a better way of life for his fellow Americans.[75]

At least one prominent Protestant also had high praise for Father Coughlin. Dr. Albert C. Diffenbach, a Unitarian, and Religious Editor of the *Boston Transcript* enthusiastically endorsed the Detroit priest's crusade for social justice:

> Apart from the scientific soundness of Father Coughlin it is admirable to have in the economic field a rebirth of free speech from the ancient Mother Church. She gives an example to all churches that is simply magnificent. Most Protestant Churches are still under the sway of the Reformation's economic individualism which in large part has brought us to our present state. . . . Whether he is right or wrong in his theoretical position for economic recovery, he is fulfilling his mission to the best of his ability.[76]

Coughlin continued his radio crusade for monetary reform throughout the winter and into the early spring of 1934. Again and again he drove home his accusation that the monied interests were responsible for the depression. In his final broadcast of 1933, he emotionally charged: "There is starvation because what little gold there is is in the hands of a few who mumble about the sacredness of man-made contracts in defiance of God-made obligations." The unemployed he characterized as "patriots wounded on the battlefield of humanity."[77] But the priest appeared confident that 1934 would see an end to this injustice:

> In the coming era both financial and industrial rights will not be respected and protected more than human rights.

It will be an age in which this so-called anarchistic individualism both in morality, in philosophy and in civilization shall of necessity give way to the fine teachings that were cradled in the crib of Bethlehem and paid for most dearly upon the cross of Calvary.[78]

Coughlin described the American financial system as a corpse and pleaded with the new Congress to bury it and replace it with a more workable system based on Christian principles.[79]

Even before his first broadcast of the new year, the priest announced a new approach to the money famine—symmetalism, the coinage of gold and silver in the same coin. This unorthodox procedure would greatly increase the base of paper currency which could thus be issued against both gold and silver. He emphatically denied that this plan was inflationary and extolled the use of silver as a boon to American Asiatic trade.[80]

Coughlin's advocacy of symmetalism brought an immediate response from James P. Warburg, a prominent Wall Street financier who was a warm friend and enthusiastic adviser of Roosevelt until breaking with the President over monetary policy. Warburg dismissed Coughlin's proposal as impractical, claiming there was not enough metal in the country for such a plan to operate successfully, and ridiculed symmetalism as just another scheme which aimed at printing-press money.[81] Father Coughlin retaliated by accusing Warburg of being a spokesman for the bankers and insinuating that he had profited from American participation in World War I. By revaluing gold and restoring silver, the priest maintained that the United States would have a base for 25,000,000,000 additional currency dollars.[82] For some inexplicable reason, Coughlin never again returned to the subject of symmetalism.

In his first radio broadcast of 1934, the Detroit priest bluntly asserted that Congress had 150 days to decide if democracy would endure in the United States.[83] Obviously, he was merely overstating the necessity for immediate monetary legislation and not threatening to overthrow the government.

Increasingly critical of all phases of the United States financial structure, he attacked the Federal Reserve System for retaining the recently nationalized gold instead of turning it over to the Treasury Department. As time went on, Coughlin became an inveterate foe of the Federal Reserve System and worked for its abolition.

While exerting tremendous pressure on the administration to coin silver, the priest still considered himself an ardent supporter of Roosevelt in the early months of 1934. Testifying before the House Committee on Coinage, Weights and Measures, Father Coughlin said:

> President Roosevelt is not going to make a mistake, for God Almighty is guiding him. . . . President Roosevelt has leadership, he has followers and he is the answer to many prayers that were sent up last year.
>
> If Congress fails to carry through with the President's suggestions, I foresee a revolution far greater than the French Revolution. It is either Roosevelt or Ruin.[84]

Coughlin's many critics invariably read a sinister meaning into such statements as his prediction that there would be a revolution "greater than the French Revolution" if Congress failed to act. There is, however, not a shred of evidence to support the charge, frequently made by *The Nation*, that the priest hoped to establish himself as the fascist dictator of the United States. That there was genuine unrest in the United States cannot be denied by any serious observer of the American scene.[85] What the priest's frightened detractors forgot to consider, however, was the emotional nature of the Detroit orator. In the old Populist tradition, he frequently gave vent to his feelings without due concern for the full implication of his words.

Shortly after testifying before the Congressional Committee, Father Coughlin visited Roosevelt at the White House for a private conference. Unfortunately, the purpose of this meeting or the issues discussed were never made public, but it is significant that the priest was still considered important enough to rate a private conference with the President. Coughlin was obviously pleased with the outcome of this meeting, for he emerged glowing with praise for Roosevelt, telling reporters that the President was twenty years ahead of his time in sociological thought.[86]

Despite his apparent hero worship of Roosevelt, Father Coughlin did not hesitate to frankly criticize New Deal measures over his radio network. Never enthusiastic about the NRA, he labeled its wage scale of forty cents an hour "slavery," but placed most of the blame for its inequities on the manufacturers who, he claimed, were attempting to "emasculate" the program.[87] Coughlin pointed with pride to the wage scale he was maintaining for the construction crew of his elaborate Shrine of the Little Flower: $.55 per hour for general laborers, $1.25 for carpenters, and $1.40 for masons. Paradoxically, for a champion of the poor, Coughlin was also severely critical of the Civil Works Administration of Harry Hopkins. While praising the agency as a temporary stopgap, he asserted that "its presence among us is a confession of past stupidity. Its continuance among us is a certain step toward fascism.[88] Apparently, the priest's anger was directed at an economic system which made such a program of government-sponsored jobs necessary.

Coughlin could not control his contempt for American businessmen who placed profit for profit's sake above all else. He urged American capitalists to forego their usual 6 per cent profit for a year and concentrate on putting the unemployed back to work, but he saw little possibility of American capitalism reforming itself: "Capitalism is doomed and is not worth trying to save."[89] The radio priest called for a new economy based on the Sermon on the Mount. In more specific terms, Coughlin advocated some form of "socialized" or "state capitalism" to solve the distribution problem. He argued that since modern capitalism had refused to reform itself there was no alternative but for the government to control credit: "Call this credit by what name you will—a bonus, a check, or an unemployment insurance. But call it what you will, credits must be issued to all." Without outlining a specific plan, the priest insisted that all Americans who are willing to work should be guaranteed an annual wage sufficient to enjoy their share of the material abundance produced by United States industry and agriculture.[90]

The following week, in a broadcast entitled the "United States Incorporated," he reiterated his demand for government control of all currency. Emphasizing that gold was not the only basis of wealth, he dramatically demanded the nationalization of all credit based upon the estimated $400,000,000,000 worth of real wealth in the United States. Coughlin also called for the early payment of the controversial veterans' bonus by an issuance of *fiat* currency. In true Bryan-Populist tradition, he maintained that nationalization of the currency was the most important single step on the road to prosperity and that unemployment would double unless this new credit system were put into operation.[91] Coughlin's new proposal that currency be based on the "real wealth,"[92] instead of exclusively on gold or silver, represented a change of emphasis rather than any significant change in his thinking on the monetary question. Formerly, as we have seen, the priest had placed great emphasis on the revaluation of gold so that more dollars could be issued against it, and his silver crusade was also motivated by the desire to increase the volume of currency by increasing the precious metals which served as the base for all paper money. But at the same time he had made it very clear that he did not regard gold as real wealth, but simply as a medium of exchange.

Reviewing the New Deal as a whole on his March 4, 1934 broadcast, the radio priest conceded that the New Deal had been "more or less successful," but he was severely critical of the Home Owner's Loan Corporation, which he said "had not functioned at all" because politics had interfered with its just application. Looking ahead to the second year of the New Deal, he predicted that the most important problem would be the struggle for a just distribution of production and credit for all.[93] On the following Sunday, Coughlin outlined his own six-point program for the solution of this problem:

1. The nationalization and revaluation of all gold.
2. The restoration of silver coinage and the nationalization of all silver.
3. The establishment of a government bank to control currency and credit.
4. The complete nationalization of all credit.
5. Legislation to extend credit not only for production but for consumption.
6. The total elimination of national government bonds.[94]

As might be expected, Father Coughlin was an enthusiastic supporter of the Fletcher-Rayburn Bill which attempted to regulate stock market abuses. In his radio address of April 8, 1934, he described the bill as an attempt to clean out "the Augean Stables of Wall Street."[95] So interested was the priest in the bill's passage that he made arrangements to have Ferdinand Pecora and Raymond Moley discuss the bill with him on his April 15 program. But when the time came for their appearance both declined, saying that since the bill was not yet out of Committee it was not the proper time to discuss it over a national network. Significantly, neither rescheduled a later appearance.[96]

Despite the failure of Moley and Pecora to appear, Coughlin's broadcast of April 15 was far from devoid of interest; he chose that particular Sunday to unveil his own plan for reforming the banking system. The priest suggested that the Federal Reserve System be relegated to the scrap heap and be replaced by a National Depository owned by the people of the United States, with branches in every city. This central agency would be a depository for privately owned national banks, and a reservoir of credit for the government. In addition, such a system would allow the government to directly issue the currency, maintain the value of the dollar, and control the flow of credit into the economy. All profits above 6 per cent would go into the United States Treasury. In an attempt to divorce politics from all financial transactions, the bank officers would be disfranchised. In the priest's view, such a bank constituted the only hope of America to endure as a free nation: "In one word I can see in the future no other organization except that of a standing army of more than 1,000,000 troops, Stalinized, Hitlerized, Mussolinized, which can hold this nation together."[97]

Despite the bitter tone of his pleas for monetary reform, Coughlin was always careful to emphasize that he loyally supported Roosevelt. The priest was understandably shocked, therefore, in April when the administration, or at least the Treasury Department, turned on him without warning. In a shrewd move to block silver legislation by an inflation-minded Congress, Secretary of the Treasury Morgenthau, with Roosevelt's full approval, published the names of all persons and organizations which had made substantial investments in silver. The idea, of course, was to discredit the motivation of many of the leading advocates of silver coinage. One of the more interesting names on the list was that of Father Coughlin's Radio League of the Little Flower which had holdings of approximately 500,000 ounces. The purchases were made by Miss Amy Collins, Father Coughlin's loyal secretary, who claimed that she invested in silver solely on her own responsibility. She insisted that the priest knew nothing of the finances of the Radio League. Coughlin, denying that he had ever owned an ounce of silver, bitterly assailed Morgenthau as a tool of Wall Street and pointedly praised silver as a "gentile" metal.[98] The priest's reputation was of course damaged by this disclosure. However, few people thought he had profited personally on the transaction, although *The Nation* gloated over Coughlin's embarrassment and denounced him as a demagogue and "perhaps the most vicious single propagandist in the United States."[99]

The silver list episode marked the first major break between Coughlin and the administration and, although the priest chose to ignore this harsh fact, Roosevelt was equally responsible with Morgenthau for the unpleasant incident. On the surface, it does not seem logical that the administration should have treated the Detroit priest in this shabby fashion. Father Coughlin had been an early, enthusiastic, and consistent champion of Roosevelt and his New Deal. It is apparent that Roosevelt, who had never personally liked Coughlin, no longer felt the same necessity to stay in the good graces of the radio orator as he had in 1932 and 1933. (Of course, it must be remembered that the President was fighting to stave off silver legislation; Coughlin, as one of the most influential silver crusaders, stood directly in his path. Ironically, Roosevelt was forced to surrender to the silver bloc only a month later in order to save the rest of his program from their obstructionist tactics; he recommended silver legislation which resulted in the Silver Purchase Act of 1934.) Although Coughlin persisted in ignoring Roosevelt's part in the affair, the incident marked a turning point in his relationship with the President. The once warm rapport between Roosevelt and the priest gradually deteriorated into polite neutrality, ending with an open break in 1935.

It is still impossible to assess Coughlin's role in the first fourteen months of the New Deal, due to the incompleteness of the data, but certain observations seem to be justified. It is clear that the priest at first considered himself an unofficial partner and spokesman of the administration, a delusion that Roosevelt deliberately chose to foster until November of 1933, when he neglected to acknowledge Coughlin's outspoken defense of the administration's monetary policy at the New York Hippodrome even though the priest had specifically requested some sign of approval on his part.[100] The Roosevelt Papers contain two interesting letters on this matter. One writer bluntly inquired if Father Coughlin was the administration's spokesman. Marvin McIntyre's reply was so noncommittal as to be almost ludicrous: "While it must be quite obvious that no one not in a responsible position is authorized to speak for the administration, it is also true, as you state, that no comments are forthcoming with reference to public utterances of individuals."[101] A retired schoolteacher wrote to Mrs. Roosevelt to ask if Coughlin's radio discourses harmonized with her husband's plans. Her letter was answered by Stephen Early in a more informative fashion: "As a matter of fact, we cannot answer your question as to whether Father Coughlin's discourses over the radio harmonize with President Roosevelt's plans. As far as Father Coughlin is concerned, he is a free agent and there is no connection whatever between the Shrine of the Little Flower and the White House. He does not seek our advice concerning what he says over the radio, nor do we offer it to him. I do not believe it has ever been possible for any one of us here, because of the pressure of work, to find time to listen in to one of Father Coughlin's radio addresses. I am certain the President has never heard one."

Father Coughlin expected the President to implement more sweeping economic reforms than the essentially conservative program of the so-called first New Deal.[102] Yet he continued to pour voluminous praise upon Roosevelt at every opportunity in the apparent belief that the President would enact the necessary reforms, if given sufficient public support.

Coughlin obviously exercised little direct influence on the administration's monetary policy, but there can be no doubt that his radio crusade for the devaluation of the dollar and the coinage of silver were contributing factors to Roosevelt's decision to carry out those measures. The priest frequently urged his vast audience to write their congressmen in support of his proposals and the fact that Roosevelt and Morgenthau were forced to resort to the publication of Coughlin's silver speculations is sufficient proof that the Detroit priest was at least partially successful in bringing pressure to bear upon the administration.

The correctness of Coughlin's monetary theories is another matter. Few economists question the necessity at that time for devaluation of the dollar, but this was not the magic formula for raising and maintaining the price level that Professor Warren and Father Coughlin had predicted. As for silver coinage, there is general agreement that the program was a fiasco, benefiting only the silver interests of the American west at the expense of both the American taxpayers and the financial structure of other nations, notably China and Mexico.[103] In all fairness, however, it must be remembered that Coughlin traveled in very respectable company when he espoused the cause of silver. Most congressmen favored some form of silver legislation, as did such nonradical personages as Raymond Moley and Walter Lippmann.

III

THE NATIONAL UNION FOR
SOCIAL JUSTICE

WITH the close of his radio season in April of 1934,
Father Coughlin temporarily faded from the national scene
until the fall, when he resumed his broadcasts. Apparently the
radio priest, who usually radiated self-confidence, was uncertain
about his future course, as he polled his radio followers in
September to determine their sentiments on the matter: "Do
you want me to preach 'Amen' both to the sins of omission
and commission which have been perpetrated in the name of
the New Deal, or . . . do you want me to oppose both reactionary politicians as well as the new type of rubber-stamp
sycophants who prefer to follow the dictates of the 'Drain
Trust' rather than the mandate of the voters?"[1] The response
to this loaded question is known only to Coughlin and his
staff, but the very phrasing clearly reveals his contempt for
the New Deal and its architects. His dilemma, of course, was
whether even his fiercely loyal audience would continue to follow his leadership if it meant deserting the extremely popular
Franklin Roosevelt. Further complicating matters was the
President's skillful handling of the situation. Roosevelt never
referred to the priest publicly and employed eminent Catholic
laymen such as Frank Murphy and Joseph Kennedy to placate
him.[2] Another indication of Roosevelt's conciliatory attitude
toward the Detroit priest was the personal attention the President gave to Coughlin's request for a naval commission for a

fellow priest. Roosevelt dispatched the following memo to the Assistant Secretary of Navy: "Will you let me know if we can do anything about this? In many ways it might be helpful."[3] Further proof that the President was not anxious to have Coughlin as an avowed enemy was the invitation extended to the priest in the autumn to visit Roosevelt at the White House. Coughlin readily accepted and tried to sell the President on the idea of providing five thousand jobs for college graduates, to be distributed through the college presidents. Roosevelt was reportedly interested in the proposal and indicated he planned to extend the CCC program to include white collar workers.[4]

It is only when one understands Coughlin's true feelings about the New Deal, his reluctance to make a complete break with Roosevelt, and the President's disinclination to feud with a popular Catholic priest that Coughlin's activities of the next three years make any sense.

Whatever the results of the Detroit priest's private poll, and his own feelings toward "Drain Trusters," he began his new broadcast year with a sweeping endorsement of the New Deal: "More than ever I am in favor of the New Deal," and pledged himself to support the New Deal as long as he possessed the power of speech.[5] Yet, one week later, Coughlin was telling his audience that the two-party system was virtually dead and helpfully suggesting that the old parties "relinquish the skeletons of their putrefying carcasses to the halls of a historical museum." The priest, as have many reformers before and since, deplored the lack of clear-cut distinctions between the Democratic and Republican parties and advocated the obvious but politically improbable solution of a new political alignment composed of genuinely conservative and liberal parties.[6] Although not yet ready to break openly with Roosevelt, Coughlin did not hesitate to place the administration on notice that the honeymoon was definitely over; he gave the Democratic party two years to solve the distribution problem or suffer "political death."[7]

The Detroit priest was deeply impressed by the steady torrent of letters he received from thousands of average Americans who were still in desperate straits despite two years of New Deal welfare programs. Coughlin was extremely proud of his huge mail and felt that it gave him infallible insight into the temper of the times: "I am not boasting when I say to you that I know the pulse of the people. I know it better than do all your industrialists with your paid-for advice. I am not exaggerating when I tell you of their demand for social justice which, like a tidal wave, is sweeping over this nation."[8]

Father Coughlin, not surprisingly, considered this "tidal wave" of protest a personal challenge to organize the discontented masses into a powerful lobby to promote his conception of social justice. On November 11, he announced the formation of the National Union for Social Justice, membership to be open to persons of all faiths who believed in the rightful necessity of social justice in the economic life of the United States. The priest had no illusions as to how his own role would be interpreted by his enemies; he accepted the possibility that he might fail and "be remembered as an arrant upstart who succeeded in doing nothing more than stirring up the people."[9]

Exhibiting the unrestrained optimism so characteristic of the reformer, the Detroit priest announced an elaborate sixteen-point program as the platform of the new national union. A careful reading of the preamble reveals that Father Coughlin's basic social philosophy was that of the papal encyclicals. A point too often ignored, however, is that the popes were extremely vague as to the methods to be employed in achieving the cherished but ever-elusive ideal of social justice. Thus, no Catholic in the United States was in any way obliged to follow the dictates of the Royal Oak pastor on this subject.

The preamble and sixteen points of the National Union for Social Justice are so essential to an understanding of Coughlin and his movement that they are reproduced here exactly as Father Coughlin first pronounced them in his broadcast of November 11, 1934:

Establishing my principles upon this preamble, namely, that we are creatures of a beneficent God, made to love and to serve Him in this world and enjoy Him forever in the next; that all this world's wealth of field, of forest, of mine and of miner has been bestowed upon us by a kind Father, therefore I believe that wealth, as we know it, originates from natural resources and from the labor which the children of God expend upon these resources. It is all ours except for the harsh, cruel and grasping ways of wicked men who first concentrated wealth into the hands of a few, then dominated states, and finally commenced to pit state against state in the frightful catastrophies of commercial warfare.

Following this preamble, there shall be the principles of social justice towards the realization of which we must strive:

1. I believe in liberty of conscience and liberty of education, not permitting the state to dictate either my worship to my God or my chosen avocation in life.

2. I believe that every citizen willing to work shall receive a just, living, annual wage which will enable him both to maintain and educate his family according to the standards of American decency.

3. I believe in nationalizing these public resources which by their very nature are too important to be held in the control of private individuals.

4. I believe in private ownership of all other property.

5. I believe in upholding the right to private property but in controlling it for the public good.

6. I believe in the abolition of the privately owned Federal Reserve Banking system and the establishment of a government owned Central Bank.

7. I believe in rescuing from the hands of private owners the right to coin and regulate the value of money, which right must be restored to Congress where it belongs.

8. I believe that one of the chief duties of this government owned Central Bank is to maintain the cost of living

on an even keel and arrange for the repayment of dollar debts with equal value dollars.

9. I believe in the cost of production plus a fair profit for the farmer.

10. I believe not only in the right of the laboring man to organize in unions but also in the duty of the Government, which that laboring man supports, to protect these organizations against the vested interests of wealth and intellect.

11. I believe in the recall of all non-productive bonds and therefore in the alleviation of taxation.

12. I believe in the abolition of tax exempt bonds.

13. I believe in broadening the base of taxation according to the principles of ownership and the capacity to pay.

14. I believe in the simplification of government and the further lifting of crushing taxation from the slender revenues of the laboring class.

15. I believe that, in the event of a war for the defense of our nation and its liberties, there shall be a conscription of wealth as well as a conscription of men.

16. I believe in preferring the sanctity of property rights; for the chief concern of government shall be for the poor because, as it is witnessed, the rich have ample means of their own to care for themselves.[10]

Aside from the monetary provisions, which many Americans considered extremely radical, there is nothing extraordinary in Father Coughlin's sixteen points. Essentially, they appear to be a mixture of midwestern agrarian reforms and the papal encyclicals of Pius XI and Leo XIII. Many of these proposals had previously appeared in the platform of the Minnesota Farmer-Labor Party.

That the sixteen points are vague there can be no argument, but then most political platforms and many constitutions are equally vague. Raymond Gram Swing professed alarm because they contained no mention of democracy, but this charge is a straw argument at best.[11] To a very great extent the sixteen points merely outlined in one document the various reforms that Father Coughlin had championed in the course of his radio career: a living annual wage, control of private property for the public good, absolute government control of all currency, a fair profit for the farmer, the right of labor to organize, and the priority of human rights over property rights.

Coughlin insisted that membership in his new organization was open to all Americans—Catholics, Protestants, Jews, and persons of any social level. It was not to be considered a political party, but a badly needed lobby of the people. The priest issued a call for five million followers to transform his sixteen points into reality by giving the National Union for Social Justice a balance of power between the two major parties. He specifically requested that professional politicians stay out of the national union: "There is not one professional politician in this nation who can conscientiously sign up with these sixteen points. . . . They have had their chance and they have failed. Too often their motto, 'to the victor belong the spoils,' is not in harmony with our motto, 'to the American public belongs social justice.' "[12] Interested members of Coughlin's radio audience were asked to write the priest a card with their name and full address. Authorized organizers for each geographical district would enroll them in a local unit. No dues of any sort were to be charged; all financial support was to be purely voluntary.

Father Coughlin left no room for doubt as to who was going to formulate the policy for the National Union for Social Justice. Even the most unsophisticated of his followers must have realized this when they heard the priest state that he personally would draw up "suitable" bills which would be submitted to Congress with full National Union for Social Justice backing.[13]

In the weeks which followed, Coughlin proceeded to elaborate on his concept of social justice and a living wage. On November 18, for example, he outlined nine principles which clarified the meaning of point two (a just and annual wage).

The essence of these nine rather wordy principles may be summed up in the statement that the government has the right to regulate both property and industry whenever it becomes necessary to insure an equitable distribution of wealth. In view of Father Coughlin's reputation as a radical, it is only fair to point out that he firmly defended the right of the individual to own private property and made the ownership of property a cherished goal of the working man.[14]

The radio priest grew increasingly critical of the inequities of American capitalism and declared it was not possible "to have a just, a living wage or an equitable price level established for the commodities of the farm or factory under the system of modern capitalism." A clear indication of how much his own position vis à vis capitalism had changed was the priest's humble admission that his previous support of capitalism was just another example of "a blind leader leading the blind."[15]

Exactly what Father Coughlin planned to substitute for the old capitalism is difficult to ascertain. What he seems to imply is a much reformed and regulated brand of new capitalism. The obvious comparison, of course, is with the "muckrakers" of the early 1900's who knew only too well what was wrong with America but left it to other minds to devise the alternatives. Since Coughlin was on record as opposing communism, socialism, and capitalism, some observers were led to believe that he was ultimately aiming at a form of American fascism. Raymond Gram Swing compared Father Coughlin to Hitler, adding: "But more nearly than any demagogue in America he has the formula for a fascist party, a semi-radical program which is 'safe' on the labor question, which guarantees the profit system, and which appeals simultaneously to agriculture, the middle class and the big employer."[16] There is nothing concrete to support this accusation. Like most reformers, or most politicians, Coughlin should not always be taken literally. It would have saved much confusion, however, if the priest had clearly stated the particular reforms he thought desirable.

However vague Coughlin may have been as to specific details, he left no doubt that he envisioned a very substantial amount of government regulation of the economy. On December 2, 1934, the radio priest announced seven principles by which the National Union for Social Justice hoped to combat the evils of capitalism and mass production; six of the seven called for direct government action.

1. We maintain that it is not only the prerogative but it is also the duty of the government to limit the amount of profits acquired by any industry.

2. We maintain that it is the function of the government to see that industry is so operated that every laborer engaged therein will secure those goods which will be sufficient to supply all needs for an honest livelihood.

3. We further maintain that it is the duty of government to secure the production of all those industrial goods —food, wearing apparel, homes, drugs, books and all modern conveniences—which the wealth of the nation, the natural resources of the land and the technical ability of our scientists are able to produce until all honest needs within the nation are amply supplied.

This principle is contrary to the theory of capitalism. Capitalism produces for a profit to the individual owner. Social justice advocates the production for use at a profit for the national welfare as well as for the owner.

4. We maintain the principle that there can be no lasting prosperity if free competition exists in any industry. Therefore, it is the business of government not only to legislate for a minimum annual wage and a maximum working schedule to be observed by industry, but also to curtail individualism that, if necessary, factories shall be licensed and their output shall be limited. For it is not in accordance with social justice that the owner of an industry will so operate his factory as to destroy free competition and thereby use his private property to the detriment of society.

5. It is the aim of the National Union for Social Justice to assist in the re-establishment of vocational groups. By this I mean that the laboring class who practice the same

trade or profession should combine in units independent, if they so choose, of the factory where they work or of the industry in which they are employed.

6. It is the aim of the National Union for Social Justice to so work towards a reform in government that the Department of Labor shall not only protect labor but shall counsel and guide it in its negotiations with capital.

7. The National Union for Social Justice contends that strikes and lockouts are absolutely unnecessary. For in the case of disagreement between employer and employee it is the business of the Public authority to intervene and settle such disputes which can be settled amicably by the parties involved. For it is our observation that both strikes and lockouts have occasioned more harm to the common good of the nation than any benefit which has been derived. But in the case of the government's neglecting its duty to settle such industrial disputes, always keeping in mind that there is no settlement without a just and living wage for the laborer and an equitable distribution of profits to all, then there is nothing left except for a united labor to refuse to sell its services at a loss just the same as it is unreasonable to expect the farmer to plow his ground and sow his seed at a loss.[17]

The first two principles are the least noteworthy; Coughlin had long preached the encyclical doctrine that the government was obligated to provide favorable economic conditions for the laboring class. Numbers 3 and 4 must have sent many businessmen scurrying for cover, as the mere thought of a planned economy was thoroughly repugnant to most Americans, who saw this step as the ultimate collapse of American individualism. Significantly, Coughlin did not specify how the government could ascertain the exact needs of the nation's consumers. It is doubtful that the Detroit priest realized the implications of government control of all production; but it must be remembered that he was speaking at a time when capitalism had been thoroughly discredited. The fifth principle, calling for the organization of trade unions along the lines of the American Federation of Labor, is somewhat confusing in view of the fact that Father Coughlin had previously chided the AFL for its indifference to the plight of the millions of unorganized industrial workers.[18] The AFL in turn had sharply criticized the priest for employing some nonunion labor on his Shrine of the Little Flower and for not having his literature printed by union printers. An attempt was made at the AFL convention in 1933 to declare the Detroit priest *persona non grata* to the American labor movement: "Resolved: That the AFL declare that the Rev. C. E. Coughlin is unfair to organized labor and is no longer entitled to financial support from any trade unionist who sincerely believes in the right of labor to organize, to deal collectively and receive an adequate wage." This proposal was defeated through the intercession of AFL President William Green, who told the convention that he considered Father Coughlin "most sympathetic and friendly to the labor movement." Coughlin defended his hiring non-union workers on the grounds that he gave work to needy individuals and had invited the union to organize them. He offered no explanation for the non-union printing but transferred his business to a union printer after the complaint.[19]

The sixth point was more of an indictment of the Department of Labor than a positive suggestion for reform; it was accompanied by a lengthy attack on labor secretaries for their icy indifference to the desperate plight of the workingman.[20] The seventh principle merely complements the sixth by calling for government intervention in labor disputes. It is clear that Coughlin envisioned compulsory arbitration, for he stated that strikes would be justified only if the government neglected its duty.[21] Thus, it appears that he advocated making labor a ward of the government. This indicates little faith in the ability of the American labor movement to protect its own interests.

Coughlin continued to make headlines. On his December 9 broadcast he attacked the American Liberty League, the financial community, and Cardinal O'Connell all in one half hour and, as if that were not enough, he also announced his own plan for a $10,000,000,000 public works project. The radio priest began by castigating the American Liberty League's emphasis on property rights to the neglect of human rights; he pointedly reminded Al Smith and John Jacob Raskob that the doctrine of the League was not the doctrine of the Catholic Church.[22] Then Father Coughlin moved on to his favorite target, the banker, and delivered his most violent assault to date, sarcastically ridiculing the banker as "civilization's tragic comedian" who not only impoverished the masses but had the gall to expect their respect and admiration.[23]

Of much greater significance than this bitter denunciation of bankers (although more vitriolic than ever, it was almost routine) was Coughlin's proposal that the government institute a mammoth public works program to guarantee steady employment for all laborers willing to work. The plan which called for an issue of *fiat* currency to finance it included the following:

1. Construction of 18,000 miles of new federal roads—approximate cost $324,000,000.
2. A thirty-year program for the reforestation of 50,000,000 square miles of timber—approximate cost $6,400,000,000.
3. The harnessing of the St. Lawrence River to gain an additional 7,000,000 horsepower, approximate cost $812,000,000.
4. Reclamation of 60,000,000 acres of agricultural land —approximate cost $600,000,000.
5. Destruction of major slum areas and construction of 900,000 homes—approximate cost $1,600,000,000.

To raise the $10,000,000,000 required to finance these vast projects, Coughlin suggested that the United States issue $5,000,000,000 against the treasury's holdings of $9,000,000,000 in metallic money and another $5,000,000,000 as purely credit money. He emphasized the fact that under no circumstances was a single dollar to be borrowed from the bankers.

So impressed was the radio priest with his own program that
he rapturously predicted the end of depressions forever. His
proposal provided for the government to give immediate employment to anyone laid off by industry. In periods of peak
business activity, the government program would slacken its
pace but would remain in existence prepared to provide useful employment, at a minimum wage of $1500 a year, for any-
one not assimilated into private industry.[24]

In retrospect, Coughlin's proposal appears to have been
merely an expanded version of what was actually accomplished under the WPA, CCC, PWA, and soil conservation
program of the Agriculture Department. One essential difference, however, was that the priest envisioned a permanent
program instead of the New Deal stopgap projects. Of course,
his method of financing was also drastically different from the
traditional procedure of floating bond issues and adding vast
sums to the national debt. Father Coughlin's inflationary
scheme probably had a respectable amount of support within
the New Deal, but most certainly not with Treasury Secretary
Morgenthau, who was obsessed with balancing the budget.
The priest's *fiat* currency idea is similar to one proposed by
Jacob Coxey to cure the depression of 1893, which was also
deemed too radical to be seriously considered.

The concluding portion of Coughlin's dramatic broadcast
of December 9, 1934, was a fighting, no-holds-barred reply to
Cardinal O'Connell of Boston, who had three times attacked
Coughlin, never by name but never leaving serious doubts as
to whom he was referring. Never before had Coughlin responded in kind, but, encouraged by Bishop Gallagher,[25] the
Detroit priest allowed his resentment full sway in a blistering
assault on the Boston cardinal:

> For forty years William Cardinal O'Connell has been
> more notorious for his silence on social justice than for any
> contribution which he may have given either in practice or
> in doctrine towards the decentralization of wealth and to-
> wards the elimination of those glaring injustices which per-

mitted the plutocrats of this nation to wax fat at the expense of the poor. Now he castigates me for doing what he was ordered to do.

William Cardinal O'Connell practically accuses me of misinterpreting the Encyclicals of both Leo XIII and Pius XI. Every word that I have written had received the imprimatur of my Right Rev. Bishop. When this is taken into consideration William Cardinal O'Connell practically accuses a brother Bishop, who for years has been famed in Michigan for his defense of the poor and for his opposition to the type of pampered evils which have been so rampant in the textile industries of New England.[26]

Coughlin made a special point of explaining that O'Connell, although a cardinal and archbishop of a large American diocese, had absolutely no authority in the Church outside of his own Boston see. Most Americans, not understanding the organizational structure of the Catholic Church, puzzled aloud at the spectacle of a cardinal powerless to silence an ordinary priest.

Demonstrating no discernible pattern at this time, Father Coughlin devoted his next broadcast to the controversial Nye Committee munitions investigation, labeling the DuPonts "Merchandisers of Murder." The priest was particularly angered to discover the close degree of cooperation between the military services, the state department, and the Delaware munitions makers. Emulating the Nye Committee in oversimplifying highly complex matters, he criticized the United States government for allowing DuPont to sell arms to Japan, a potential enemy of the United States.[27]

Continuing to manifest an amazing (if bewildering) flexibility, Coughlin followed his broadcast on the "Merchandisers of Murder" with a savage attack on the Mexican policy of President Wilson. Whatever his intentions, the priest revealed a woeful lack of knowledge of Wilson's motives, and of the facts of history. Coughlin's version was that Wilson's policy was motivated solely by the desire to secure oil leases for the United States. Huerta was the hero in the priest's estimation; Wilson, Daniels, Villa, Carranza, and Calles were the arch-villains. Father Coughlin was gravely concerned by the growth of communist influence in Mexico, and insisted that it was Wilson's responsibility for refusing to support Huerta. The Mexican revolutions and American response to them are far too complex to be discussed in a few sentences, but even Wilson's critics usually concede his concern for the Mexican people; no responsible critic charges Wilson with intervention to protect American oil interests. In fact he is generally castigated for being oversolicitous of the Mexican people at the expense of American business interests. Josephus Daniels provoked the priest's ire because as Wilson's Secretary of Navy he cooperated in the assault on Vera Cruz and as Franklin D. Roosevelt's ambassador to Mexico he praised the atheistic school system of the revolutionary government. Coughlin was particularly incensed at reports that the Mexican government was openly teaching sexual perversion in the public schools in order to eradicate all belief in a Christian code of morality. The only charitable explanation for this terribly unfair attack on Woodrow Wilson is that the radio priest was the victim of his own ignorance of American history. It is logical to conclude that other programs were as badly researched. Unfortunately, all too few of Coughlin's listeners knew even as much history as their leader; they were prepared to accept anything he said, even his ridiculous accusation that the United States government had "aided and abetted the rape of Mexico" from the time of Wilson down to and including the administration of Franklin Roosevelt.[28]

On his final broadcast of 1934, Father Coughlin reverted to his favorite theme and reiterated his demand that Congress assert its constitutional prerogative and nationalize all currency. The priest added no new arguments to his case for drastic currency reform but shocked many of his loyal listeners by announcing that he saw no hope for modern capitalism or modern democracy in America. Never before had Coughlin used such pessimistic language about the democratic process. As he saw it, the United States would have to succumb to communism, fascism, socialism, or Hitlerism or else construct a new system based on social justice. The priest rejected communism because it was godless, socialism because it went too far in the nationalization of industry, fascism and Nazism because they were repugnant to American ideals of democracy and republican institutions. America's only salvation, therefore, was social justice: "Against all these systems . . . there stands an economic system known as social justice. Seeking no compromise, enticing no man by vain promises, it writes down a platform for today, with principles of truth, of justice, of humanity."[29]

This is a prime instance of Father Coughlin's vagueness. The Detroit priest offered a moral principle as both a political and economic system. No specific details were given as to the operation of the economy. If communism, socialism, and fascism were all great evils to be avoided, how could industry operate unless by private capital? Yet capitalism stood condemned. Nothing whatsoever was said about a new form of government to replace democracy; somehow social justice was to serve as both a political and economic system, but the priest did not disclose what changes were to be made. Whatever Coughlin really meant to say, this broadcast added weight to his critics' charges that he did not think things through. It is all too easy to say that capitalism must go, but the responsible critic must posit a workable alternative. In the light of Coughlin's past and future statements it would appear that he really meant that the principles of Christian social justice must be applied to American capitalism by means of sweeping government controls. But this is not what he said on December 30, 1934, and many people then and later were confused as to his intentions. Unfortunately, as is frequently the case with agitators, well-intentioned or otherwise, Father Coughlin allowed his words to flow faster than his ideas. Very few Americans would place themselves on record as opposed to social justice, but very few would agree as to the meaning of the term.

Having written off both "modern" democracy and "modern" capitalism, Coughlin continued to confuse friend and foe alike by beginning the new year of 1935 with lavish praise of Roosevelt's state of the union message. The President called for renewed efforts to fight the depression, none of which involved the destruction of capitalism or democracy. But the radio priest hailed Roosevelt's message as the beginning of a new era in America: "January 4, 1935, brings to an end the economic principles of individualism hitherto taught in practically every American university. . . . Such outworn and impractical economic phrases as 'free competition' and 'rugged individualism' and 'laissez-faire' today are seeking a resting place in the limbo of archaic falsehoods." Coughlin was more than gratified to hear the President say: "In most nations social justice, no longer a distant ideal, has become a definite good, and ancient governments are beginning to heed the call."[30] But he also did not hesitate to capitalize on the President's candid admission that the first two years of the New Deal still found "our population suffering from old inequalities, little changed by sporadic remedies." The priest gleefully retorted: "For two years Mr. Roosevelt was so conservative that he gave ear to those men whose policies were most responsible for effecting the depression." Coughlin chided the President for having allowed private control of currency to continue side by side with the expensive relief program that it made necessary. Most galling of all to Father Coughlin was the fact that the government borrowed the money for these projects from private bankers.[31]

The Detroit priest also had kind words for Roosevelt's new public works program, which he interpreted to be a permanent system along the lines he himself had recently proposed. But Coughlin was still convinced that money and the control of credit were at the root of the economic problems and implored Roosevelt to finance this new program with United States greenbacks rather than long-term interest-bearing bonds. He pointed out that the Roosevelt administration had already borrowed $8,000,000,000 in its first two years and stated that it would cost the nation $14,400,000,000 by the time all the compound interest was paid. But whatever his disappointment over the method of financing relief and public works, Coughlin emphasized that he was still a staunch supporter of Roosevelt:

> My friends, there is no one who wishes this New Deal to succeed more than I do. Thus more than a year ago I coined the phrase "Roosevelt or Ruin" because I believed in him when he openly avowed that he would drive the money changers from the temple and hand America back to the Americans.
>
> Today I believe in him as much as ever. Today it is "Roosevelt and Recovery" provided he veers neither to right nor left.[32]

The Detroit priest's cordial attitude toward Roosevelt was amazingly short-lived, for on January 27 he unleashed a full-scale attack on the administration-supported proposal to have the United States join the World Court. His opening sentence eloquently reveals the emotional tone of this impassioned plea: "My Friends: If I am properly informed—Tuesday of this week—Tuesday, January 29—will be remembered by our offspring as the day which overshadowed July 4. The one date was associated with our independence. The other with our stupid betrayal."[33] Coughlin conceded that most of the Senators favoring the bill were sincere, but insisted that they were acting in ignorance of the true facts. What were these facts? Simply that the World Court and its parent, the League of Nations, were both organized by international bankers and their cohorts. The priest professed to have learned this from informants "who sat in at the secret sessions when the abortion of the League of Nations was cradled by those determined to protect injustice."[34]

Coughlin's main line of attack was the traditional isolationist, nationalist argument that the United States should refrain from any participation in European affairs and should never surrender one iota of its sovereignty for any reason. To support this view the radio priest, like virtually all isolationists of this period, appealed to the foreign policy statements of Washington and Jefferson without revealing any understanding of their context and true meaning.

Realizing himself how confusing his sudden assault on the administration must appear, Father Coughlin attempted to separate his disagreement on foreign policy from the economic field by stating that he would still uphold the administration in its attempt to achieve social reform. But at the same time he professed surprise that attention would be turned to foreign affairs when the domestic situation was still so unsettled. He made it absolutely clear that the National Union for Social Justice was a "national" organization in every sense of the term.[35]

The Court fight came to a roaring climax with a special nationwide broadcast on Monday, January 28, wherein Coughlin reiterated his charges against the World Court in a dramatic last-ditch effort to defeat the measure. On this same program, Msgr. John A. Ryan, Newton Baker, Senator Joe Robinson of Arkansas, Senator Joe Bailey of North Carolina, and Gen. J. F. O'Ryan of New York all spoke in favor of United States participation in the World Court. Msgr. Ryan's appearance was an apparent effort to remind Catholics that Father Coughlin was not an official spokesman for the Catholic Church.[36] The administration's pro-Court strategy fell flat, however, as Coughlin's talk brought a torrent of anti-Court telegrams upon the divided Senate; these appeared to have influenced just enough votes to prevent the Court treaty from receiving the necessary two-thirds majority. Some assistance must be credited to William Randolph Hearst whose newspaper chain was also vigorously opposed to United States participation. As *The New York Times,* a leading proponent of the World Court, expressed it: "Intensive propaganda, which Democratic leaders declared originated with Father Coughlin and the Hearst newspapers and was finally expressed in 40,000 telegrams in the last two days, played an important part in the defeat."[37] Coughlin was understandably jubilant at this turn of events and issued a statement congratulating an aroused citizenry for saving American sovereignty. His claim of two hundred thousand telegrams containing over one million names was considerably higher than the *Times* estimate, but most historians credit his influence as having been extremely important, if not decisive.[38] Further proof that Coughlin's efforts had hit home was Senate Majority Leader Robinson's charge that Father Coughlin had joined in the campaign to terrify Court advocates by issuing propaganda that was "unfair, unjust, and unreasonable."[39]

The priest's decisive role in defeating American participation in the World Court gave him new confidence in his ability to influence the cause of legislation by manipulating public opinion, and he became more impatient than ever with Roosevelt's failure to enact sweeping monetary reforms. Thus, only one month after praising Roosevelt for launching a new era of social justice, Coughlin bluntly asserted that the administration was "wedded basically to the philosophy of the money changers," and was "engaged in keeping America safe for the plutocrats." These charges were based, he said, on the administration's failure to (1) restore the coinage and regulation of money to Congress alone, (2) issue United States greenbacks, and (3) halt government borrowing from bankers.[40]

The Detroit priest was so impressed by his surprise victory in the World Court fight that he professed to believe that his followers were strong enough to exercise the same measure of control over future legislation: "Through the medium of the radio and the telegram you possess the power to override the invisible government; the power, at the risk of their political lives, to direct your representatives on individual matters of legislation."[41] What Father Coughlin failed to realize in the flush of victory is the simple fact that the United States was in the midst of a period of extreme isolationism in 1935; the anti-World Court faction merely needed an articulate leader to rally around. The priest filled this void admirably, but he deluded himself into believing that he had created a large part of the anti-World Court sentiment, when his real role was one of giving voice and direction to a relatively silent but sizable opposition. Father Coughlin was probably unaware of Roosevelt's halfhearted efforts on behalf of the World Court; the priest assumed that the President had given unequivocal support to the measure, and this accounts for much of the significance he attached to the defeat of the treaty. The radio priest was soon to learn that there was a vast difference between leading people who already agreed with his point of view and persuading the public that his social justice program was the sole remaining hope for America.

No particular event can be said to mark Coughlin's definite break with the administration, but this open assertion that Roosevelt was in league with the money-changers was his first direct attack on Roosevelt. Before this attack, the priest had confined his criticism to policies or subordinates. Even this criticism was general, directed at the entire administration, but it nonetheless included the President.

Despite the supreme self-confidence he exuded, Father Coughlin did not delude his followers into thinking that monetary reform would be as easily achieved as the World Court's defeat. Instead, he warned them to be prepared to be ridiculed as "nit-wits and morons" and to hear the social justice program disparaged as "the brainchild of a demagogic crackpot." As for himself, Coughlin asserted that "I would rather be a crack-pot for social justice than a hired 'yes man' and an internationalist for the present policies of this administration."[42]

Having prepared his followers for the worst, the priest proceeded to give them concrete evidence of their difficulties by announcing that the National Union for Social Justice was already $41,000 in debt and desperately in need of financial assistance. Coughlin bluntly asserted that he could not continue his activities in behalf of social justice unless sufficient funds were rapidly forthcoming to pay the expenses of the National Union. He emphasized that he had held the expenses of the organization to a bare minimum by allowing the National Union for Social Justice the free use of the office facilities of the Radio League of the Little Flower.[43] His impassioned plea for financial support did not go unheeded. Just one week later he announced that several thousand letters had poured in containing donations.[44] In the course of his appeal for funds he mentioned that over five million people had already signed the sixteen-point program of the national union. There is no way to check these figures (Coughlin has consistently refused access to his files), but there is little reason to doubt this figure; his great radio popularity is conceded by even his most vitriolic critics.[45]

On this same February 3 broadcast the Detroit priest elaborated on the meaning of part of his sixteen-point program for social justice. Although the third point clearly called for the nationalization of "banking, credit, currency, power, light, oil and natural gas, and our God-given natural resources," Coughlin explained that he did not actually advocate the nationalization of anything but money. What he really intended was for the government to regulate the rates and profits of public utilities. This, of course, is exactly what government agencies such as the Federal Power Commission and the Interstate Commerce Commission were supposed to be doing. It would have made more sense for Coughlin to have simply advocated tighter federal regulation, if that is what he meant. He also suggested that the federal, state, or municipal governments build their own power plants in competition with private enterprise.

On the subject of monetary control, the priest stressed that it was not his purpose to drive out of business any banker who was willing to cooperate and loan genuine United States currency "instead of manufactured money." Repeating his demand for a central bank, Father Coughlin sarcastically labeled the Federal Reserve System the "Gibraltar of the Plutocrats" and called for a union of farmers, laborers, small businessmen, and professional men to overthrow it.[46]

Concerning the ninth point in the National Union for Social Justice platform, which demanded a fair profit for the farmer, Coughlin announced his wholehearted endorsement of the Frazier-Lemke bill to make the farmers independent of the bankers and accountable only to the United States government. The priest also asserted that he would support any effort the farmers made to organize for the purpose of securing a just share of the fruits of their labors.[47]

On his next broadcast, continuing to elucidate his vague social justice platform, Coughlin engaged in his most bitter criticism of the President. He recklessly charged the Roosevelt administration with having communist leanings; in the same breath he reiterated his accusation that it was a tool of capitalism. Roosevelt was damned on the one hand for refusing to nationalize the banks and castigated on the other for "sovietizing" the American economy. Even the priest admitted that this was a bewildering paradox, but insisted he could demonstrate the validity of his charges. It seems that he read a *New York Times* dispatch that the federal government had taken out charters for several government corporations in Delaware. "The Corporation is to have perpetual existence," a legal phrase, Father Coughlin interpreted to mean that the Roosevelt administration expected the depression to endure forever. But this was not the major cause of his vexation. What really attracted Coughlin's fire was an attempt to obtain a charter for "The Public Works Emergency Leasing Corporation." This charter would have given the PWA authority to acquire private property and businesses. The Detroit priest insisted that this meant the government was assuming the right to confiscate private businesses at the PWA's discretion.[48] For the record, it should be noted that "The Public Works Emergency Leasing Corporation" charter was withdrawn shortly after it was granted.

Having given up all hope that the administration would enact the sweeping financial reforms he deemed so vital to the nation's full recovery, the radio priest produced his own monetary reform bill, "The Banking and Monetary Control Act of 1935," later known as the Nye-Sweeney Bill. This plan called for a Bank of the United States of America with forty-eight directors, one elected member from each state. Each director was to serve for a twelve-year term, with one-sixth being elected every two years. They were not to be on the payroll of any other government agency or private enterprise during their term of office. The new bank was to be the direct fiscal agent of Congress and control all monetary aspects of the United States government. Under this new system all currency issued was to be United States bank notes and all other notes were to be exchanged for these within one year's time. The headquarters of the Bank of the United States of America was to be in Washington, D.C., but branch offices were to be established in every state. The new bank was authorized to purchase all the stock of Federal Reserve Banks in United States Bank notes, after which the old Federal Reserve Banks would become branch banks of the new Bank of the United States. Private banks were to continue in operation but were considered to be engaging in interstate commerce and thus subject to federal jurisdiction under the new banking law. They would be required to gradually build up their reserves to a point where they would actually have 100 per cent of all demand deposits. Another feature of the bill was a provision for the Board of Directors to maintain the so-called "commodity" dollar. The directors were to be guided in their monetary control policy by data supplied by a new Bureau of Statistics which was to be formed by transferring the Bureau of Labor Statistics from the Labor Department to the new Bank and consolidating it with the statistical departments of the Treasury Department, the Comptroller's Office, and the Federal Reserve System.[49]

Coughlin quickly followed up his Central Bank scheme with a proposal to solve the concentration of wealth problem by taxing big business into submission. His plan called for a graduated tax upon annual industrial profits of 2 per cent on the first $1,000,000, 3 per cent on the next million, 4 per cent on the third million, and so on; at $10,000,000 taxes would be so drastically increased that it would not be profitable to operate much above this point. Capital wealth would also be taxed: the first $5,000 would be exempt, but after that level the tax would rise to such high amounts as to preclude the amassing of more than $10,000,000. This far from radical program was aimed at checking the unhealthy centralization of industry and wealth which then prevailed in the United States.[50] Adolph A. Berle and Gardiner C. Means in their authoritative study, *The Modern Corporation and Private Property*, estimated that the two hundred largest corporations controlled over half of the nation's wealth.

Having confounded his critics by devoting two successive broadcasts to positive suggestions for reform, Coughlin devoted his March 3 broadcast to disparaging the first two years of the New Deal. The priest sarcastically suggested: "The first two years of the New Deal shall be remembered as two years of compromise, two years of social planning, two years of endeavoring to mix bad with good, two years of surrender, two years of matching the puerile, puny brains of idealists against the virile viciousness of business and finance."[51]

The radio priest specifically criticized Roosevelt for not using the Sherman law to curb the centralization of business and for his failure to nationalize the monetary system. The NRA also came in for its share of abuse with the priest repeating a charge frequently raised by the agency's critics, that prices rose more than wages under NRA. In substance, however, Father Coughlin objected more to the method of financing New Deal projects than to the programs themselves; even relief programs were attacked because they served to swell the income of the bankers who loaned the government the necessary capital at compound interest.[52]

In addition to his impatience with compromise, Coughlin also displayed the average American's contempt for intellectuals, as was evidenced by his use of the term "puerile idealists" to describe New Dealers and "virile" to describe the American businessmen. This is a strange choice of words, for some of Coughlin's other statements show that the priest considered himself an idealistic reformer.

So savage was Coughlin's indictment that administration spokesmen, referred to by *The New York Times* as Democratic senators and cabinet members, took the position that they should not dignify the priest's accusations by replying to them.[53]

Not so fastidious, however, was General Hugh Johnson, who took to the airways on March 4 and unleashed a free-swinging, no-holds-barred attack upon Father Coughlin and Huey Long, the colorful Senator from Louisiana. The vitriolic Johnson denounced Coughlin and Long as leaders of the lunatic fringe and charged that they were both a menace to the nation. The unpredictable former NRA chief, making special reference to Coughlin's Roman Catholic priesthood, directed the Royal Oak cleric to get out of politics if he wished to continue in his priesthood. Johnson implied that it was intolerable for a priest to engage in politics in a Protestant country such as the United States. He also made pointed reference to Coughlin's citizenship: "There comes burring over the air the dripping brogue of the Irish-Canadian priest." The erratic general warned the American people that a political alliance had already been formed between Huey Long and the "political padre" which did not augur well for the future of American democracy: "These two men are raging up and down this land preaching not construction, but destruction—not reform but revolution, not peace but—a sword. I think we are dealing with a couple of Catilines, and that it is high time for someone to say so."[54]

Outside of the Coughlin camp, reaction to Johnson's low-road approach was generally favorable. Arthur Krock reported in his New York Times column that Johnson's talk had given new courage to many in Washington who had begun to fear the power of Coughlin and Long. The staid Times editorially thanked Johnson for denouncing "two would-be political tyrants," but conceded that Johnson would restrict the liberty of critics if given full rein.[55] Business Week also praised the Johnson approach as the only way to stop Coughlin and called for a rapprochement between the Roosevelt administration and the business community in order to protect the country from this type of extremist.[56] A dissent was printed in Commonweal, the liberal Catholic weekly; very critical of Johnson's attack, it defended Father Coughlin's right as an American citizen to speak out on public affairs, regardless of the fact that he was a Catholic priest.[57]

NBC offered the Detroit priest equal time to answer Johnson and Coughlin eagerly accepted. In addition to proudly proclaiming his American citizenship and defending his right as a citizen to speak out on politics, the radio priest emphasized that he had not personally benefited from any of his activities. Johnson had insinuated that Coughlin had supported silver only to line his own pockets. The priest admitted that his Radio League had made $12,000 on silver futures, but far from being on the defensive, he asserted that this only demonstrated the complete confidence that he had in President Roosevelt. Having defended himself, Father Coughlin then proceeded to turn the full power of his own rare talent for vituperation on General Johnson. He termed him "a political corpse," "the chocolate soldier," and "the first great casualty of New Deal experimentation." Coughlin also devoted a substantial portion of his speech to attacking Johnson's World War I boss, Bernard Baruch. The priest insisted that Johnson was simply the mouthpiece of Baruch and Wall Street; he suggested that it was more than mere coincidence that Baruch's middle name was Manasses, the same name as that of the ancient prince who had the prophet Isaiah killed for criticizing him. Father Coughlin, of course, saw himself as the modern Isaiah criticizing Baruch and other international bankers for their greedy manipulation of the monetary system. Baruch was particularly culpable because of his reported influence with Hoover and Roosevelt.[58]

The most extraordinary part of Coughlin's response to Johnson was his flat denial that he had broken with Roosevelt at the time of the silver list uproar in the spring of 1934:

An entire nation knows that his statement is palpably untrue. . . . My friends in this audience, I still proclaim to you that it is either "Roosevelt or Ruin!" I support him today and will support him tomorrow because we are neither going back to the individualism of the past nor are we going forward to the communism of the future. But I am not that type of false friend who, mangling the very meaning of the word friendship, praises policies like NRA when criticism is required or betrays my millions of supporters throughout this nation by preaching to them the prostituted slogan of "Peace, Peace," when there is no peace.[59]

Reaction to Coughlin's reply to Johnson was not long in coming. NBC announced that it received three hundred phone calls praising Coughlin's efforts. Bernard Baruch issued a dignified statement to *The New York Times* which ignored most of Father Coughlin's charges, but revealed that his middle name was Mannes and that he had never at any time been a banker. Arthur Krock made Baruch's case his own and charged that the priest had gotten his facts twisted, that very little of Baruch's advice had been accepted by either Hoover or Roosevelt, making his influence almost negligible.[60] Johnson himself retaliated with a prepared statement to the press in which he denounced Father Coughlin and Huey Long as public enemies 1 and 2; he promised a full reply at a later date. There is no record of Johnson's making such a reply, but on March 12 Johnson announced that he planned to recruit "thinking citizens" to speak out against Coughlin and Long. This project apparently never got beyond the idea stage.[61] A lighter note was struck by Mayor Harry Bacharack of Atlantic City, who offered Father Coughlin and Johnson $3,500 each to debate their differences in the resort's spacious Convention Hall.[62]

The only member of the administration to attack Coughlin publicly was Secretary of the Interior Harold Ickes. Speaking at an Associated Press luncheon in New York, the irascible Ickes bluntly labeled both Long and Coughlin "contemptible." A master of sarcasm, Ickes referred to the Detroit priest as "the cloistered individual whose rich but undisciplined imagination has reduced politics, sociology and banking to charming poetry which he distills mellifluously into the ether for the entrancement of mankind."[63] Public reaction to this speech, which was carried over a national radio network, was divided. Ickes noted in his diary that he received a heavy volume of mail both for and against Long and Coughlin, but he failed to indicate whether or not a majority favored his criticism.[64] One man who did not appreciate it was Franklin D. Roosevelt, who told Jim Farley that Ickes' reference to Coughlin "was very unwise."[65]

Father Coughlin's alleged association with Huey Long is the most puzzling aspect of the priest's controversial excursion into politics. Long had established himself as a virtual dictator in his native Louisiana. He rapidly became a national figure with a large following by advocating a Share-the-Wealth plan whereby every American was to receive $5,000 a year income from a soak-the-rich tax scheme. With his popularity increasing rapidly, the Louisiana demagogue created much alarm within administration circles. At Jim Farley's behest, the Democratic National Committee conducted a straw vote in the summer of 1935, which indicated that a third-party ticket headed by Long in 1936 would draw three million or more votes.[66] The Democratic chieftains assumed that these votes would be taken from the Democratic total and would thus pose a real threat to Roosevelt. It was clear then that any addition to Long's strength, such as a union with Father Coughlin's followers, was something to be avoided at all costs. Many commentators spoke of the threat posed by their collaboration, but very little is known of their true relationship. The most bizarre story connecting the two appeared in *Newsweek*. According to this unsigned article, Father Coughlin had persuaded Long to give up his heavy drinking, in order to increase his effectiveness.[67] Professor T. Harry Williams, who is preparing a biography of Long, says that the two men met several times in Long's Washington hotel. He believes that Long planned to use Coughlin in his movement.[68] When the Louisiana Senator filibustered against the administration's $4,800,000,000 relief bill, *The New York Times* reported that Long was widely believed to be conspiring with Coughlin to block Roosevelt's program. Their alleged plan called for Long to stall the bill's passage until Father Coughlin could bring the full weight of his radio influence against it.[69] Coughlin's failure to make a key issue out of the relief program gives the lie to this story. A *Times* story four days later is indicative of how little was really known of the Long-Coughlin relationship: it reported a split between the two men after Coughlin had reiterated his support for the administration Long was so bitterly assailing.[70]

Whatever the possibilities of a Long-Coughlin coalition, both men were considered to be serious threats to American democracy in 1935. One of the best known journalists and radio news commentators of the day, Raymond Gram Swing, contended that the Detroit priest and the Louisiana Senator were the advance agents of American fascism. Swing viewed with alarm their ever-increasing popularity. (He noted that when radio station WCAU in Philadelphia conducted a poll to determine whether it should carry Father Coughlin or the New York Philharmonic, the priest triumphed by a staggering 187,000 to 12,000 vote.) Swing considered Coughlin the greater evil, claiming he was actually fascistic in his thinking while Long was merely leaning in that direction. The popular radio commentator maintained that General Johnson's joint attack actually brought the men and their followers closer together, as well as creating additional support for them. Without indicating the source of his information, Swing claimed that the Roosevelt administration had tried to persuade Johnson to eliminate his references to Coughlin.[71] Swing was not alone in his fears. *The Christian Century* attacked Long and Coughlin and denounced their approach to reform as fascism.[72] Even the London *Times* joined the anti-Coughlin chorus and predicted that "if Roosevelt does not succeed in restoring prosperity, the American people will turn to Long and Coughlin and their quack remedies."[73]

Hamilton Basso, writing in *The New Republic,* sounded a more rational note. He described Father Coughlin's National Union for Social Justice as a potential fascist organization but was not as critical of Coughlin's motives as other journalists. Basso feared that the priest was truly confused as to the method of translating the National Union for Social Justice program into reality and might stumble into fascism on the way.[74] The editors of *The New Republic* took somewhat the same view; they denounced Coughlin as a dangerous demagogue, not because he promised too much, but because they felt that he was utterly incapable of carrying out his promises.[75]

Norman Thomas, now a venerable patriarch of the American Socialists but then in his most active role as perennial Socialist candidate for President, challenged both Father Coughlin and Huey Long to debate the issue of American fascism "for which you are preparing in both your programs and your methods."[76] Hugh Johnson also was among those who put a fascist label on Father Coughlin. Appearing at a government-businessmen's conference at Princeton, Johnson noted that it was impossible to distinguish between the quotations of Father Coughlin and Adolf Hitler.[77] As might be expected, the editors of *Business Week* castigated Coughlin, contending that his National Union for Social Justice was named in honor of Hitler's National Socialists.[78] The most vicious attack on the priest as a fascist was an article in *Forum* by the Rev. Daniel Colony, a Protestant Episcopalian minister, who compared Father Coughlin and his National Union for Social Justice to Hitler and his Storm Troopers. Colony did not confine his attention to the priest but bluntly accused the Catholic Church of quietly advancing the fascist cause in the United States. The minister maintained that the Church's silence on Coughlin was tacit approval of his actions. The Catholic Church, Colony contended, was weak and declining and desperately hoped to eliminate competition by holding the favored place in a fascist regime in the United States.[79]

In view of the suspicion with which the Catholic Church is often regarded in the United States, it is easy to imagine the confusion with respect to Father Coughlin. Here was a

Catholic priest with a radio audience of several million people, organizing an important political force, the National Union for Social Justice, which many thought would evolve into a political party. Believing that the Church was a rigidly organized, smooth-functioning, monolithic machine, many sincere individuals assumed that Father Coughlin must be acting on direct orders from the Vatican. The simple truth is that the Catholic Church is a very loosely knit organization with large measures of local autonomy. Every bishop, subject only to the Pope, is supreme in his diocese. Since Coughlin's bishop backed him all the way, the criticism of fellow priests or even members of the hierarchy such as Cardinal O'Connell had no official effect. It is true that the Vatican has the power to intervene in extreme cases, but only rarely is such an extraordinary step taken.

There can be no possible doubt that Father Coughlin enjoyed the full support of his immediate religious superior, Bishop Michael James Gallagher of Detroit. The bishop went out of his way to make his position clear in a public statement in the spring of 1935: "I pronounce Father Coughlin sound in doctrine, able in application and interpretation."[80] Evidence that the Catholic Church itself was badly divided on the Coughlin issue at this time appeared in the *Ecclesiastical Review,* a monthly for Catholic priests. The Rev. Edward V. Dargin, canonist for the Archdiocese of New York, published an article stating that Father Coughlin was violating the law of the Church by participating in politics. Father Dargin contended that Canon 83 of the Third Plenary Council of Baltimore forbade any participation by a Catholic priest in politics. The New York cleric was careful not to question the zeal or integrity of the Detroit priest; he simply stated that Coughlin, no matter how dedicated to social justice, was violating an important law of his Church by mixing in politics. Knowing the animosity which existed between Father Coughlin and Father Dargin's superior, Cardinal Hayes, it is difficult to believe that the New York priest acted spontaneously.[81] Whatever enthusiasm the anti-Coughlin forces might have enjoyed while contemplating an official crackdown was soon extinguished when the Vatican announced that no charges were pending against Father Coughlin and no action would be taken.[82] The next issue of *Ecclesiastical Review* carried a rebuttal to Father Dargin's argument by Msgr. William F. Murphy of Detroit who contended that canon law did not specifically forbid political action by a priest and maintained that the disputed Canon 83 was not meaningful because it had never been observed. Thus, he concluded, Father Coughlin had not violated canon law in any way.[83] As could be expected, the *Michigan Catholic,* official paper of the Detroit Archdiocese, defended Father Coughlin's position and emphasized his role as a great teacher of social justice rather than a political figure.[84]

Why did vociferous malcontents like Huey Long and Father Coughlin attract such enthusiastic followings during the administration of so popular a reform president as Franklin D. Roosevelt? The answer lies in the deep economic distress still endured by countless Americans in 1935 and Roosevelt's middle-of-the-road policies which antagonized both right and left. Despite all the efforts of the New Deal programs, there were still ten million Americans unemployed in 1935, and a perplexingly large number of Americans failed to qualify for any form of government relief. The President had only to read his mail to see signs of serious discontent on all sides. Typical of the pathetic and desperate quality of some of the letters to him in March of 1935 are the following: "If you listened in today to Father Coughlin's talk over the radio, you will have an idea of what the people who are forgotten are ready to fight for. All we need is a leader. We might better be dead, than living as we are, you have failed us so far."[85] "I know the truth and the truth is you have deceived the working man of the United States, and favored the Big Business and Huge Corporations and let the Poor Working Man go starving, or go to Hell. I loved you and you have betrayed."[86]

Of course, not all of the Coughlin-inspired mail was negative. Some people wrote to tell Roosevelt that they still supported him despite Father Coughlin's attacks.[87] Elzey Roberts, publisher of the *Saint Louis Star-Times*, graphically spelled out his own fears about the Coughlin situation to the President: "A power has arisen in this country greater than that of government itself. Therefore to my way of thinking, the new power, unless checked, will itself become government. I would describe this power as a demagogue with a foundation of discontent to stand on, and a radio to talk through." He continued: "The demagogues are impatient, and by use of their new weapon, the radio, they are turning the usual patience of the people into impatience that merely awaits a strong enough leader to break out into direct actions."[88] Roberts later revealed that he had squelched an anti-Coughlin editorial "because the tens of thousands of Father Coughlin's followers among our readers are so emotionally worked up that an appeal to reason seems vain."[89] Another alarming letter that came to Roosevelt's attention was from Daniel J. Tobin, boss of the Teamsters' Union, who wrote to Jim Farley that the Coughlin movement was not "a thing to be sneezed at." Tobin explained that he himself had criticized the priest only to be bombarded with letters of protest from irate Coughlinites.[90]

There is clear evidence that Roosevelt was fully aware of the political danger inherent in Coughlin's agitation of the discontented masses. In the spring of 1935, the President appointed Frank Murphy as unofficial liaison to placate the Detroit priest.[91] Murphy was a member of Father Coughlin's parish and they were reputed to be good friends, but it would appear that it was primarily a friendship of political convenience. No details were ever revealed about Murphy's unofficial activities as special envoy to Royal Oak, but it is obvious that he failed to reconcile the two men.

Roosevelt's own silence at this period was puzzling to many. He was generally recognized as the best radio speaker in the nation and had enjoyed great success with his "Fireside Chat" technique. The President himself provides the answer in a letter to Ray Stannard Baker:

> There is another thought which is involved in continuous leadership—whereas in this country there is a free and sensational press, people tire of seeing the same name day after day in the important headlines of the papers, and the same voice night after night over the radio. For example, if since last November I had tried to keep up the pace of 1933 and 1934 the inevitable histrionics of the new actors, Long and Coughlin and Johnson, would have turned the eyes of the audience away from the main drama itself. . . . Individual psychology cannot, because of human weakness, be attuned for long periods of time to a constant repetition of the highest note in the scale.[92]

The adroit use of psychology was only part of the reason for the President's silence. One of his most respected biographers, Arthur Schlesinger, Jr., makes the point that Roosevelt was simply unprepared to act in the first months of 1935 and could not speak out forcefully until new policies were formulated. For two years the New Deal had ridden on the crest of the first "100 Days," but by 1935 the two bulwarks of the early period, the AAA and the NRA, had failed to achieve all that had been expected of them and were under threat of Supreme Court action. At this time, Roosevelt was slowly feeling his way toward a leftward course; his obvious hesitation made the administration extremely vulnerable to attack from the Longs and Coughlins.[93]

Despite his disavowal of any plans to form a third party by joining forces with Huey Long or anyone else, Father Coughlin began to act more and more the role of a man with definite political ambitions. Coughlin told Walter Davenport, who interviewed him for *Colliers* in the spring of 1935, that he still looked to Roosevelt for political leadership rather than Huey Long. The priest emphatically denied that he was involved in any third party movement: "I have given the matter no thought at all. What would it be? A gathering of political malcontents with personal grudges to air?" Davenport predicted that Coughlin would support Roosevelt in 1936.[94]

Instead of ending his radio talks in early April as had been his custom, the priest arranged for thirteen weeks of additional air time beginning on April 28.[95] To further increase his influence, Coughlin initiated a series of spirited public rallies to stimulate enthusiasm for the National Union for Social Justice and to make it an effective pressure group. Appropriately, the first such meeting was held in Detroit; fifteen thousand people flocked to Olympia Auditorium to hear the Royal Oak orator officially launch the Michigan chapter of the national union. Coughlin again disclaimed any intention of organizing a new political party but bluntly asserted: "It is our intention to drive out of public life the men who have promised us redress, who have preached to us the philosophy of social justice and then having broken their promises, practice the philosophy of plutocracy."[96] The priest vehemently denied entertaining any thought of a fascistic system: "We disavow racial Hitlerism. We turn our backs upon industrial fascism."[97] As usual, Father Coughlin was more eloquent in denouncing present evils than in outlining future reforms. He did, however, endorse six important measures then being considered by Congress: (1) Frazier-Lemke farm mortgage bill, (2) Wagner Labor Bill, (3) Wheeler Holding Company act, (4) Nye Munitions Bill, (5) Nye-Sweeney coinage bill restoring to Congress the sole right to coin money, and (6) veterans' bonus. The radio priest also revealed that he would retire from active political affairs as soon as the National Union for Social Justice was properly under way. Speakers sharing the platform with Father Coughlin were Louis Ward, his close friend and biographer who was also his lobbyist in Washington; Edward Kennedy, the Secretary of the National Farmers' Union; William Collins of the AFL; Senator Elmer Thomas (Democrat, Oklahoma); Senator Gerald P. Nye (Republican, North Dakota); Representative William P. Connery, Jr. (Democrat, Massachusetts); Representative Thomas O'Malley (Democrat, Wisconsin); Representative Martin Sweeney (Democrat, Ohio); and Representative William Lemke (Republican, North Dakota). The presence of Edward Kennedy of the National Farmers' Union was interpreted to mean that Father Coughlin was giving his endorsement to that group rather than Milo Reno's National Farmers Holiday Association.[98]

Coughlin did not attack the President personally, but he was obviously declaring political war against the Roosevelt administration—and indirectly against its chief. But Coughlin still preferred to maintain the fiction that he was essentially for Roosevelt and only opposed certain of his subordinates. Whether he did this to avoid alienating many of his own followers who were also strong supporters of Roosevelt, or because he simply shied from irrevocably breaking with a man he had so fervently supported, is very difficult to say. As with most human motivation, the real answer probably is a complex combination of factors.

Shortly after Father Coughlin's Detroit triumph, a new crop of rumors sprang up to the effect that he was joining forces with Huey Long. There was speculation that representatives of Coughlin would meet with Long at a farm rally in Des Moines, Iowa, sponsored by Milo Reno and the National Farmers Holiday Association. Coughlin emphatically denied this, stating that neither he nor any representative would attend the Des Moines rally and confirmed the report that he favored the National Farmers' Union over Reno's group.[99] In spite of this announcement, *The New York Times* reported that two advisors of the Detroit priest did attend the Des Moines meeting, but had refused to sit on the platform.[100] Significantly, both Long and Reno singled out Father Coughlin for praise at the meeting, leaving little doubt that they would welcome a fusion movement. Undaunted, the priest continued to deny having sent any observers to the meeting and again insisted that the National Union for Social Justice was not a political party.[101]

Coughlin's extended radio series opened rather inauspiciously on April 28 with Louis Ward substituting for the priest, who was reported to be resting.[102] Father Coughlin spoke for himself the following week and once again denied any thought of a third party, insisting: "We are above politics and above politicians." The bulk of this talk, however, was devoted to his endorsement of the Patman soldiers' bonus bill, which provided for an issue of greenbacks to finance the bonus payments, as contrasted with the more conservative Vinson bill, which called for the traditional bond issue. Attempting to emulate his success with the World Court issue, Coughlin urged his listeners to bombard Congress with letters in behalf of the Patman bill. Thousands of them did just that, and the Patman bill was passed by a large margin.[103] Although this would seem to indicate that Father Coughlin's influence was still potent, there was some truth in what columnist Walter Lippmann wrote at the time: "We will never get a real test of his influence until he decides to stake his influence on a question that isn't going to be decided his way anyhow."[104] Despite a radio warning from Coughlin that the administration would be committing political suicide if it opposed the Patman bill, Roosevelt vetoed the measure.[105] Surprisingly, the priest appeared more hurt than angry at Roosevelt's veto. He smugly described it as the President's "most foolish political move."[106] The issue became, indirectly, a personal duel between Roosevelt and Coughlin when the President made a rare personal appearance before Congress to ask that his veto be upheld. The House listened respectfully and promptly voted to override the veto by a 322-98 margin.[107] When the Senate sustained the President's veto, the priest admitted that the bonus cause had received a setback but advised against a bonus march as "imprudent, inefficient and provocative of trouble."[108]

Father Coughlin staged his second national union rally in Cleveland, Ohio, on May 8. A crowd estimated at twenty-five thousand heard the priest attack the Eccles bill, the administration-backed bank reform bill, as a measure aimed at making the President the financial dictator of the United States. As could be expected whenever the subject of finance was considered, Coughlin seized the opportunity to criticize the Federal Reserve System, scornfully describing it as "a marriage license between a prostitute who has wrecked our home and the government who has deserted his wife, the American people."[109] The Eccles bill had as its main objective one of Father Coughlin's cherished goals: direct control of the money market by the federal government rather than by private bankers. But Marriner Eccles, newly appointed Chairman of the Federal Reserve Board, wished to utilize the existing system with significant changes, whereas Coughlin demanded that the Federal Reserve be scrapped and be replaced by a government-owned Central Bank. Ironically, Roosevelt and Morgenthau both endorsed government ownership of the Federal Reserve stock, but the President made no attempt to convince Congress of this view.[110]

One of the most colorful events in Coughlin's controversial political career was his Madison Square Garden appearance of May 22, 1935. The priest arrived in New York early and consented to a news conference. In the course of it he denied all personal political ambition and indicated there was still a slim chance that he might stand by Roosevelt: "I sincerely hope to be able to support Mr. Roosevelt again. I said I hope. He has given expression to the greatest social philosophy that has ever been initiated by any country. Now we have hope that he will put it into practice."[111]

The next evening twenty-three thousand enthusiastic Coughlinites jammed Madison Square Garden to hear their leader attack the capitalistic system and the Roosevelt administration. Every mention of Roosevelt, Bernard Baruch, James Warburg, or the House of Morgan brought a resounding chorus of boos from the crowd. The President was attacked not only for vetoing the veterans' bonus but for tolerating such a pitifully low wage scale for relief workers as $19 a month. Such wages, the priest declared, not only served to lower an already inadequate standard of living but actually encouraged the growth and spread of communism among the discontented poor. Coughlin struck hard at Roosevelt's contention that the soldiers' bonus was class legislation, insinuating that the President was quite willing to approve special class legislation to serve the bankers' interest.

Father Coughlin briefly summarized the National Union for Social Justice platform as follows: (1) protection for small businessmen and industrialists, (2) production at a profit for the farmer, and (3) a just and living annual wage for the laborer. The national union was going to achieve these ends, not as a political party, but as a well-organized articulate lobby of the people. He insisted that all these reforms would be enacted in the regular American constitutional manner as opposed to any sort of dictatorship, communist or fascist. What Coughlin proposed was a union of farmers, laborers, and small businessmen to work within their respective parties to nominate social justice candidates in the primaries. Appearing on the speakers' platform with the radio priest were James E. Van Zandt, national commander of the VFW, who spoke on the bonus question, and Representative John V. Truax of Ohio, who made a brief speech praising Father Coughlin.[112] Analysis of Coughlin's New York remarks shows that he still hoped to avoid a complete break with Roosevelt by pressuring the administration via the World Court and soldiers' bonus procedure of government by telegram. While Coughlin spoke before twenty-three thousand at the Garden, a crowd of one hundred attended an anti-Coughlin rally at Columbus Circle under the auspices of the West Side Council Against War and Fascism.

Coincident with Father Coughlin's appearance in New York City, a criticism of the priest's Central Bank scheme appeared in the respected Jesuit weekly, *America*. Father Wilfred Parsons, one of the most distinguished Catholic journalists in the nation, attacked the Nye-Sweeney bill as not only allowing all the "old evils" of bad banking but compounding the confusion by adding additional weaknesses. As if this were not enough, Father Parsons went on to criticize Father Coughlin for pushing "doubtful economic legislation" instead of concentrating on reforming the minds and souls of men. The Jesuit expressed the fear that his fellow priest was actually harming the cause of social justice by dragging it into politics.[113] Coughlin's response was to assail Parsons at the Madison Square Garden national union rally as "a fellow priest already notorious for playing into the hands of unclean motion picture producers."[114] Thus Father Coughlin made no attempt to meet Father Parsons' criticisms but struck out blindly at the Jesuit with a ridiculous accusation. By contrast Parsons calmly replied: "I am deeply disappointed that Father Coughlin had no other answer to make to my impersonal and objective appraisal of his theories."[115]

In the June 1 issue of *America* Parsons continued his criticism of Coughlin's monetary theories and emphasized that Coughlin's ideas were his own and not those of the Catholic Church. The Jesuit editor, while admiring Coughlin's earlier efforts for social justice, was deeply concerned about his present course: "For years Father Coughlin has done incomparable service in calling attention to the evils of our economic system. Let me say I have always admired him for it. But the situation today is changed. He is now offering plans based on monetary theories which, to say the least, are untried." He continued: "The danger is that they will distract his followers from the much more necessary work of the reform of industry, where the trouble really lies. If people begin to look for prosperity and justice in some easy magic of monetary reform, the long hard job of social justice in the factory will be overlooked and that will be tragic."[116] Further indication that Coughlin was causing alarm within his own Church was a new attack from his old clerical enemy, Cardinal O'Connell of Boston. Addressing the Massachusetts Catholic Order of Foresters on the day following the national union's Madison Square Garden rally, the Boston prelate struck out at what he termed "hysterical voices." Although the cardinal did not refer to the radio priest by name, it was evident to all that he was referring to Coughlin: "And all those disturbing voices, the yelling and screaming, are so unbecoming to anyone who occupies the place of teacher in Christ's Church, that even the quality of their voices betrays them. They are hysterical. And no priest of God, no teacher of the Christian Church even permits himself to be hysterical. The matter is too serious."[117]

In the first weeks that followed his Garden appearance, Father Coughlin managed to stay in the news quite regularly. In his radio series he had restrained praise for the NRA and advocated the continuation of its good points after all the provisions tending toward monopolistic practices had been dropped. As a matter of record, Coughlin's criticism of the NRA as an instrument of business consolidation was a widely shared feeling.[118] When the Supreme Court struck down the NRA as unconstitutional, the radio priest was furious and compared the court's action to the Dred Scott decision, pleading that labor and agriculture "should not be crucified upon the interpretation of an obsolete law." It was his judgment that Congress should redefine the meaning of interstate commerce by constitutional amendment, if necessary, but that business had to be prevented from continuing to exploit the workers and the poor. Coughlin gave his full support to the Wheeler-Rayburn Public Utilities Act which was aimed at destroying holding companies which could not clearly prove the economic necessity of their existence. The priest also continued to insist that Congress restore to itself the right to coin money; he warned that his way meant "Roosevelt and Recovery" while any other path meant "Roosevelt and Ruin."[119]

Despite the pressure of national union affairs, Father Coughlin found the time to support an independent labor union among the auto workers of Detroit known as the Automotive Independent Workers Association, which was reported to have between seven and nine thousand members in July of 1935, mostly in the Chrysler plants. The priest addressed a mass meeting of the new union in Detroit and announced an annual wage of $2,150 as the auto workers' goal. The capital for such a guaranteed wage was to come partly from the manufacturer's profits and partly from raising the price of cars. This is one instance where the priest could not be accused of generalizing; he even stated the exact amount of the annual wage. The problem of seasonal employment was serious in Detroit and Father Coughlin was close to the scene, having a working-class parish in a suburb of the auto capital.[120] Later in the summer he again addressed the independent auto union and pledged them the full support of the national union, which he now claimed had nine million members.[121]

In July, August, and September of 1935, it appeared that the radio priest was taking a breathing spell to consolidate his organization or to rechart his political course. He had planned another public rally in Soldiers' Field, Chicago, but was denied permission to rent the field by the Chicago Park Board. Coughlin took his fight to the courts and won an initial victory in the lower court, only to have the Park Board win its appeal and maintain its right to bar him. The priest received some unexpected but ineffective help from the Communist party in Chicago, which sent a representative to testify on his right to be heard. This petty action of the Chicago Park Board is difficult to defend in view of their allowing American fascists to conduct rallies on the same field.[122] The suspicion that Father Coughlin was temporarily curbing his activities in mid-summer is given credence by the fact that Louis Ward, Coughlin's Congressional lobbyist, left Washington on July 29 with Congress still in session. In addition, the priest made no real effort to fight for the Nye Amendment to the Omnibus Banking Bill. Coughlin's own bank reform measure, the Nye-Sweeney bill, was never seriously considered because of the great number of money bills then before Congress. It was decisively defeated, 59 to 10.[123] *The New York Times* interpreted these events to mean that Father Coughlin was postponing his plans for making the National Union for Social Justice a truly potent political lobby of the people.[124]

In August Coughlin came out of political obscurity long enough to pay a triumphant visit to Mayor Curley and the

Massachusetts Legislature. He received a very enthusiastic welcome from both the House and Senate, but Mayor Curley candidly revealed in his autobiography that he personally did not have much regard for the Detroit priest.[125] Any plans that Coughlin may have had to join forces with Huey Long in the 1936 election were shattered by the bullets that destroyed the Louisiana Senator on September 10, 1935. Whatever their relationship had been, Father Coughlin appeared deeply disturbed by the assassination, calling it "the most regrettable thing in modern history." The priest revealed that he himself had received a warning of a plot to kill Long by tampering with his car. He did not indicate what action he took, but the assumption was that he relayed the information to Long. Coughlin received the news of Long's death while in New York to visit his friend Joseph Kennedy, Chairman of the Securities Exchange Commission. It seems that Kennedy was trying to work out a reconciliation between Coughlin and Roosevelt, and arranged for the priest to visit the President at Hyde Park. The two men met just a few hours after Long's death, an event which certainly must have had great significance for both of them. Nothing is known about the nature of their conversation. Roosevelt told reporters that the visit was "social" and Coughlin declined to comment, saying that courtesy to his host precluded any statement from him.[126] Whatever was said, the visit failed to accomplish a reconciliation and the two continued to drift farther apart.

Coughlin's prolonged inactivity, combined with Long's death, gave credence to a rumor that the priest was going to scrap the National Union for Social Justice and support Roosevelt. So widespread did this rumor become that Father Coughlin deemed it necessary to telephone a denial to *The New York Times:* "I am neither supporting Roosevelt nor opposing him. I am determined to support principles, and not men. The major principle is the nationalization of credit."[127] This was rather a strange statement from a man who had coined the phrase "Roosevelt or Ruin," but it revealed his almost pathetic reluctance to break completely with the President he had so devotedly supported in 1932 and 1933. Only two weeks after denying he opposed Roosevelt, Coughlin opened a new radio series with an ultimatum to Congress to enact social justice legislation or face political annihilation at the polls. Mincing no words, the priest declared that "hunting season for members of Congress is on." While continuing to disclaim any third party intentions, Coughlin announced that he was compiling a record of every representative or senator "either to applaud him as a patriot or lash him as a Benedict Arnold." Unless the American people removed the members of Congress "who had lost sight of their duty as representatives of the American people," Coughlin predicted, his own slogan of "Roosevelt or Ruin" would have to be changed to "Roosevelt and Ruin." In this same broadcast the Detroit priest warned Americans that the stage was being set for another world war because the United States government had "secretly, though unofficially, condoned the sanctions of Great Britain" against Italy for her aggression in Ethiopia. Coughlin interpreted this to mean that the United States was going to fight a war to preserve the British international bankers, as he claimed had been the case in 1917. For some inexplicable reason the priest championed the unpopular cause of Italy.[128] His critics contended that this was clear proof of his fascist sympathies, but it was probably more a case of an emotional Irishman so obsessed with hatred of Great Britain that he would side with virtually any cause the British opposed. As was clearly revealed earlier by his opposition to the World Court, the Royal Oak orator was a complete isolationist in foreign affairs, which would make him automatically suspicious of any form of cooperation between the United States and Great Britain.

After the many bitter attacks Coughlin had made on the administration, few people could have been surprised when the open, irrevocable break between the radio priest and the Roosevelt administration came on November 17, 1935, just one year and six days after the founding of the National

Union for Social Justice. Apparently confident of the loyalty of his followers, Coughlin informed his radio audience in characteristically blunt fashion that the principles of the New Deal and social justice were "unalterably opposed." The Roosevelt administration, he charged, had embraced two conflicting extremes, communistic tendencies and plutocracy, and was no longer deserving of support. Thus ended one of the most bizarre political alliances of the 1930's.[129]

IV
THE UNION PARTY

EVEN AFTER Father Coughlin had finally broken with the New Deal, he was reluctant to appear as an implacable foe of Roosevelt's recovery policies. Thus, on the broadcast following his blunt repudiation of the New Deal, the priest shifted his attention to the realm of foreign affairs. He bitterly accused Roosevelt's roving ambassador, Norman Davis, of secretly pledging United States assistance to the League of Nations in imposing sanctions on Italy for her aggression against Ethiopia. Coughlin predicted that such meddling in the affairs of other nations would lead to a general war by 1937.[1]

When the Detroit priest returned to the subject of the New Deal on December 1, he adopted a more moderate tone, contending that he had no desire to obstruct the New Deal but wished only to perfect it. What he opposed, Coughlin said, were its extravagant experiments and reactionary tendencies. The priest conceded that Roosevelt's election prevented a revolution of the discontented in 1932, but declared that the President was not "the only man who can save America."[2] It is obvious that Coughlin was unsure of his future course at this time. His followers were first told that the principles of the National Union for Social Justice and the New Deal were "unalterably opposed," but two weeks later they were informed that their leader did not want to destroy the New Deal, but to perfect it. What is there to perfect about "unalterably opposed" principles? This kind of illogical statement occurred with embarrassing frequency in Coughlin's broadcasts, revealing an extremely confused state of mind.

Shortly after his split with Roosevelt, there were persistent rumors that the radio priest was going to join forces with Dr. Francis E. Townsend, an elderly California physician, whose pension scheme attracted widespread support in the 1930's. When Townsend visited Coughlin at Royal Oak, it appeared that an alliance had been arranged. But the California doctor emphatically denied that any had been made or even contemplated. He did say that the Detroit priest had sanctioned his old age pension plan.[3]

Coughlin received an indirect rebuke at this time from Cardinal Mundelein of Chicago, who, on the occasion of receiving an honorary degree from the University of Notre Dame, made the following statement:

> We are not in politics, neither the Church nor I. . . . No individual Catholic Bishop or priest, no organization of laymen or Catholic newspaper has the right to speak for the 20,000,000 Catholics in this country in the matter of politics, only the Bishops of the country together, in conference, or in council, and they have not done so, and so we do not wish our words to be interpreted in that sense.[4]

Mundelein, like O'Connell, did not mention Father Coughlin by name but his meaning was obvious. Thus, the three most respected members of the Catholic hierarchy in the United States, the cardinals, Mundelein, O'Connell, and Hayes, had all spoken out against Father Coughlin's participation in politics, but none of them, despite their high ecclesiastical rank, had jurisdiction over the Detroit priest. Coughlin ignored Mundelein's statement but continued to deny that his national union was a political party: "We do not believe in establishing a third party which will only add to the confusion." The priest called for twenty thousand volunteers to spearhead the fight against communism. He was extremely vague concerning the role of these volunteers outside of pledging to fight communism wherever it appeared in America.[5] Whatever Father Coughlin had in mind, he triumphantly announced one week later that he had received forty thousand volunteers.[6] Nothing more was ever said about this auxiliary group. Apparently deciding that he had to increase his direct communication with the public if he hoped to exert any significant influence, Coughlin announced on his final broadcast of 1935 that he planned to inaugurate a weekly newspaper if one million listeners would send him a write-in vote of confidence. As might be expected, the proposed paper was "to interpret the news" rather than report it. In the same talk the Detroit priest took violent exception to a statement by the National Association of Manufacturers that recovery would come only when the government ceased to regulate industry. Coughlin labeled the NAM position as "the damnable philosophy of the ancient Bourbons of France," and claimed that such a policy would bring on an even worse depression, which would be settled by a bloody revolution.[7]

In January, Coughlin boasted that he had organized National Union for Social Justice units in 302 of the nation's 435 congressional districts, a clear warning to all congressmen that his lobby of the people meant business.[8] *The New York Times,* clearly annoyed by Coughlin's political activities, ran an editorial belittling his influence as a radio speaker. But one wonders why the editorial writer was so irritated by the radio priest if he really had no influence. The petulant journalist even cast aspersions as to the size of Father Coughlin's audience: "Incidentally, who ever counted these countless millions?"[9]

Despite Coughlin's bitter denunciation of the Roosevelt administration, the priest visited the President at the White House on January 8 and was granted a forty-minute private conversation with Roosevelt. No details were released to the public, but the President did reveal that Coughlin had shied away from politics, preferring to discuss plans for his new church in Royal Oak.[10]

In February, the Detroit priest began a frenzied, ill-fated

crusade for passage of the Frazier-Lemke bill. This was a farm mortgage bill jointly sponsored by Senator Lynn Frazier and Representative William Lemke, both of North Dakota. The measure provided for the federal government, acting through the Farm Credit Administration and the Federal Reserve System, to purchase all farm mortgages and allow the farmers to gradually liquidate them at 1½ per cent interest. The government was to finance the mortgage purchases by floating a special bond issue. The Federal Reserve Board would be obligated to purchase any bonds not bought by private interests and to deliver Federal Reserve notes equal to the value of the bonds, but not to exceed $3,000,000,000. In simple terms, this was interpreted to mean a $3,000,000,000 issue of paper money to put the government in the farm mortgage business on a gigantic scale. To many harassed farmers who were still paying usurious interest rates on their mortgages and losing their farms at the fantastic rate of two thousand a day, the Frazier-Lemke bill seemed to be their only salvation. To nonfarm groups, however, it appeared to be the traditional agrarian demand for soft money in a time of economic distress.[11]

Father Coughlin vigorously defended the unorthodox financial provisions of the Frazier-Lemke bill and maintained that the bonds issued would have the real wealth of the United States behind them, the fields with their crops, the farm buildings and machinery, etc. Coughlin's theory of money was that it was not real wealth, but only a medium of exchange. Thus, he contended that the government could and should create the $3,000,000,000 needed for the Frazier-Lemke bill, since this money would be backed by $20,000,000,000 of farm real estate.[12]

The Frazier-Lemke bill had substantial support; the legislatures of thirty-three states had adopted resolutions advocating its passage and a sizable number of congressmen were known to be supporters of the measure. But, as any casual student of American government knows, it is an extremely difficult task to steer a bill onto the floor of Congress for a vote if it is opposed by the party in power. The majority party's representatives on the appropriate committees can usually tie up controversial bills in committee and thus avoid the risk of an embarrassing defeat for the administration. The Frazier-Lemke bill was accorded the usual treatment; Representative John O'Connor of New York exerted every effort to bottle up the controversial farm bill in the powerful Rules Committee he headed.

When this evasive strategy became painfully evident to Father Coughlin, the priest dispatched his close friend and lobbyist, Louis Ward, to discuss the situation with Col. McIntyre, one of Roosevelt's closest assistants. McIntyre's version of this conversation, as recorded in an office memo, was that Ward demanded that the administration release the Frazier-Lemke bill or face violent attacks from Coughlin on his broadcasts. Outraged by this crude attempt at blackmail, McIntyre tersely informed Ward that he would not even present such a proposition to the President. The Roosevelt aide also told Ward that neither he, Roosevelt, nor Farley knew anything about what was happening to the Frazier-Lemke bill on Capitol Hill,[13] a statement difficult for students of the era to accept at face value.

Having failed to intimidate the administration, Coughlin kept his word and bitterly berated Roosevelt on his radio program. He demanded that the President endorse the bill or take responsibility for its death in committee. Coughlin insisted that Roosevelt had pledged himself to support the principles of the Frazier-Lemke bill in a 1932 campaign speech at Sioux City, Iowa, and had betrayed the trust imposed in him by the farmers: "Not once had you intervened for the bill which you promised to sustain. . . . Meanwhile 32,000,000 residents of farm states of America, defrauded of their hire, raised their voices to highest heaven for vengeance which God will not deny."[14]

Coughlin also castigated O'Connor as "a servant of the money changers" and ordered the New Yorker to release the Frazier-Lemke bill or resign from Congress. The priest accused O'Connor of cowing House members into removing their signatures from a petition the bill's supporters were circulating to force the measure out onto the House floor for discussion.[15]

Roosevelt shrewdly adhered to his personal policy of remaining silent during Coughlin's attacks, but this did not prevent Congressman O'Connor from attacking the Detroit priest. O'Connor denied that he had attempted to coerce anyone into withdrawing his signature from the Frazier-Lemke petition and denounced Father Coughlin as "a disgrace to any church." The volatile New Yorker, who was himself a Roman Catholic, dispatched a blistering telegram to the radio priest: "Just read your libelous radio rambling. The truth is not in you. You are a disgrace to my church and any other church and especially to the citizenship of America which you recently embraced. You do not dare print what you said about me." He angrily continued, "If you will please come to Washington I shall guarantee to kick you all the way from the capitol to the White House with clerical garb and all the silver in your pockets which you got from speculating in Wall Street while I was voting for all the farm bills. Come on!"[16]

The not-so-decorous House was in an uproar when Representative Martin Sweeney of Ohio, a close friend of Coughlin, read O'Connor's telegram (to loud applause) and shouted, "He accepts your challenge and will be here at 10 o'clock tomorrow morning [February 18]." It was announced later on the same day that Father Coughlin would not arrive in Washington until February 26.[17]

In the exchange which followed, Representative O'Connor continued his bitter personal assault on the Detroit priest:

Every decent Catholic in America has been ashamed of him since he came to this country. There isn't a clergyman of the Catholic Church except one (Bishop Gallagher of Detroit) that I know of who has approved of his desecration of the cloth by his intrusion into politics.

I personally never heard a Catholic priest talk politics from the pulpit. In the old days of prohibition and the KKK the cry of many of us to Bishop Cannon was "Back to the pulpit, Stay where you belong."

Just because Father Coughlin is an egomaniac he thinks he can run the government. He stepped into the bonus and world court issues, but had as much to do with Congressional action on them as any elevator operator in the Capital.

When he saw the Frazier-Lemke petition needed only four signatures he stepped into that.

He is ineligible to run for President, but most people would welcome his attempt to run for any other office.

While purporting to be for the bonus, he told American Legion commanders that he was for the economy bill; that the soldiers had too much already.

In a conference with fifteen Senators last year after the House had passed the Patman [bonus] bill, one of his aides started to dictate what kind of bill the Senators should introduce and when they made certain suggestions this man said "Father Coughlin will not let you propose any such bill."[18]

O'Connor claimed that the real beginning of his feud with Father Coughlin occurred in January of 1935, when Representative Sweeney requested that Coughlin be allowed the use of a caucus room in the House Office Building. The Commission on the House Office Building, of which O'Connor was a leading member, turned down the irregular request on the grounds that the priest could well afford to rent an office. At this point, O'Connor continued, he was informed that he would hear from Father Coughlin about the matter.[19]

The New York congressman was certainly somewhat less than candid when he denied blocking the Frazier-Lemke bill, protesting that he was but one of fourteen congressmen on the Rules Committee. No doubt modesty made him hesitate to admit that he was the chairman of the Committee and as such might have some small influence with the other members. O'Connor openly admitted that he was against the Frazier-Lemke bill as an inflationary measure and claimed, in addition, that the insurance companies, not the farmers, would gain most, since they held the mortgages. He accused the radio priest of killing the bill's chances by his extreme attacks on its opponents.[20]

At first Father Coughlin refused to comment on O'Connor's attack, but he was merely holding his fire until his next radio broadcast. O'Connor himself moderated his criticism somewhat by admitting he was disrespectful of Coughlin's status as a clergyman; but the congressman insisted that the priest had given him ample provocation and that he would not retract his remarks.[21] O'Connor was joined in his feud with Father Coughlin by Representative Patrick J. Boland of Pennsylvania, who compared the Detroit priest with Judas, and denounced him as a demagogue.[22]

Coughlin's congressional defense was handled by Representative Sweeney, who accused O'Connor of stirring up intolerance by raising the issue of a priest in politics. At one stage, Sweeney dramatically turned to the House Chaplain, Reverend James Shera Montgomery, and Representative James Eaton of New Jersey, a former minister, and asked: "Is it politics for a man of Christ to rise on Sunday in a pulpit or by a microphone and beg to change an economic system that allows children to go to garbage cans in search of food?" The congressman continued, "Thank God for men like him who have the courage to stand on Sunday and speak to unseeing millions, 30, 40, 50 million people about this situation."[23]

Another interesting development was the offer of Kid McCoy, former light-heavyweight boxing champion and paroled killer, to fight O'Connor as a substitute for Father Coughlin. This friendly gesture, which was not accepted, was counterbalanced by the harsh words of President James Roland Angell of Yale University who took the occasion of the annual alumni day address to single out Father Coughlin for a blistering reproach: "A recently naturalized foreign priest . . . is allowed to pour out weekly over the radio, under the blessed name of social justice, the most poisonous and inflammatory economic and social nonsense."[24]

In reality, there was never any possibility of a physical showdown between the congressman and the priest. Bishop Gallagher was willing to back Coughlin to a fantastic degree, but he would have been totally derelict in his duty if he had sanctioned the participation of one of his priests in a public brawl. When questioned by the press, the bishop disclosed that he planned to take no action on the matter and predicted that both sides would cool off. But he left little doubt that he was still supporting Coughlin to the limit, commenting that "a Representative ought to know the only way to answer argument is by counter-argument and not by little-boy tactics." Actually, the bishop did not appear unduly disturbed about the affair, as this humorous jibe at Representative O'Connor demonstrates: "Moreover it is presumptuous of Representative O'Connor to assume he can kick Father Coughlin all the way down Pennsylvania Avenue."[25] It was announced without comment on February 26 that Father Coughlin was canceling his trip to Washington.[26]

Although Coughlin was not permitted to meet O'Connor on the field of physical combat, he was obviously under no other restrictions; he devoted his entire radio broadcast of February 23, 1936, to the incident. The priest justified his conduct by stating that he was defending not himself, but the National Union for Social Justice. Coughlin answered O'Connor's denial of pressure tactics by jubilantly reading the following telegram from Representative Theodore L. Moritz, of the Thirty-second District of Pennsylvania: "I was persuaded to remove my name from the Frazier-Lemke petition by Congressman John J. O'Connor, Chairman of the Rules Committee. He said I was embarrassing the President by supporting this petition."[27]

Father Coughlin eloquently defended his participation in politics in a condescending, sarcastic manner: "My dear John, is it politics to plead for the poor? Is it politics to emulate the gentle Master who castigated the Scribes and Pharisees in ancient days because 'they devour the homes of widows and orphans.' " He continued, "In fear and trembling, I ask you, John, is it politics to attempt, even at an infinite distance, to follow in the footsteps of Him Who, when reason and prayer had failed, drove the money changers from the temple by physical force? John, if these be politics, I humbly submit that I am a politician."[28]

In March, the Frazier-Lemke furor subsided somewhat, but Coughlin continued to fight hard for the bill through his new medium, a weekly newspaper appropriately called *Social Justice,* the first issue of which appeared on March 13. The Detroit priest had first broached the subject of a weekly newspaper in a December, 1935, broadcast. At that time he requested that a million of his followers write him a vote of confidence. Only Father Coughlin and his aides know what response he received to this request, but it is logical to assume that he must have obtained substantial evidence of support before venturing into so costly an enterprise as a weekly newspaper. Coughlin's financial problem was compounded by the fact that he was determined to operate the paper without advertising of any nature.

The priest completely dominated the new paper in its early period. Those articles not actually authored by him were written by close associates who were in total accord with their chief's ideas. E. Perrin Schwarz, city editor of the *Milwaukee Journal,* wrote to Coughlin expounding his views on what type of newspaper the priest should publish and was astounded to hear Coughlin parrot his suggestions in one of his Sunday broadcasts. He was even more surprised when Coughlin telephoned the next day and offered him the editorship of the new weekly. Schwarz quickly accepted and remained on the paper until its inglorious demise in 1942.[29]

With the launching of *Social Justice,* Father Coughlin redoubled his efforts to organize the National Union for Social Justice into a potent political force. Still denying all intentions of starting a third party, he nevertheless urged his supporters to concentrate their energies upon congressional elections. The first issue of *Social Justice* contained an article, apparently written by the priest, entitled "Voters Are Being Fooled Over The Political Sham Battle." It ridiculed the presidential election as a meaningless exercise in political futility: "We can afford mediocre Presidents, but a blundering and venal Congress would be fatal to our right to life, liberty and the pursuit of happiness."[30]

Originally, the National Union for Social Justice was organized in local units of no less than 100 members. Each unit elected a president, as did each congressional district. The activities of each state organization were to be directed by an elected state supervisor. The national leadership consisted of twelve regional supervisors under the national president, Father Coughlin himself. When some organizers, particularly in rural areas, found it very difficult to recruit 100 members, the priest changed the minimum unit membership to 50 in towns of 1,000 or more and to 25 in communities of less than 1,000. No single unit was to enroll more than 250 members.[31]

It was recommended that local unit meetings be held at least once a month, at which time the unit president would read the members a special message from Coughlin. The members were strongly urged to devote a substantial part of their meeting to a serious discussion of one or more of the sixteen principles of social justice. A strenuous effort was made in *Social Justice* to push Coughlin's own financial treatise, *Money: Questions and Answers,* as discussion material.[32]

It is clear from even a casual reading of *Social Justice* that all did not run smoothly in the early months of the national union. For example, there was considerable grumbling over the mandatory recitation of the social justice pledge at the end of each meeting. This was the troublesome formula: "I pledge to follow the example of Jesus Christ Who drove the money changers from the temple because they exploited the poor." It seems that Jews, atheists, and agnostics, and even a few Catholics and Protestants, objected to the reference to

Christ. Coughlin insisted that it remain unchanged, maintaining that Christ was referred to only as "One Who had the interests of the downtrodden at heart." There was also grave concern that outsiders might occasionally sit in on one of the meetings. It was recommended that a sergeant-at-arms be appointed for each unit to check membership cards before admitting people to the hall. Coughlin also gave orders that the units were to be addressed only by fellow members of the national union who were approved by the state officers. In addition, no mass meetings of any kind were to be conducted because it was feared that the membership might be swayed in direction "if some silver tongued politician were allowed to speak at a mass meeting of its members."[33] This last stricture was ironic in the light of Coughlin's own persuasive oratory.

The first financial report of the national union was filed on April 20 in accordance with the provisions of the Corrupt Practices Act. This report revealed that the national union had raised $101,060 in the previous two months, but that most of this sum ($76,692.17) was simply borrowed from the Radio League of the Little Flower, and an additional $2,000 from Father Coughlin's parish. Thus, only $22,368.39 had actually been contributed. Of this amount, only $925 was made up of donations of $100 and more.[34] If this report is accurate, and there is no reason to believe otherwise, it would seem clear that Father Coughlin had no large financial backers and did indeed rely upon the nickels, dimes, and dollars of the poor. The Radio League of the Little Flower also supplied free office space, machinery and clerical help, indicating the dependence of the fledgling National Union for Social Justice upon the older organization. Although it obviously did not disturb Coughlin, there is a serious question as to the propriety of using the resources and funds of the Radio League of the Little Flower for political purposes, since the donations were not solicited or donated for any such political purpose. The loan was presumably repaid, but the large expenditure in services provided was not. In all fairness, the radio priest could persuasively argue that these funds were used to further the cause of social justice, which was why he was broadcasting in the first place. The $2,000 loan from parish funds is more difficult to justify, since we have his word that the parish was short of funds. If there was any surplus parish money, it should have been placed in a sound bank to draw interest. From the statement Coughlin filed, it is clear that all the money was spent on legitimate expenses of the national union. It is generally conceded that he did not use any of the vast funds he accumulated to enrich himself.

Coughlin repeatedly exhorted the National Union for Social Justice units to endorse only candidates who had openly supported the sixteen points of the national union. Political affiliation was not a factor in the selection of candidates to endorse, but the priest stipulated that no member of the national union was to receive the endorsement of the organization. To qualify for endorsement, the candidate was expected to publish his pledge to support the principles of social justice at least three times. The central office of the national union, which was really Father Coughlin himself, reserved the right to disapprove the choices of congressional districts.[35]

The first congressional district meeting of the national union was held on April 5. In attendance were the officers of the local units and elected delegates who represented units of 100 or more members. The highlight of the meeting was a radio talk by Father Coughlin, who used the occasion to castigate both political parties for their failure to reform the monetary system: "Both have wedded their destinies to those of the international banker. Both subscribe to the common policy of financial slavery for the inarticulate masses."[36] Contrary to his earlier pronouncements, the priest informed his followers that a congressional candidate would not have to formally endorse social justice but should be judged on his past record. Once endorsed, however, the candidate was obligated to accept the support of the National

Union for Social Justice in writing and pledge himself to work for congressional control of the currency.[37]

Coughlin professed to believe that American democracy was in danger of collapse because of the appalling indifference of vast numbers of American voters. In an early issue of *Social Justice,* he predicted that "by 1940 we will be able to gauge whether or not America will remain as a democratic state."[38] As the Detroit priest envisioned it, the role of the national union was that of a civic-minded third force which could compel the selection of good candidates from both parties by ignoring party labels and supporting men on their individual merits: "The stupidity of voting for a person because he waves the Republican black banner of reaction or because he flaunts the pink pennant of New Deal Democracy is outmoded."[39] At the same time, the radio priest advised his followers to retain their regular political affiliations, since this was essential to their playing an active role in the primaries.[40]

Although Father Coughlin tried to make it absolutely clear that the national union was only to make congressional endorsements, some eager Republican candidates for county offices in St. Clair County, Illinois, circulated an advertisement announcing their support by the national union. When the *St. Louis Post Dispatch* immediately rebuked Coughlin for meddling in local politics, the priest indignantly denied any connection with the St. Clair County Republicans and the paper published a retraction.[41]

The first test of the national union's ability to influence the selection of congressional candidates came in the Pennsylvania primary of April 28. With less than a week to organize, the National Union for Social Justice nevertheless endorsed candidates in twenty-four of Pennsylvania's thirty-four congressional districts, of which twelve emerged victorious. It is impossible to assess the true influence of Father Coughlin in this election without an intimate knowledge of the political situation in the twenty-four districts involved. Of the twelve national union winners, ten were incumbents, a fact which also tends to lessen the significance of their endorsement, since the incumbent is almost always the organization candidate of his respective party. An exception to this general pattern was the victory of Michael J. Stack, incumbent Democrat of Philadelphia. The party organization repudiated Stack, but he won renomination with the aid of the national union. The national union also claimed credit for the defeat of two Democratic incumbents, William E. Richardson of Berks County and J. Twining Brooks of Pittsburgh. There is no question that the national union played an important role in the Pennsylvania primary, but an analysis of its true significance must await a closer study of Pennsylvania congressional politics of that period.[42]

Social Justice, however, revealed no such scholarly reservations in boasting of the national union's success in Pennsylvania. The May 8 issue proclaimed in banner headlines: "Victories in Pennsylvania Spur National Union's Fighters in Ohio—Nominate Twelve Candidates—Unseat Two Congressmen." For added effect, the paper optimistically claimed that most of the twenty defeated endorsees would run as independents and were virtually assured of election.[43]

Encouraged by its impressive showing in Pennsylvania, the national union entered the Ohio primary with great expectations. Coughlin claimed a quarter of a million followers in Ohio and there was ample time to organize a concerted effort since the election was scheduled for May 12. In the weeks preceding the primary, the pages of *Social Justice* brimmed with glowing accounts of national union activity and optimistic forecasts of the great victory which the organization would win. Of particular interest was the twentieth district where Representative Martin Sweeney, Father Coughlin's congressional champion, was engaged in a bitter battle for political survival. The Democratic organization in his Cleveland district was determined to drop him from the slate and the national union was equally resolved to renominate him.

Proof of the great significance attached to the Ohio primary was Coughlin's decision to campaign personally in the state.

The priest addressed an enthusiastic crowd of twenty thousand at Toledo on May 8; but his major effort was made in Cleveland on May 10, where twenty-five thousand heard him denounce machine politics and urge a return to real democracy. Coughlin exuded confidence, predicting victory in one-half of the congressional districts. This speech was carried over the priest's radio network as his regular Sunday broadcast. To insure complete coverage of Ohio, Coughlin's regular outlets WGAR, Cleveland, and WLW, Cincinnati, were supplemented for this occasion by WBNX, Columbus, and WSPD, Toledo.[44]

Coughlin's efforts in Ohio paid substantial dividends as National Union for Social Justice candidates won nominations in thirteen of the eighteen congressional districts in which they had entered candidates. In two districts, both candidates were national union endorsees. Of the fifteen victorious candidates, twelve were Democrats, only three were Republicans. Something Father Coughlin and his enthusiastic followers preferred to overlook was that seventeen of their thirty-two candidates lost. Of the seventeen defeated only six were Democrats; eleven were Republicans.[45]

Unquestionably, Coughlin scored an impressive victory in Ohio, but a truly accurate estimate of his influence is impossible without detailed knowledge of political conditions and personalities in the eighteen Ohio congressional districts. *Social Justice,* of course, claimed a great victory for the national union: "Smashing Success in Ohio Primaries Added To National Union Victory Roll."[46] But *The New York Times* was almost equally impressed: "Not only did the National Union for Social Justice score a triumph over incumbent lawmakers, but apparently fifteen of its thirty-two endorsees were nominated with the possibility of the sixteenth being added by the late returns." The article continued: "The strength of the National Union for Social Justice was one of the big surprises of the state-wide primary."[47] The *Cleveland Press* also acknowledged the national union's strength in Ohio: "The Coughlin organization demonstrated impressive strength in yesterday's primary. Nowhere was Coughlin's influence more effective than Cuyahoga County. Congressman Sweeney was one of its beneficiaries, as was Congressman Crosser. . . . In no other state primary held thus far were the Coughlin forces so well organized and active as Ohio." The article further stated: "The large measure of success that resulted from their efforts will undoubtedly stimulate organization in other states. Politicians can look forward to a fall campaign, therefore, complicated by a new and important factor of a sort they have not had to contend with for years."[48]

Although Coughlin had devoted most of his attention in the spring to organizing the national union and to the Pennsylvania and Ohio primaries, he continued to wage a relentless campaign for the Frazier-Lemke bill. The Frazier-Lemke petition finally received the necessary 218 signatures on April 30 and the bill was scheduled for debate on May 11.[49] Whether this was attributable to Father Coughlin's efforts is still a matter of conjecture. It is very possible that some congressmen signed the petition merely for the sake of putting an end to all the agitation. The opposition to the bill centered their attention on what they termed its inflationary aspects but some eastern representatives declared they would support such a bill if an amendment were added to include Eastern homeowners in the program. *The New York Times* and *Social Justice* agreed that the turning point in the debate came when Speaker Joseph W. Byrns read a letter from AFL President William Green, asserting labor's opposition to the measure as inflationary and requesting all friends of labor to vote against it.[50] The bill went down to a crushing 235-142 defeat, the responsibility for which the Detroit priest laid squarely upon the shoulders of the AFL chieftain. Coughlin described Green as an "honest" but "incapable" labor leader who through ignorance had allowed himself to be used as a tool of the money interests.[51] A final attempt to pass the Frazier-Lemke bill in the Senate as an amendment to the Guffey Cash Act failed by a 34-17 vote in July.

It was immediately evident that Coughlin was not going to

take the defeat of the Frazier-Lemke bill lightly. In a May 29 *Social Justice* editorial entitled "The Last Straw," the radio priest savagely attacked the opponents of monetary reform in both parties who had defeated the bill and strongly suggested the possibility of future retribution:

> With the defeat of the Frazier-Lemke bill the last straw has fallen upon our wearied backs. The last hope for financial reform under the New Deal has vanished. Approximately 150 members of Congress have been driven, politically and economically, into no man's land. Untold numbers of American citizens who believe in democracy and the high purpose of this nation have been driven with them. . . . These 150 Congressmen and their millions of constituents will not remain bewildered in no man's land nor will they return in desperation to the New Deal which is nothing more than the Old Deal turned inside out. Take this determination for what it is worth.[52]

In the wake of Coughlin's primary successes in Pennsylvania and Ohio and his angry resentment over the Frazier-Lemke defeat, a fresh crop of rumors emerged to the effect that the priest was going to form a new political party by merging his followers with the Townsendites and the Share-the-Wealthers now under the leadership of the Rev. Gerald L. K. Smith. The latter gave this rumor considerable impetus by his public statement that the political tactics of Jim Farley were forcing the organizations to consolidate their strength.[53]

Coughlin himself compounded the confusion by strongly hinting at the formation of a third party in the May 29 issue of *Social Justice*. His "Weekly Letter," a regular back-cover feature of the paper, began with the question "Where Do We Go From Here?" and implied that the primary victories in Pennsylvania and Ohio were but the forerunners of bigger and better things to come. It was his concluding paragraph, however, which raised political eyebrows around the country. "Within two or three weeks, I shall be able to disclose the first chapter of a plan, which if followed out, will discomfort the erstwhile sham battlers, both Republican and Democrat. We must go to victory from the primaries."[54]

Attracted by the news potentialities of Coughlin's statement, both *The New York Times* and *New York Sun* tried to persuade the radio priest to clarify his intentions. He informed both papers that he was not considering the formation of a third party. In a telephone interview with *The New York Times*, the Detroit priest said he could not support Roosevelt in any case, but would consider supporting the Republicans if they reformed and nominated a good candidate, but he left no doubt that he did not deem Alf Landon, Governor of Kansas and frontrunner for the Republican nomination, worthy of consideration. In the event of a Roosevelt-Landon race, the priest insisted, he would concentrate his efforts on the congressional races and bide his time until the 1940 presidential election.[55]

Father Coughlin replied to *The New York Sun* by telegram: "I have not contemplated the launching of a so-called third party. A renovated Republican party possessing a contrite heart for its former misdeeds and an honest standard bearer in whom I could repose complete confidence are all that are necessary to convert this nation from ruinous Rooseveltism." The telegram continued, "Otherwise the re-election of Roosevelt is inevitable, with the result that our liberties will be likewise exploited."[56]

The irrational nature of Coughlin's hostility toward the New Deal was never more clearly manifested than in his "Weekly Letter" of the June 5 *Social Justice*. After reiterating at some length his familiar charge that Roosevelt had reneged on his promise to reform the monetary system, the radio priest dramatically attempted to link Roosevelt with communism: "The opposing lines are already drawn. The Roosevelt administration, on one hand, bent on communistic revolution: on the other, a public opinion progressively enlightened, as never before, on matters of monetary finance." Coughlin went on to accuse Roosevelt of establishing a personal dictatorship in order to install regimentation with little interference. Roosevelt was not wholly damned, however; the priest conceded that the President was probably not fully aware of his administration's drift toward communism, but was "being driven by sinister influences he does not fully comprehend."[57] Elsewhere in the paper, Coughlin had identified one of these "sinister influences" as Rexford Guy Tugwell, one of Roosevelt's top braintrusters. The priest assailed Tugwell as "a premier parlor pink" and the "number one meddler in the private affairs of people victimized by capitalism gone vicious."[58] Coughlin was to repeat these same preposterous charges throughout the presidential campaign of 1936.

Despite such bitter criticism of the New Deal, the priest continued to deny all third-party intentions. But between denials he gave every indication that he was about to launch a new political movement. In the June 12 issue of *Social Justice* he urged all readers to stand by for future developments of great significance: "The activities of the National Union will increase tremendously immediately following June 16th or 17th. Approximately at that time I shall lay down a plan for action which will thrill you and inspire you beyond anything that I have ever said or accomplished in the past." He continued, "Already the plan is completed. The statement is prepared. The element of time prevents my mentioning it at this moment." Clearly hinting at the possibility of a new party, Father Coughlin asked his followers to have complete faith in his judgment for the next six months and to await patiently the full explanation of his future conduct which would be found weekly in *Social Justice*. He also announced that no congressman who had opposed the Frazier-Lemke bill could be endorsed by the national union.[59]

Shortly after Coughlin's "standby" message appeared in *Social Justice*, the Maine primaries were held. Despite the ironclad conservative Republican control of the state, the national union had worked diligently to nominate three candidates favorable to the social justice program. Although only one of the three, James C. Oliver, a South Portland Republican, actually won, *The New York Times* gave Coughlin credit for the near-record turnout in Maine and expressed genuine surprise at his strength within the Republican party.[60]

Only a few days before his June 19 broadcast, the first of a special summer series, the radio priest admitted to a *New York Times* reporter that he considered a third party near, but denied that he himself would play an active role in its formation and absolutely refused to speculate upon the identity of possible candidates. Not so discreet was the brash Gerald L. K. Smith, who stole Coughlin's thunder by announcing that a coalition had already been formed of Father Coughlin's followers, his own Share-the-Wealth movement, Townsendites, and supporters of Representative William Lemke of North Dakota. Dr. Townsend at once denied having made any commitments but indicated he would be willing to consider a third party if the occasion presented itself.[61]

It was generally assumed that Coughlin was going to name his own presidential candidate and launch the new party on his first summer broadcast, but there was a great deal of confusion over the identity of the candidate. The full story has not yet been revealed, but *The New York Times* implied that Father Coughlin had so much difficulty over the selection of an acceptable candidate who would be willing to make the race that it appeared for some time that the priest would have to broadcast without a candidate.[62] In view of Coughlin's close association with William Lemke during the long, unsuccessful struggle for enactment of the Frazier-Lemke bill and Smith's premature announcement of the new political alliance, the *Times* story would appear to be nothing more than journalistic speculation.

Whatever the backstage machinations might have been, Coughlin took to the airways on June 19 and announced his support of Representative William Lemke for president on a new Union party ticket. Although he said little that was new, the talk revealed his deep sense of personal betrayal by Roosevelt. Even with allowances for oratorical effect, it is still a rather moving speech:

At last, when the most brilliant minds among the industrialists, bankers, and their kept politicians had failed to solve these questions on the principles upon which the Old Deal had operated, there appeared upon the scene of our national life a new champion of the people, Franklin D. Roosevelt. He spoke golden words of hope to the people. Never since the days of the gentle Master and His Sermon on the Mount were such humanitarian principles enunciated. . . . The thrill that was mine was yours. Through dim clouds of the depression this man, Roosevelt, was, as it were, a new saviour of his people. . . . It is not pleasant for me who coined the phrase "Roosevelt or ruin"—a phrase based upon promises—to voice such passionate words. But I am constrained to admit that "Roosevelt *and* ruin" is the order of the day because the money changers have not been driven from the temple.[63]

The Republicans were also castigated in colorful Coughlin fashion: "Alas! These Punch and Judy Republicans, whose actions and words were dominated by the ventriloquists of Wall Street, are so blind that they do not recognize, even in this perilous hour, that their gold basis and their private coinage of money have bred more radicals than did Karl Marx or Lenin. To their system of oxcart financialism we must never return."[64]

America's hope, Coughlin contended, lay in nominating a man not bound to either party who could be counted on to reform the currency. Such a man, the priest maintained, was Bill Lemke. Actually, Father Coughlin did not nominate the North Dakota congressman, but simply declared him "eligible for endorsement by the National Union for Social Justice" and invited the support of the Townsendites, farmers, laborers, and all other groups. The Detroit priest attempted a rather forced comparison between Lemke and the Union party of 1936 and Lincoln's Union party of 1864 whence he derived the new party's name: "In 1864 when Lincoln proposed to abolish physical slavery there was established a 'Union Party.' In 1936, when we are determined to annihilate financial slavery, we welcome the 'Union Party' because it has the courage to go to the root of our troubles." Lemke himself was described as "a man who had made promises in the past and has kept them."[65] For vice president, the priest revealed that Lemke had chosen Thomas C. O'Brien of Massachusetts, former district attorney of Boston and counsel for the Brotherhood of Railroad Trainmen. Theoretically, the new party had a balanced ticket: Lemke was a Westerner, a Protestant, a Republican, a representative of the farm interest, O'Brien was an Easterner, a Catholic, a Democrat, and a representative of labor's interests.

Father Coughlin addressing a mass meeting in Detroit

With English Socialist
Dr. Hewlett Johnson,
Dean of Canterbury

Calling at the White
House — early in 1936

Wide World Photo

Acme Photo

With Dr. Francis E.
Townsend before ad-
dressing the Townsend
Old Age Pension
Convention

Acme Photo

Father Coughlin with his constant companion, Pal

With Governor Curley in
Boston after anti-Roosevelt
speech, June, 1936

Delivering "Scab President" speech in Detroit, October, 1936

Police escort after Madison Square
Garden address to 20,000

Father Coughlin in 1935

Delegates cheer nomination of Father Coughlin for first president
of National Union for Social Justice. Convention has just endorsed
Lemke and O'Brien as candidates for president and vice-president
of the U.S., 1936

Acme Photo

Union Party candidates William Lemke, left, and Thomas C. O'Brien with Father Coughlin at the N.U.S.J. Convention

Discussing the bank situation with Attorney General Patrick O'Brien of Michigan

Wide World Photo

Father Coughlin at 65, at the Shrine of the Little
Flower in Royal Oak, Michigan, in 1956

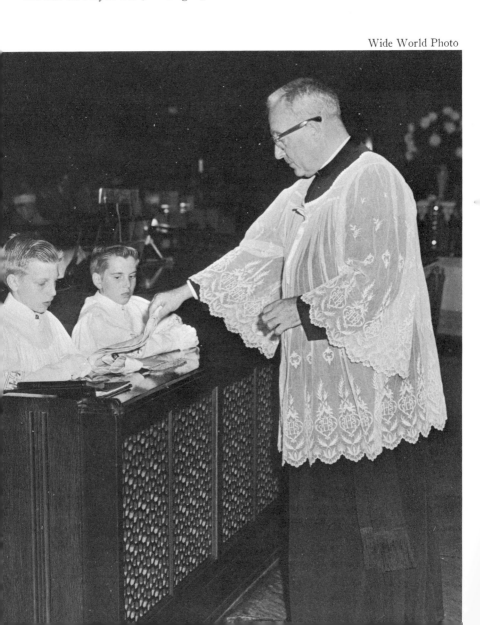

V

LEMKE FOR PRESIDENT

WILLIAM LEMKE was probably as good a candidate as the Coughlin forces could muster. He was thought to have strong support in the farm belt due to his consistent championing of farm legislation. He had received a great deal of favorable publicity in his unsuccessful fight to enact the Frazier-Lemke farm mortgage bill. Lemke, born in Stearns County, Minnesota, grew up in Tonner County, North Dakota, near the Canadian border. After working his way through the University of North Dakota, he journeyed east and repeated the process at the Yale Law School. He then became involved in a land speculation venture in Mexico that was a complete fiasco. The young Dakota lawyer considered Wilson's failure to recognize the Huerta regime the cause of his Mexican debacle and wrote a bitter attack on Wilson's Mexican policy, *Crimes Against Mexico*, which appeared in 1915.

Following the collapse of his Mexican land scheme, Lemke returned to North Dakota and became extremely active in politics. He was one of Arthur Townley's most energetic assistants in the organization of the Non-Partisan League in 1915. Lemke was a registered Republican but had no deep affection for the Grand Old Party, running under its banner solely because his own Non-Partisan League dominated that party in North Dakota. He was respected as a hardworking, conscientious representative of the farmers' interests. Lemke had previously served as attorney general of North Dakota during the controversial governorship of Lynn Frazier. He was re-

127

called, along with Frazier, in 1921 in a dispute over the operation of the Bank of North Dakota. In 1922 Lemke made an unsuccessful bid for the governorship, losing by twenty thousand votes. He was first sent to Congress in 1932, and reelected in 1934. From all accounts the North Dakotan lacked personal magnetism and was almost completely overshadowed by the colorful personality of his sponsor, Father Coughlin. Lemke was obviously not very confident of his presidential prospects, as he remained a candidate for reelection to Congress on the Republican ticket.

Thomas C. O'Brien, the vice-presidential nominee, was an obscure Massachusetts Irish-Catholic politician. In true Horatio Alger fashion, O'Brien had worked his way through Harvard as a railroad baggage man. In addition to serving as the district attorney of Suffolk County, he was also the regular counsel of the Brotherhood of Railroad Trainmen. Like Lemke, O'Brien did not put all his political eggs in one basket; he was also the Coughlin candidate for senator against Mayor Curley and Henry Cabot Lodge, Jr. O'Brien was such a political nonentity that it is difficult to escape the conclusion that he was tapped by Coughlin solely because he was an Irish Catholic from Massachusetts.

As with many other important matters relating to Father Coughlin, the inside story of the Union party's origin remains an enigma. For months the Detroit priest had denied any thought of a third party; then, in a complete reversal, he launched a new party only a few short months before the election. The decision to support a presidential ticket was so ill-timed that it strongly suggests that Coughlin acted on impulse while still smarting from the Frazier-Lemke bill defeat. He did reveal in *Social Justice* that friends of Lemke had approached him concerning Lemke's candidacy "many weeks ago." Coughlin disclosed he had agreed with them that Roosevelt must be removed because "it was realized how impossible future congressional activities would be unless a sympathetic President occupied the Chair of the White House and permitted Congress to fulfill its Constitutional function." The

Royal Oak priest insisted that Lemke's candidacy had not altered his own position or that of the National Union for Social Justice: "Let no idle rumor deceive you that the National Union is amalgamating with the Townsendites, the Share-the-Wealthers, the AFL, the Socialist Party or any other organization. Independent of every organization we upon our own initiative are preparing to endorse Federal candidates." The priest continued: "If these other organizations, independent of us, determine to endorse them, that is their business. If they choose to take the same step which we have taken, that is their responsibility."[1]

Never was Father Coughlin's authoritarian control over the national union revealed more clearly than in his endorsement of Lemke on his own initiative without so much as consulting the officers of his own organization. It is true that he qualified his action to some extent by saying that he found Lemke "eligible for endorsement by the National Union for Social Justice," but no one doubted that the national union convention, scheduled for August, would merely ratify the priest's choice. Dramatic proof of Father Coughlin's hold upon his followers is the fact that twelve thousand telegrams endorsing Lemke arrived within a few hours of the priest's talk. Thus we have the ironic spectacle of Coughlin using dictatorial tactics to nominate a man to defeat Roosevelt because the President had become a dictator. But history is replete with examples of reformers who overthrew dictatorships only to establish their own brand of authoritarianism.

For reasons known best to himself, Father Coughlin had failed to consult with either Townsend or Smith before making his own announcement of support for Lemke. At first it appeared that the radio priest was going to be forced to go it alone, as both Townsend and Smith were reported to have serious doubts about supporting Lemke. Both said they would have to consult their followers before taking any action.[2] Townsend was undoubtedly sincere, but Smith, having already announced a marginal coalition with Coughlin, was apparently procrastinating in the hope of wringing certain concessions from Lemke. Eventually, both men actively campaigned for Lemke.

Whatever limited possibility of success Lemke enjoyed was clearly contingent upon the active cooperation of the national union, the Townsend clubs, and the Share-the-Wealth movement. Coughlin claimed to have 5,000,000 members in his national union, Smith boasted that he controlled 3,000,000 votes, and Townsend with 5,000,000 members maintained that he could influence 20,000,000 votes.[3] But as the November election was to prove, there is a vast difference between potential support and actual votes.

Reaction to the Union party's birth followed a fairly predictable course. Senator Elmer Thomas, a close associate of Coughlin in the 1934 silver crusade, declared himself still in favor of monetary reform as suggested in the Union party platform, but avoided the real issue of Lemke's candidacy.[4] The irrepressible renegade Republican from Idaho, William Borah, endorsed the money and labor planks of the new party and praised Lemke as a man for whom he had great respect, but refrained from actually supporting the new party.[5] President Roosevelt's personal reaction to the Union party threat was not officially recorded, but the usually reliable *New York Times* reported that the President had telephoned party leaders assembled in Philadelphia for the Democratic convention and had discussed the course of action the party should pursue with respect to Lemke and Coughlin. The strategy decided upon, according to the *Times*, was for Roosevelt to make an intensive appeal to the farm vote by strengthening the farm plank and directing many of his campaign speeches to the farmer. The *Times* reported that some Democratic leaders were afraid that Lemke would draw enough votes away from Roosevelt to give Landon a chance of capturing certain key western states—Minnesota, North Dakota, South Dakota, and Montana.[6] Despite the lack of documentation, there is reason to believe that the Democrats took the Union party as a serious threat in the 1936 campaign, at least in the early stages. For the record, however, both party chairmen, Jim Farley and

John D. Hamilton, refused to comment on the significance of the Lemke ticket. The most prompt and direct response to Coughlin's new party came from David Lawrence, Democratic State Chairman of Pennsylvania, who immediately wired all Democratic county chairmen to preempt the name of the National Union for Social Justice so that Coughlin's followers would be confused when they attempted to vote for Lemke. This rather unsportsmanlike tactic was easy to employ in Pennsylvania where the law required only five voters in a county to sign a petition to place a slate on the ballot.[7] Coughlinites solved the dilemma by running Lemke on the Royal Oak ticket in Pennsylvania.

Newspaper comment on the new party was universally critical; not a single important paper supported Lemke. The *New York Herald Tribune* called the Union party a "serious menace" to the administration and predicted it would hurt the Democrats more than the Republicans.[8] *The New York Times* maintained that it was too early to predict the importance of the new party in the outcome of the race but accurately prophesied that the Union party would have serious difficulty getting on the ballot in most states.[9] The *Philadelphia Bulletin* conceded that Father Coughlin's party might possibly play a vital role in 1936 but shared the view of many observers that Lemke was overshadowed by the Royal Oak priest.[10] *The New Republic* speculated that Lemke, with the support of both Father Coughlin and Dr. Townsend, might poll enough votes in certain strategic states to swing them away from Roosevelt to Landon. The liberal weekly had no quarrel with the Detroit priest's program as outlined in the Union party platform, but it doubted Coughlin's ability to carry it out without recourse to fascism. The magazine had been a strong advocate of a national Farmer-Laborer party, but its hopes were dashed by the failure of the Farmer-Laborer convention, meeting at Chicago in May, to name a presidential candidate.[11] Just one week later *The New Republic* published an article by its regular political columnist, T.R.B., stating that the Union party marked the entrance of the Catholic Church into American politics. The writer gave three reasons to support his controversial thesis: (1) Coughlin was the logical choice to organize Christian Socialism in America; (2) the Vatican was losing influence all over the world and was relying more and more on the United States; (3) many American Catholics opposed Roosevelt on religious grounds: his son's divorce, his wife's support of birth control, and his appointment of the supposedly anti-Catholic Josephus Daniels as ambassador to Mexico had alienated many Catholics.[12] A writer in another influential liberal weekly, *The Nation*, took the view that the Union party would hurt Landon more than Roosevelt. The editors correctly saw Roosevelt as the only issue in the election. Thus, to *The Nation*, Lemke's candidacy simply meant that some anti-Roosevelt votes would go to the North Dakota congressman instead of the Kansas governor.[13]

The Union party platform,[14] was nothing more than a rehashing of the National Union for Social Justice sixteen points, except for the glaring omission of any reference to nationalizing "power, light, oil, natural gas and other natural resources," as specified in point three. Since Coughlin had already accused the Roosevelt administration of drifting into communism, point three simply was not expedient in 1936. Notable by their absence were the programs of the Townsendites and the Share-the-Wealthers. The aged were vaguely promised "reasonable and decent security" in the sixth plank. Only indirect sympathy was shown to the share-the-wealth idea in the fourteenth plank which recommended "a limitation upon the net income of any one individual in any one year." Like most political manifestos, the Union party platform was extremely vague. As could be expected, it called for enactment of Father Coughlin's central bank scheme, the direct control of all coinage by Congress, and the recall of all interest-bearing bonds. Other key points were a guaranteed annual wage for all who were willing to work and a promise of production at a profit for the farmer. Aside from the monetary provisions, no hint was given as to how any of these goals were to be achieved.

Soon after Father Coughlin's "nominating" speech of June 19, Lemke and O'Brien both came to Royal Oak to plan their battle strategy with Coughlin, another strong evidence of the priest's dominant role. Little is known of this meeting except for Coughlin's announcement that Lemke's candidacy did not change the congressional endorsements already made by the national union. Only in areas where there were no acceptable Democrat, Republican, or Farmer-Laborite candidates in the race would a Union party candidate be placed on the ballot. An important new condition was attached to all candidates receiving the support of the national union: they were forbidden to support either Roosevelt or Landon. But they were not obligated to support Lemke; silence could be their discreet way out of their dilemma. It was also disclosed that Chicago had been selected as the Union party's national headquarters and that Representative Usher Burdick, an independent Republican from South Dakota, had been named national chairman.[15]

Another interesting political development at this time was the entrance of Louis B. Ward, Father Coughlin's close friend and Washington lobbyist, into the Michigan Democratic primary race for United States senator. As could be expected, Coughlin enthusiastically supported Ward's candidacy in *Social Justice*.[16]

The Union party campaign, as such, officially opened July 4 when Father Coughlin journeyed to Brockton, Massachusetts, and assailed the Roosevelt administration before ten thousand enthusiastic supporters. The Detroit priest castigated Roosevelt for "out-Hoovering Hoover" by saddling the American people with $35,000,000,000 of public debt. He also used the occasion to support O'Brien's bid for the United States Senate against Henry Cabot Lodge and James Michael Curley.[17] From Massachusetts, Coughlin traveled to Trenton, New Jersey, where he conferred with twelve hundred national union officials and promised to return in the fall if they could guarantee a crowd of a hundred thousand.[18] One result of Coughlin's New Jersey visit was the appeal of twenty National Union for Social Justice representatives to Governor Hoffman to call a special session of the Legislature to amend the election laws to make it possible for Lemke's name to go on the ballot. The governor refused. From Trenton Coughlin moved on to Philadelphia and consulted with seven hundred National Union for Social Justice aides on the role they were to play in the campaign.[19] Continuing his whirlwind tour of key states, the priest appeared before eighty national union leaders in Chicago and predicted that Lemke would carry Rhode Island, Massachusetts, Pennsylvania, and Michigan. Defending his own platform as very conservative, the Detroit priest contended: "The only radicals I know are Democrats, Republicans, and Socialists."[20]

The Union party needed the enthusiastic support of the Townsendites, and so Father Coughlin secured an invitation to speak to the national convention of the Townsend movement, which was held in Cleveland in mid-July. Appearing at his oratorical peak, Coughlin held his elderly audience of ten thousand spellbound for half an hour as he eloquently persuaded them to support Lemke. The priest reminded the Townsend delegates that their beloved leader had already endorsed Lemke and assured them they would not lose their identity by supporting the Union party. At the dramatic climax, Coughlin asked all those who supported Lemke to stand. No one in the hall remained seated. Intoxicated by the oratorical spell he was casting, Father Coughlin ripped off his coat and Roman collar and hysterically accused Roosevelt of being both a "liar" and "a great betrayer" for not having fulfilled his pledges to reform the monetary system. The initials F.D.R., the priest shouted, really stood for Franklin Doublecrossing Roosevelt. He also challenged the President on the support he was receiving from the American Communist party, the insinuation being clear that Roosevelt must be doing something to deserve their assistance.

Another high point of the radio priest's appearance was a semi-vaudeville routine, with Congressman Sweeney of Ohio as his straight man. The priest summoned Sweeney to the speaker's rostrum and had the congressman publicly reiterate his loyalty to the National Union for Social Justice:

> Coughlin: Although the National Union for Social Justice has endorsed you as a Democrat, are you aware that if you support Roosevelt, you lose that endorsement?
> Sweeney: I have answered by my criticism of Roosevelt during the last four years. I know he is a doublecrosser. I stand with the National Union.

So willing were the faithful to be converted that even this ludicrous theatrical stunt seemed to impress them.

Unquestionably, the Townsend convention marked Coughlin's greatest oratorical triumph. He completely won the Townsendites and stampeded them into an enthusiastic though unofficial endorsement of the Union party ticket. Prior to the convention both Townsend and Smith, although freely admitting they favored Lemke, had withheld their full support, apparently fearful of backing a hopeless cause. Coughlin's warm reception and convincing oratory seemingly turned the tide in Lemke's favor. The high-water mark of the Coughlin-Townsend-Smith partnership came at the close of Coughlin's address when the three posed amiably for photographers. The priest playfully poked the Rev. Smith in the ribs, threw his arms around Dr. Townsend's shoulders, and informed the world that they stood together in their crusade for Lemke.

Coughlin's powers of persuasion appear even more potent when it is realized that the very same audience had wildly cheered Roosevelt when Gomer Smith, the Townsend senatorial candidate from Oklahoma, had previously praised the President for saving the United States from communism.[21] Congressman Lemke also spoke to the delegates, but his pedestrian oratory was anticlimactic, following as it did on the heels of such dramatic speakers as Gerald L. K. Smith and Father Coughlin. Lemke assured the oldsters that he was in favor of old-age revolving pensions, but did not commit himself specifically to the Townsend Plan.[22]

Despite Coughlin's impressive victory at Cleveland, harmony

did not reign within the Townsend movement. Dr. Townsend appeared far from enthusiastic over the new partnership and challenged the priest to offer constructive suggestions "if he was really eager to save the country."[23] But in view of Coughlin's previous disparagement of the Townsend Plan (the May 22 *Social Justice* had ridiculed the principles of the Townsend clubs as "absolutely not practical"), it was quite an achievement for the two men to get together on any basis. One Townsendite congressman, Martin F. Smith of Washington, actually spoke against Lemke at the meeting and pleaded with his fellows not to endorse the North Dakotan: "We are not going to lose with Lemke. We are going to triumph with Townsend." He was also rewarded with tumultuous applause by the same audience which would so enthusiastically receive Father Coughlin's plea for Lemke on the following day.[24] The receptivity of the Townsendites to any and all spellbinding orators, regardless of conflicting principles, reveals their total lack of objectivity. Discontented, often destitute, the Townsendites were ready to believe anyone who appealed to their emotions and promised them succor. Thus they were putty in the hands of an emotional orator of Coughlin's great talents.

One disgruntled Townsendite, Gomer Smith, unsuccessful in his convention effort to hold the Townsendites for Roosevelt, bought radio time in the Southwest to warn his followers that Townsend was being tricked by Coughlin and Gerald L. K. Smith, neither of whom really intended to work for the Townsend Plan. Smith was particularly vehement about the Detroit priest, describing his talk at Cleveland as "the most radical and un-American speech I have ever heard."[25]

As might well be expected, the spectacle of a Roman Catholic priest labeling the President of the United States "a liar" before ten thousand people at a public political rally caused a furor in the nation's press. Many Americans felt that the priest had at last overreached himself and would finally be curbed by his Church. As fate would have it, Coughlin's religious superior, Bishop Michael Gallagher of Detroit, was in New York at the time preparing to embark for Rome and a visit to the Pope. When reached for an interview, the bishop defended his subordinate unequivocally: "There are a lot of people who would like the Church to discipline Father Coughlin because they would like him out of the way, but as far as I am concerned, and he is directly under my authority, he is working along the right path and he has my support."[26] Speculation continued, however, that the Vatican was about to crack down on the Royal Oak pastor. *The New York Times* on July 24 carried a report that Bishop Gallagher was going to Rome primarily to discuss Father Coughlin. Another story to the effect that the Apostolic Delegate to the United States was preparing a special report on the Detroit priest was promptly denied by that diplomat. Coughlin's public apology to Roosevelt on July 23 served only to add more fuel to the rumors. The *Times* reported that it had learned from a "reliable source" that the Vatican had reached Coughlin by radio and ordered him to apologize.[27] In his apology, the priest explained that his speech at Cleveland had been extemporaneous and he had used the term "liar" in the heat of impassioned oratory. If he had spoken from a prepared text, he contended, the term would never have been used. Coughlin added that he had received a phone call from Dr. Townsend on the night before asking his help to prevent Gomer Smith from taking over the convention and that this accounted for his no-holds-barred approach.[28] In the text of the apology, the priest proudly reminded the President of his early support and demonstrated once again that he considered himself partly responsible for Roosevelt's election: "I was one of the first, and not one of the least, to help you attain the presidency." Coughlin went on to say that he still had high regard for the President as a man and a fellow citizen but not as President. He even conceded that Roosevelt was probably well-intentioned.[29]

Bishop Gallagher, arriving in Rome a few days after Coughlin's public apology, was once again besieged by reporters. He reaffirmed his faith in Father Coughlin and emphatically denied any Vatican intercession. The bishop put himself on record as agreeing with Coughlin that Roosevelt had not carried out promises he had made to enact monetary reforms.[30] The Detroit prelate insisted that he had never discussed Father Coughlin's political activities with the Pope and had not come to Rome to do so at that time.[31]

The "liar" speech also served to break the silence of Democratic Chairman James A. Farley, who had hitherto refused to comment on the Union party. Farley expressed the view that Father Coughlin had hurt himself more than anyone else by his violent attack on the President, and wrote off the Union party as an insignificant factor in the campaign.[32]

Undaunted by the international furor he was creating, Coughlin continued to stump for Lemke and to stir up new controversies. On July 25 he spoke to a crowd of twenty thousand at Hamburg, New York, and bitterly denounced Governor Herbert Lehman, who was running for reelection, for vetoing a school bus bill which would have provided public transportation for pupils of all schools.[33] Addressing fifteen thousand farmers at Harrison, North Dakota, on July 26, the priest was quoted as advising them to repudiate their debts if Lemke lost the election. When harshly criticized for advocating fiscal irresponsibility, Coughlin replied that he had been misquoted because of the poor public address system. What he had really said was that farmers would have no choice but repudiation unless some aid was extended to them. He challenged Eastern newsmen to visit the Dakotas and investigate the desperate plight of the farmer in an area that was fast becoming an "American Sahara."[34] When reporters questioned Bishop Gallagher on Coughlin's alleged suggestion of debt repudiation, the bishop, as ever loyal to his subordinate, praised him for calling the public's attention to the miserable lot of the American farmers, who were losing their farms at a rate of two thousand a day.[35]

Almost forgotten in the raucous turmoil generated by Coughlin's activities, and drawing few headlines, was the hapless presidential candidate of the Union party, William Lemke. Launching his campaign in the West the last week in June, Lemke made speeches at Burlington, Iowa, and Moorhead,

Minnesota, emphasizing monetary reform as the only solution to the farmer's ills and the nation's.

Coughlin continued to hit the campaign trail during the month of August, and his attacks became increasingly bitter. He told ten thousand people at Worcester, Massachusetts, that Landon was a "menace" and predicted a revolution if the Kansas Governor were elected President. The violence of his attack on Landon was somewhat surprising; he usually reserved that kind of treatment for Roosevelt.[36] On the following day at New Bedford, Massachusetts, Coughlin reverted to form and centered his fire once again on the President. Going from the merely extreme to the ludicrous, he clearly labeled Roosevelt a communist: "As I was instrumental in removing Herbert Hoover from the White House, so help me God, I will be instrumental in taking a Communist out of the chair once occupied by Washington." This charge was repeated at Providence, Rhode Island, on the same day.[37]

The real highlight of the campaign, as far as Coughlin was concerned, was the national convention of the National Union for Social Justice held at Cleveland, August 13-16, where the priest's followers finally got their chance to ratify the nomination of Lemke. Not to be outdone by other conventions, the national union sent ten thousand delegates to Cleveland to represent a membership estimated by *Social Justice* at six million. The atmosphere resembled that of a religious revival rather than a political meeting. The faithful eagerly snapped up 11,500 portraits of the radio priest at 25 cents each.

There was no mistaking the fact that Father Coughlin was their leader and could have anything he wanted from this convention. The keynote address was given by Senator Rush Holt of West Virginia, who dramatically extolled the virtues of the sixteen-point program of the national union without any reference to the Union party. Holt, who was not even a member of the National Union for Social Justice, reportedly took the speaking assignment only after it had been refused by Senator Thomas of Oklahoma and Senator McCarran of Nevada.

After a tumultuous welcome, Coughlin was, to no one's surprise, unanimously elected President of the National Union for Social Justice. The priest was nominated in almost reverent tones by Miss Helen E. Martin of the Bronx, New York, and warmly seconded by Louis Ward and a long list of other national union officials. As expected, the priest had little difficulty securing Lemke's endorsement. One delegate, John O'Donnell of Pittsburgh, protested and was promptly ejected from the hall as a troublemaker. Only the intercession of Father Coughlin prevented his suffering a severe beating from the enraged mob. O'Donnell, whose lone negative vote made the official tally 8,152 to 1 in favor of Lemke's endorsement, claimed to be an admirer of Father Coughlin, but objected to seeing the delegates made victims of mob psychology. From all contemporary reports, the Detroit priest's handling of the convention could be used as an outstanding exhibit in any college course dealing with mob psychology. Coughlin was their messiah, and these people came prepared to obey humbly his every wish. There was little real discussion on anything; Coughlin had already appointed himself their president before the delegates voted him the honor, and he had already selected Lemke for them. There was nothing that remained for the delegates but the formal ratification of their leader's actions.

Aside from O'Donnell's "betrayal" there was only one other discordant note in the proceedings. Walter P. Davis, Grand Marshal of the Convention, tried to bar Dr. Townsend and the Rev. Smith from speaking at the meeting. Mr. Davis was quickly overruled by Father Coughlin who upheld his invitation to the aforementioned gentlemen, but carefully arranged their appearances so that he himself would have the last word at a giant outdoor rally in Cleveland Municipal Stadium. Townsend and Smith spoke to the National Union for Social Justice on Saturday afternoon after the convention had officially adjourned. Both received cordial receptions but said nothing of real significance. Of more importance was Coughlin's self-styled "lecture" to a group of reporters during the final business session of the convention. The priest challenged all Jews to adopt the Christian view of "love thy neighbor as thyself" in place of the old Hebrew law of "an eye for an eye, a tooth for a tooth." Coughlin tried to explain how the unjust treatment of the Jews by the Christians had forced the Jews into becoming money-lenders because gold was the only form of wealth that the persecuted Jews were able to carry with them. After building quite a strong case against Christians for the cruel treatment they inflicted upon the oppressed Jews, he suddenly switched and implied strongly that the time had come for the Jews to mend their ways and act like good Christians. All things considered, it was a very confusing performance, but it is difficult to escape the conclusion that it revealed definite hostility to Jews on the part of the priest, conscious or not. Severely criticized by the *Detroit Jewish Chronicle* for this speech, Coughlin absolutely denied any anti-Semitism and took pains to show that he had been equally critical of gentile money interests such as the House of Morgan. It is entirely possible that the priest did not intend any slur upon the Jewish people. It would have been sheer folly on his part to alienate so numerous a group during a presidential campaign.

The climax of the convention was an outdoor rally at Cleveland Municipal Stadium on Sunday afternoon. A highly partisan crowd of forty-two thousand ardent Coughlinites heard the Detroit priest renew his promise to fight for monetary reform and deplore the lack of Christian charity in the operation of the government. Buoyed by the tremendous enthusiasm of the convention, he rashly threw caution to the winds and boasted: "If I don't deliver 9,000,000 votes for William Lemke, I'm through with radio forever." Before he could complete his talk, Coughlin dramatically collapsed and had to be assisted from the platform. Congressman Sweeney, who had been at the side of the priest throughout the convention, later announced that Father Coughlin was suffering from heat prostration and nervous indigestion.

Both Lemke and O'Brien appeared before the same crowd and received loud and enthusiastic welcomes. Lemke exuded confidence, flatly predicting victory for the Union party: "We are going to win. The Union Party's bid for the Presidency and the Vice Presidency of the United States will not be a campaign of defeatism." O'Brien attacked AFL chieftain William Green for his opposition to the Frazier-Lemke bill and prophesied that most of labor would reject the leadership of Green and support the Union party. Thus ended one of the most unusual conventions ever held in the United States. *Commonweal* aptly described Father Coughlin's convention as "the emotional high water mark of American political history."[38] Certainly, the National Union for Social Justice convention could not be considered a normal democratic process in the traditional American sense. Even the presidential candidate, William Lemke, admitted that "it was a closed corporation," but added philosophically that "a lot of things are closed corporations." It was just this form of "limited" democracy that convinced many contemporary observers that Coughlin was planning a form of fascist dictatorship in the not too distant future.[39]

There was little doubt that the national union had become a major financial enterprise by the summer of 1936. In his financial report to the delegates, Father Coughlin revealed that he had received $684,444.30 since establishing the organization on November 11, 1934, and had spent $718,237.82 in the same period, mostly on radio time and staff salaries. The deficit was made up by a loan of $52,000 from the Radio League of the Little Flower.[40]

Despite the outward show of harmony, strong rumors persisted that all was not well with the triumvirate of Coughlin, Smith, and Townsend. It was thought that the three men would make some public appearances together, but Coughlin refused to commit himself to any such joint campaigning. He was reported to have protested against Townsend and Smith "tagging after me in this campaign." One observer predicted the probable dissolution of the partnership in the middle of the campaign.[41] But whatever differences existed were smoothed over, at least on the surface, and all three men continued to work for Lemke right up to election day.

It should be emphasized that Father Coughlin refused to allow his National Union for Social Justice to endorse the Union party as such; only Lemke and O'Brien were endorsed as individuals. Coughlin explained that he did not want to connect his organization with any political party, but would place his trust solely in individuals. Despite its noble beginnings, he feared that the Union party might go the way of the Democratic and Republican parties in the years to come. Another reason which may have crossed his mind was his own position as a Catholic priest. Both his Church and American tradition frowned upon a Roman Catholic cleric playing an active role in politics; it was undoubtedly essential for him to remain formally aloof from a political party. As president of the National Union for Social Justice he was merely the head of a group dedicated to better government which had decided to endorse candidates for United States President and Vice-President as well as for Congress.[42]

The many critics of the Detroit priest, who had long demanded that the Vatican censor his conduct, got their wish in early September when the Vatican newspaper *Osservatore Romano* openly rebuked Coughlin for his violent criticism of the Roosevelt administration. The paper said, in part, that "an orator who inveighs against persons who represent the supreme social authorities with the evident danger of shaking the respect that the people owe to these authorities, sins against elementary proprieties. The impropriety is greater as well as more evident when he who speaks is a priest." Bishop Gallagher was also an indirect target of the paper's ire. Referring to Bishop Gallagher's alleged statement that "the Holy See fully approved Father Coughlin's activities," the Vatican editor claimed that this did not "correspond with the truth"; he pointedly added that the bishop knew "quite well what he was told on the subject." *The New York Times* claimed that "high Vatican circles" stressed that the rebuke in *Osservatore*

Romano should not be interpreted as blanket disapproval of all Father Coughlin's activities. Actually, they said, the Vatican enthusiastically approved of Coughlin preaching the social encyclicals, but was disturbed that his attack on President Roosevelt might undermine respect for all authority and lead to chaotic conditions such as those experienced in Spain.[43]

On the day following the American publication of the Vatican paper's censure of Coughlin, Bishop Gallagher arrived at New York City on his return from Rome. Reporters flocked to interview the Detroit prelate on his reaction to *Osservatore's* criticism. The occasion was enlivened by the presence of Father Coughlin, on hand to greet his superior, and several hundred ardent supporters of Coughlin who staged an enthusiastic demonstration for him. Openly pleased at this show of loyalty for his favorite, Gallagher told the dockside crowd: "It's the voice of God that comes to you from the great orator of Royal Oak. Rally round it!"[44] The Detroit bishop reiterated his denial that the Vatican had disciplined Coughlin. Apparently more irritated than impressed, he explained that *Osservatore Romano* was not the official newspaper of the Vatican nor even the semiofficial spokesmen. The status of the Vatican newspaper is very confusing; although it is definitely not the official voice of the Catholic Church, it is generally assumed that the paper reflects Vatican policy on current issues. Most Americans, however, assume that the paper's articles are the official pronouncements of the Church; this is why the attack on Coughlin was looked upon as an official crackdown on the Royal Oak priest.

Father Coughlin attempted to put his superior on record as favoring his National Union for Social Justice platform and agreeing with his criticism of Roosevelt and Landon, but the bishop shrewdly sidestepped such leading questions: "As far as my present knowledge of the candidates goes, President Roosevelt is the best of them. Landon is out for the gold standard and would put us back where Hoover left us. I don't know much about Lemke."[45] Bishop Schrembs of Cleveland, who had made the trans-Atlantic voyage with Gallagher, also defended Father Coughlin: "Father Coughlin's stand on money is in accordance with the Pope's encyclical *Quadragesimo Anno*. If you read that you will find it is more radical than Father Coughlin himself."[46] Two days later, Bishop Gallagher arrived in Detroit and was again besieged by the press. Once again he categorically denied that the Vatican had ordered him to discipline Father Coughlin, but admitted for the first time that someone in Rome had discussed Coughlin: "There was an inconsequential individual who tried to find a flyspeck in the beautiful picture I painted of Father Coughlin's activities, but I explained that the flyspeck had already been erased and this individual apologized." Gallagher emphasized that Coughlin's activities had not been the subject of any official discussion.[47] *The New York Times* carried a story on September 6, the same day that "Vatican Prelates" had announced that Coughlin was being allowed to continue his activities if he refrained from attacking those in authority. *Time* speculated that Papal Delegate to the United States Amleto Cicognani had been given special orders to watch Father Coughlin closely.[48]

In the midst of all the uproar, Coughlin held his most successful mass meeting at Riverview Park, Chicago. A tremendous crowd of more than eighty thousand people paid fifty cents admission to hear their leader denounce the Roosevelt administration. Breathing defiance at his critics, Coughlin scoffed at the persistent reports that he had been reprimanded by Rome: "Don't let them deceive you that the Vatican has cracked down on Bishop Gallagher or me. If they cracked down, I wouldn't be here this moment and you know it." The most interesting feature of a rather badly organized speech was his comparison of the New Deal with a slick magazine with a fancy cover that hides the inferior content:

Mr. Roosevelt is the beautiful cover on the New Deal magazine. But what do we find when we open it. The first article is by Henry Morganthau, the lover of the international bankers. The second article is by Rexie Tugwell, the communist and handshaker with Russia. The third article is by Mordecai Ezekiel, the modern Margaret Sanger of the pigs. The fourth article is by Henry "Plow Me Down" Wallace, etc. . . . Last but not least, we have "Three-Finger" Jim Farley, Postmaster General, chairman of the state committee, of the national committee—three fingers—one for each pie.[49]

Despite all the denials by Coughlin and Gallagher, the rumor persisted that the Vatican had rebuked Coughlin and was carefully observing his actions. It was now reported by both *The New York Times* and the *New York Herald Tribune* that the Vatican had circulated a statement to all the news services emphasizing that the *Osservatore Romano* article actually did express the view of the Church.[50] No definite source was given for this new information. It is difficult to evaluate such news stories; if they had not appeared in reputable papers, it would be wisest to discount them as sensational journalism, but many significant news developments are first announced through incognito "high sources," "reliable sources," "good authorities," "responsible spokesmen," etc. Dealing with the Catholic Church is more complicated than seeking news from regular sources, however; even a good reporter could easily be confused by speaking to a highly titled monsignor who was merely expressing his own personal viewpoint.

If Father Coughlin had been muzzled by the Vatican, he apparently was not aware of it, for he continued to heap abuse upon Roosevelt. In his opening radio talk of the fall season, he accused the President of currying "favor for [sic] the leaders of communism."[51] On September 13, Coughlin made a dramatic appearance at Ebbetts Field before an enthusiastic crowd of twenty-two thousand, who paid as much as $1.65 for the chance to see their idol. Many contemporary observers were disturbed by the military escort provided Father Coughlin by veterans' organizations at some of these public rallies, apparently seeing too much resemblance to Hitler's National Socialist party. The faithful followers of the radio priest got their money's worth at Ebbetts Field. Coughlin once again attacked what he termed the pagan industrial system of the United States, and scornfully ridiculed the NRA, WPA, AAA, PWA, and the entire New Deal. For good measure he accused David Dubinsky, founder and president of the International Ladies Garment Workers' Union, of raising $5,000 for the Spanish communists, strongly implying that Dubinsky was a communist.[52]

Coughlin's Brooklyn performance provided the pattern for the priest's entire campaign; it was almost totally negative in nature, with Roosevelt receiving the bulk of the abuse. Frequently, his advocacy of William Lemke for President appeared to be almost an afterthought. A *New York Times* reporter in attendance clocked the attack on the New Deal at one hour, compared to a five-minute denunciation of Landon and a two-minute endorsement of Lemke.[53] A few days later at New Haven, Connecticut, Coughlin again linked Roosevelt with communism: "Unless the flirting with communistic tendencies begun by the present administration is halted, the red flag of communism will be raised in this country by 1940. . . . The Communists are coming out for Mr. Roosevelt and he lacks the courage to denounce them."[54] A few days later at Des Moines, Iowa, the priest again injected the communist issue, claiming that Roosevelt had surrounded himself with communist advisers and was personally enamored of communism. His Des Moines speech also contained a strong hint that he was not nearly as optimistic about Lemke's chances as he tried to appear. Referring to the Union party, he said: "It is a banner which likely will be trailed in the dust of defeat. . . . Gladly I prefer to uphold a losing cause which is right rather than a winning cause which is wrong."[55] He told reporters in Des Moines that Lemke needed only 6 per cent of the vote to prevent either Landon or Roosevelt from obtaining a majority in the electoral college.[56]

As Coughlin continued to excoriate Roosevelt, rumors once again were rife that he was about to be silenced by the Vatican, which was reportedly very much annoyed that he had failed to heed its first warning in *Osservatore Romano*. *The New York Times* claimed that certain "Vatican prelates" who were the paper's source of information still insisted that the editorial in *Osservatore* accurately reflected the thinking of the Pope.[57] Coughlin, as usual, reiterated his contention that he was only doing what Pope Pius XI had commanded all priests to do, namely, championing the cause of social justice as outlined in the encyclicals, and was not anticipating any Papal rebuke.[58] Once again Bishop Gallagher rallied to the defense of his protégé and denied knowledge of any plan to discipline Father Coughlin.[59]

Even the extraordinary loyalty of Bishop Gallagher was put to the test during the campaign. Speaking extemporaneously to a conference of Catholic study clubs in Detroit, the bishop was quoted as attacking William Lemke and the money plank of the Union party: "President Roosevelt has a much better background to work out these monetary problems than this man from the Dakotas. . . . I am sure Father Coughlin thinks if Lemke gets in he can control Lemke. Well, he couldn't control Roosevelt. The money plank is dangerous because it nationalizes credit and gives the government too much control."[60] Obviously chagrined by this unexpected development, Coughlin devoted page 1 of the October 5 issue of *Social Justice* to a not altogether satisfactory attempt to deny that there had even been any difference of opinion between the bishop and himself. Banner headlines proclaimed that Gallagher had approved Lemke's financial program. The priest insisted that his superior had been misquoted deliberately, but Gallagher neatly sidestepped the whole issue of what he had said and declared that since Lemke had now clarified the monetary plank by stating that it referred to wholesale credit instead of retail credit, he saw no objection to it.

It is very likely that the bishop, not fully understanding Lemke's platform, said some things that he had not intended for national consumption. When political furor ensued and these remarks were used against his favorite, Gallagher was only too glad to discover that Lemke's money program was essentially that of Father Coughlin.[61] It is highly significant that the bishop never did come over to the Lemke camp and openly admitted he preferred Roosevelt. The whole incident reveals a remarkable lack of intellectual rapport between two men generally considered to be extremely close; it also demonstrates that the bishop, while loyally supporting Coughlin's right to speak out on political issues, was still able to make his own political judgments. This should also give pause to those who insisted that Lemke's candidacy was part of a sinister Catholic plot to take over the country; surely Coughlin's own bishop would have supported Lemke, if such had been the case.

Father Coughlin and the National Union for Social Justice proved to be a potent political force in the September Democratic primaries of Michigan and Massachusetts. Louis B. Ward, Coughlin's lobbyist, came extremely close to defeating the organization candidate in Michigan for senator, Prentiss Brown. The original returns showed Ward trailing by only 4,032 votes. The National Union for Social Justice financed a recount, only to have Ward lose by 3,799 in the final tally. Even though Ward failed to defeat Brown, it was a tremendously impressive showing of the national union's strength in Michigan, and political observers admitted they were "shocked" at the size of his vote.[62] In Massachusetts, Thomas C. O'Brien, the Union party candidate for vice president, polled 37,000 votes in the Democratic primary, running against the popular Irish-Catholic mayor of Boston, the irrepressible James Michael Curley. It was really no contest; Curley polled 246,000 votes, and another Democrat 104,000.

What is truly remarkable, however, is that O'Brien's name was not even on the ballot; all his votes were procured by means of stickers which had to be distributed before the voters got to the polls. O'Brien also received 6,000 votes on the Republican ticket. Undaunted by his defeat, O'Brien ran on the Union party ticket in the November election and drew

enough votes away from Curley to allow his Republican opponent, Henry Cabot Lodge, Jr., to win the election. Curley
claimed that Coughlin had promised to support his Senate
bid before O'Brien entered the race, but relations between
the two men, which had never been cordial, deteriorated
drastically. They were soon exchanging bitter personal insults.
The exact cause of the Curley-Coughlin feud has not been
ascertained, but Boston, with its huge Catholic population,
was described by Curley himself as "the most Coughlinite city
in the United States," and there wasn't room for two such
dynamic personalities in the same city. Curley tried unsuccess-
fully to get O'Brien out of the race. A telephone call to
Father Coughlin asking him to persuade O'Brien to withdraw backfired by increasing Coughlin's ire: the priest wired
O'Brien to stay in the race and advised Curley to quit. The
Boston Mayor even offered to pay O'Brien $10,000 to get out
of the race, but to no avail. Father Coughlin apparently
attempted to trap Curley in an awkward political dilemma:
back Roosevelt and lose national union support in a Catholic
area or drop Roosevelt and lose regular Democratic support.
Curley remained loyal to Roosevelt.[63]

October brought another important development on the
ecclesiastical front: the Vatican suddenly announced that
Cardinal Eugenio Pacelli, Papal Secretary of State, was going
to make an extended tour of the United States. No reason was
given for his American visitation, but it was assumed by the
American press that the cardinal was coming to investigate
the political activities of Father Coughlin. *The New York
Times* also carried a story that Pacelli was coming on a good-
will mission to assure Roosevelt that the Catholic Church was
not opposed to his policies and to seek his aid in the Church's
crusade against communism.[64] Pacelli arrived in the United
States October 8, but refused to answer any questions about
Father Coughlin. Naturally, this was widely interpreted as
confirming the original speculation that he had been sent to
investigate the Royal Oak priest.[65] After Pacelli had been in
the country three weeks without commenting on Coughlin,

The New York Times stated that it was "reported authoritatively" that the Vatican was planning to crack down on Coughlin after the election when Pacelli had made his report to the Pope.[66] The Pacelli visit remains an enigma; the Vatican has never revealed whether the cardinal's mission had any connection with Father Coughlin's activities. Certainly, the timing of the visit in the midst of the presidential campaign lends weight to the assumption that Coughlin was indeed the *raison d'être* of Pacelli's sudden interest in the United States. But this is speculation, not history; the historical record shows that Pacelli did visit the United States in October of 1936, and that this was interpreted by many as a move on the part of the Vatican to obtain a first-hand report on Coughlin's activities.

If Pacelli acted as a moderating influence on Coughlin, as claimed by the leftist *New Masses*,[67] there is little real evidence of it in the radio priest's speeches. He was still as critical of Roosevelt as ever. His choice of words could be classified as more moderate, he did not use insulting language like "liar" and "great betrayer," but he still associated Roosevelt with communism at every opportunity. No longer claiming victory for Lemke, he now repeated his encouragement to his followers to remember that Lemke needed only 6 per cent of the total vote to throw the election into the House of Representatives.[68]

Early in October the presidential campaign took an unusual twist when Msgr. John A. Ryan attacked Father Coughlin over a nationwide radio hookup provided by the Democratic National Committee. Pulling no punches, Ryan labeled Coughlin's charges of communism against Roosevelt as "ugly, cowardly, and flagrant calumnies," and criticized Coughlin's monetary theories as 90 per cent incorrect. Ryan not only defended Roosevelt against the charge of communism but also such favorite Coughlin targets as David Dubinsky, Sydney Hillman, Rexford Tugwell, and Felix Frankfurter. As for Roosevelt's policies, Ryan declared they were only "mild installments of too delayed social justice." Urging the workers to vote for Roosevelt, Ryan emphasized the absurdity of

Father Coughlin's trying to pin a communist label on the President, who had received honorary degrees from two leading Catholic universities, Notre Dame and Catholic University: "Indeed, the charge of communism directed at President Roosevelt is the silliest, falsest, most cruel and most unjust accusation ever made against a President in all the years of American history." Ryan added that he himself had frequently been called a socialist because of his ideas on social justice and a living wage.[69]

Coughlin's response to Ryan was to deny that he had ever called Roosevelt a communist; he had used the word "communistic" to refer to Roosevelt's theories. But he still maintained that the President adhered to some theories that were communistic.[70] The radio priest devoted an entire broadcast to answering Msgr. Ryan, the sarcastic title of which was "A Reply to a Right Reverend Monsignor: Spokesman for the Democratic Political Party." The Royal Oak pastor insisted that many New Deal agencies were similar to the Russian communistic system and attacked New Deal financing as "a new kind of usury," charging that thirty-three cents out of every dollar went to finance New Deal programs. Father Coughlin acknowledged Ryan's pioneering role in the field of social justice, but emphasized that the present day demanded a different approach. Quoting directly from Pope Pius XI's *Quadragesimo Anno* on the money question, Coughlin attempted to demonstrate that his crusade against the private control of money and credit was in direct accord with the Papal directive.

> This power becomes particularly irresistible when exercised by these who because they hold and control money, are able to govern credit and determine its allotment, for that reason supplying, so to speak, the life-blood to the entire economic body and grasping, as it were, in their hands the very soul of production, so that no one dare breathe against their will.[71]

What Coughlin intended to show was that the encyclical

clearly stated that there could be no real progress made in the equitable distribution of wealth until private control of money was abolished. Supremely confident of the loyalty of his followers, the priest asked his listeners to send him an expression of approval or disapproval of his position and promised to retire from public life if a majority voted against him. Although Coughlin promised to make public the results of this mail poll, there is no record of his having done so. The odds were all in his favor, however, since most of those listening to the radio priest may be presumed to have been favorable to his message.

Whatever the content of the mail received at Royal Oak, there is no doubt that Msgr. Ryan was on the receiving end of much savagely critical correspondence. The Catholic University professor reported that of twelve hundred letters from Father Coughlin's followers, only fifty could even be classified as courteous.[72] Like their leader, the Coughlinites simply refused to admit that there could be such a thing as an honest difference of opinion, and resorted to invective as a substitute for logic. Even a cursory examination of the letters Ryan received reveals that the writers were generally poorly educated people who had blindly placed all their hope for a better future in Father Coughlin and were appalled to hear a fellow priest criticizing their leader. There was a definite note of anticlericalism running through the letters; many resented the economic security enjoyed by the clergy at a time of widespread hardship for the poor. As one writer expressed it:

Would to God that we had a few hundred Father Coughlins willing and courageous enough to fight for the poor instead of so many monied clerics who are constantly having trips here, there and abroad—new machines each year or two and what not while the poor are told to raise families and then left to fight for their existence alone.

No wonder Father Coughlin says Communists are not born—but made. You and many of our clergy will help to make plenty.[73]

The letters also bear witness to the fact that Father Coughlin was not only trusted but also loved by many of the pathetically large minority of unfortunates not properly aided by the New Deal relief measures who felt that no one cared whether they lived or died. As one ardent admirer of Coughlin wrote: "When I had neither food nor shelter for my lovely family the thought of him kept me sane, gave me hope and courage, but God forgive you because I don't think I ever will."[74] Many of the letter-writers assumed that Ryan had been paid by the Democrats to discredit Coughlin: "Your church is making a racket of politics. You must have got your hand greased either by Farley or the WPA President." The letter continued, "You are upholding a government that is paying $55 a month to keep a family of six. Do you live on that, no you do not, you have a pocket full of money the latest car while babies cry for milk. Oh I know you will laugh at my spelling and writing but you won't laugh when God has you before him."[75]

Msgr. Ryan, far from laughing at the spelling of these anguished correspondents, was deeply disturbed about what he considered the harm that Father Coughlin had done to people by exploiting their misery. Ryan would not have been human if he had not been hurt by these attacks on him. Here was a man who had fought for social justice throughout a long and fruitful career, generally recognized as the leading scholarly proponent of Catholic social dogma in America, being castigated for his indifference to the plight of the workers. But Msgr. Ryan was not a great radio orator and did not possess a nationwide following numbering in the millions. Probably only the small percentage of Catholics who attended Catholic colleges had ever heard about his pioneering work. In the early phase of Coughlin's radio career, Ryan had lavishly praised the Detroit priest; at one point he had even stated that Father Coughlin was "on the side of the angels" in his crusade for social justice. But when Coughlin became more extreme and broke with the Roosevelt administration, Ryan, himself an enthusiastic New Dealer, was deeply disturbed because he feared that Coughlin's efforts might cause Roosevelt's defeat in 1936, and that in that event American Catholics would be blamed for this, with unfortunate repercussions which would take years to overcome.[76]

Ryan's own emergence into politics received a mixed reception in the Catholic press. The *Baltimore Catholic Review* suggested, with tongue in cheek, that both Ryan and Coughlin would be performing a great service for their Church if they joined a Trappist monastery and remained forever silent.[77] *Commonweal,* however, sprang to the defense of Ryan, stating that he was motivated by his love for social justice rather than the partisan politics of the New Deal. The magazine was bitterly critical of Father Coughlin: "The rank wizardry of his illogical, yet crudely fascinating oratory may continue to obsess the unthinking portion of his diminishing audience, but the appeal to reason made by Msgr. Ryan will be increasingly heeded by those Catholics who use their heads."[78]

Msgr. Ryan was not alone in his concern over the unfortunate effect Coughlin's actions were having upon the Catholic situation in America. Many Catholics, both lay and clerical, made their feelings known in letters to Roosevelt or in public statements. Typical of the response of ordinary lay Catholics to Father Coughlin's "liar" speech was the following: "As Catholics and American citizens, my family are bitterly ashamed at Father Coughlin's ungentlemanly . . . and unwarranted attack on you."[79] Another in the same vein from a Philadelphia woman read as follows: "I am a Catholic woman but I am ashamed of his [Coughlin's] speech and his actions, his picture and yours were in my living room, some time ago I removed his, I could not stand to look at him. There are many thousands of Catholics who think as I think."[80] The captain of the Harvard football team of 1919, William Murray, an Irish Catholic, wrote: "I decry the utterances of this madman Coughlin. . . . Please allow some prominent Catholic laymen to organize the intelligent thinking Catholics to offset the horrible statements Coughlin has made."[81] Such a group was organized by a former Massachusetts congressman and Acting Assistant Attorney General John

A. Conry, but nothing was heard from it after the announcement of its organization.[82]

Two very prominent Irish-Catholic Democrats who publicly deplored Coughlin's attack on the President were John B. Kelly, the millionaire Democratic City Chairman of Philadelphia, and Joseph P. Kennedy, the Boston financier who served as the first chief of the Securities Exchange Commission and later as a controversial ambassador to England. Kelly, long noted for his bluntness, lived up to his reputation by a frontal assault on the Detroit priest: "Father Coughlin has by his own words and actions disgraced the cloth of the priesthood both by his attacks on the President of the United States and by remarks made by him about prelates of his own church."[83] Kennedy was more indirect in his criticism. Without mentioning Coughlin by name, he struck out at the Royal Oak priest's attempt to label Roosevelt a communist: "If there were any semblance of communism, or dictatorship, or regimentation in this country, the words 'liar' and 'betrayer' would have been used only once."[84] The Securities Exchange Commission chief was in a very awkward position when Coughlin became such a bitter foe of the administration. Kennedy was a good friend of the radio priest and had used his mutual friendship with Coughlin and Roosevelt to try to reconcile the two men. The Boston Democrat was on record as late as August 16, 1936, as boasting of his friendship with Coughlin.[85]

With the notable exception of Archbishop Francis Beckman of Dubuque, Coughlin was not supported publicly by any member of the Catholic hierarchy other than his own superior, Bishop Gallagher of Detroit, and even he refused to back Lemke. As indicated earlier, Cardinal O'Connell of Boston was bitterly opposed to Coughlin; less direct critics were Cardinal Mundelein of Chicago and Cardinal Hayes of New York. These three ecclesiastical dignitaries, the top ranking members of the Catholic hierarchy in the United States, were significantly on record against Father Coughlin long before his Union party venture of 1936. But as the campaign of 1936 became more heated, other Catholic prelates felt obliged to comment publicly on Coughlin's unorthodox conduct. Included in this group were Bishop Schrembs of Cleveland, a friend of Coughlin's own bishop, who, while defending the right of clergymen to speak out on political issues, deplored the tactics employed by Coughlin: "But as far as party politics is concerned, it is not wise to get actively in it in a vicious way, using vicious language or indulging in personalities. Personally, I do not like to see a clergyman starting out on a political campaign."[86]

Another member of the hierarchy who demonstrated concern over Coughlin's political activities was Archbishop McNicholas of Cincinnati, who was visibly distressed by the violent tone of Coughlin's attack on the Roosevelt administration in a Cincinnati speech. The radio priest had suggested that it might be necessary to resort to bullets instead of ballots in the event an "upstart" dictator established one-party government in the United States. The reference, though vague, was obviously to Roosevelt. Unimpressed with the danger of an American dictatorship, the Cincinnati prelate rebuked Coughlin for raising such a dangerous straw argument: "There is no excuse for inciting in the people a spirit of violent rebellion against conditions which do not actually exist and may never exist."[87] Bishop Noll of Fort Wayne, Indiana, was another prelate who placed himself on record as an opponent of Coughlin. Annoyed at seeing a journalist link his name with the radio priest, the bishop clarified his position: "I certainly cannot conceive just what is the source of your information, because I doubt whether any Catholic Bishop has criticized him more."[88] Even more negative than Noll was Bishop Mahoney of Sioux Falls, South Dakota, who revealed his sentiments in a telegram to Roosevelt after the "liar" speech: "In the name of the priests and people of the diocese of Sioux Falls, South Dakota, I wish to protest against reference to you by clerical vulgarian."[89]

A most significant indication of the attitude of the Catholic clergy to Father Coughlin's attacks on President Roosevelt was the following letter of the Rev. Maurice S. Sheehy, Assistant Rector of Catholic University, to Marvin H. McIntyre, July 18, 1936:

> At a meeting in the Waldorf-Astoria in New York last night, four bishops, three monsignori, another priest and I, discussed for four hours the attack of Father Coughlin on the President. We decided how this action might be handled most effectively. We have taken action. . . . "We wish to have nothing to do with those engaged in the political campaign and the identity of the members of this group is not to be made public. However, you are free to tell the President his friends are not ignoring the calumnies of Father Coughlin."[90]

Msgr. Sheehy wrote in 1959 that two of the bishops referred to in this letter were Bishop Thomas O'Reilly of Scranton and Archbishop James H. Ryan of Omaha, both deceased. Msgr. Sheehy did not feel it discreet to reveal the names of the participants still living, but he did attempt to summarize the general trend of thought at the meeting: "I think the attitude of the bishops I met in regard to Father Coughlin at that time was that if he projected himself into the field of politics he should not be protected from abuse because he was a priest." Msgr. Sheehy continued, "Most of the bishops and priests I knew were vehemently opposed to any priest going on the political platform, stripping himself of his Roman collar, as Father Coughlin did once at Cleveland, and risking the prestige of the priestly office in matters economic and political, as did Father Coughlin."[91] Unfortunately, we have no Gallup Poll of Catholic clergy to indicate how widespread this negative reaction was among the lower clergy. But Msgr. Sheehy estimated that 103 of the 106 American bishops voted for Roosevelt in 1936.[92] It is perfectly clear that the radio priest did not represent a concerted political effort on the part of the Catholic Church in America.

Most Catholic publications approved of Coughlin's early crusade for social justice, but deserted him when he began to attack the Roosevelt administration. *America* and *Common-weal,* two representative national Catholic weeklies, became outspoken critics of Coughlin soon after he turned against the President. Other publications, such as *The Catholic World,* strove to be neutral, but the ultraconservative *Brooklyn Tablet* remained loyal to Coughlin to the bitter end, as did his own diocesan paper, the *Michigan Catholic.* Thus, if there was a Catholic "party line" on Father Coughlin, the Catholic bishops and editors of the United States did not know it.

October continued to be a trying month for Father Coughlin. John Barry of the *Boston Globe* charged that the priest attacked him in a rage over an interview the reporter had conducted in Boston. Coughlin contended that Barry had tried to force his way into a private meeting and became violent when asked to leave. *The New York Daily News,* always eager to promote a lively scandal, published a picture of the priest in the act of punching Barry. *Social Justice* carried a reasonably convincing denial and accused the *News* of deliberately faking the picture. Whatever the real story, the incident did little to enhance Coughlin's already damaged priestly dignity.[93]

To add to the priest's embarrassment, John H. O'Donnell of Pittsburgh, the lone dissenter to Lemke's endorsement at the national union convention, filed suit for $1,000,000 of National Union for Social Justice funds, which he claimed Coughlin had misused for political purposes, and demanded the priest's ouster as president of the national union. Coughlin's reaction to this charge was characteristic; he suggested that it was part of Jim Farley's effort to discredit him.[94] O'Donnell's charges were obviously ridiculous; the funds collected by Father Coughlin were clearly designated as donations to pay the expenses of his radio time and publications. All the money was freely sent by people who approved of Coughlin's program and were eager to assist their leader in propagating it. The suit was later dropped. O'Donnell's motivation remains obscure, but the whole affair appears too ludicrous to have been the work of a clever politician like

Jim Farley. As if this were not enough aggravation for one week, the next day Father Coughlin was showered with feathers by a demented heckler while delivering a speech at a Detroit national union rally. In a matter of seconds, the athletic Coughlin had thrown his assailant and pinned him to the floor, unassisted. The angry crowd of loyal Coughlinites threatened to kill their leader's oppressor, but the priest intervened. At this same rally Coughlin announced his support for the Republican candidate for governor of Michigan, rather than for his former close friend, Frank Murphy. Murphy had not only failed to heal the breach between Coughlin and Roosevelt, but had thoroughly alienated the Detroit priest by yielding to Roosevelt's pressure and heading the Michigan Democratic ticket.[95]

As the campaign drew to a close, Coughlin appeared to be taking a more realistic attitude; he began to express doubt that 1936 was the year for a social justice triumph. He intimated that the national union might have to endure a martyr's fate in 1936 but would definitely triumph in 1940.[96] For the most part, Coughlin's speeches in the last few weeks contained nothing new; he still concentrated all his efforts on criticizing the New Deal for failing to solve the depression by monetary reforms and for flirting with communism. One notable exception, however, was his radio talk of October 24 when he injected foreign affairs into the campaign by contending that the real issue in the election was peace or war. Roosevelt, the priest claimed, was dragging the United States into the League of Nations through the back door by playing a leading role at such international conclaves as the recent Pan American Conference at Buenos Aires. Such a course of action would surely lead to war in two or three years, since the League, in Coughlin's view, was a menace to world peace. The priest sharply criticized Morgenthau's handling of the First World War debt problem and predicted that the United States would finance England and France in the next war also.[97] At Cleveland two days later, Father Coughlin assailed the WPA as a "scab army" and labeled Roosevelt a "scab

President." The priest demanded a $150 monthly wage for all WPA workers, arguing that the government should pay salaries comparable to those of private industry.[98] Coughlin's last great public rally was a dramatic affair staged at the scene of one of his earlier forensic triumphs, the New York Hippodrome. Six thousand enthusiastic Coughlinites solemnly pledged themselves to secure ten votes for the Republican candidate for governor of New York, William F. Bleakley, in his race against Herbert Lehman, and also for Senator John A. Hastings, the Republican opponent of John J. O'Connor in the sixteenth congressional district of New York. Coughlin's antipathy toward Lehman, as noted earlier, was partly attributable to the former governor's opposition to a bill providing free bus transportation for Catholic school pupils; O'Connor, of course, was the chairman of the Rules Committee who had blocked action on the Frazier-Lemke bill. The priest did not ask his New York followers to pledge themselves to Lemke, since the Union party ticket could not secure a place on the New York ballot because of the complicated election laws of that state. This was a staggering blow to the Lemke cause; Coughlin confessed in a New York interview that failure to get Lemke on the ballot in New York had ended all hope for the North Dakotan. But the priest stoutly refused to concede a Roosevelt victory; he now predicted a Landon victory.[99]

Coughlin ended the campaign as he had begun it, with bitter slashing attacks on Franklin Roosevelt at New York, Scranton, and Newark. In his final broadcast of the campaign, from Flushing High School in Queens, he apologized for calling Roosevelt a "scab president." But in the same address, Coughlin declared that "a vote for Roosevelt was a vote for 273,000 socialists and David Dubinsky and 78,000 communists who sent funds to Spain to massacre helpless nuns and priests."[100] At Scranton, on the following day, he referred to the President as "the upstart president" and the "reviver of the divine right theory" and pronounced the New Deal "more vicious than the old deal."[101] Appearing at Newark on the same day, Coughlin told an audience of eight thousand that there would be twenty million unemployed if Roosevelt were reelected.[102]

As the campaign drew to a close, *The New York Times* reported that Bishop Gallagher had said some disciplinary action might be taken against Coughlin after the election. The bishop had been so disturbed by the "scab president" epithet that he had "suggested" an apology.[103] Apparently fearful of any future repetition of Coughlin's embarrassing performance, Gallagher announced that he would not allow any of his priests to participate in the next campaign.[104] Nonplussed by all the uproar, Coughlin procured a telegram from Gallagher saying he had no intention of interfering with the radio priest. The bishop also clarified his previous remarks; what he really meant to say was that he would not allow all the priests in his diocese to participate in politics since few were well-informed on political matters.[105]

Although there can be little doubt that Roosevelt was strongly tempted to reply in kind to Coughlin, the President was too astute a politician to run the unnecessary risk of alienating large numbers of Catholic voters. Actually, he did not feel that the radio priest posed a serious threat in 1936, although the President and Democratic Chairman Farley had both been seriously concerned in 1935 about the possibility of a Coughlin-Long coalition the next year.[106] The simple yet effective strategy devised by Roosevelt was to allow his friends within the Church, such as Msgrs. Ryan and Sheehy, to defend his cause among Catholics, and to ignore Coughlin. When Harold Ickes ridiculed Lemke and accused the Union party of being a front for the GOP, Roosevelt criticized Ickes for directly attacking Father Coughlin.[107] Another effective Rooseveltian touch was to recall Frank Murphy from the Philippines to be the Democratic candidate for governor of Michigan, in an apparent effort to weaken Coughlin's influence in his own bailiwick.[108]

As for the Republicans, they simply ignored Coughlin while believing, or at least hoping, that the Union party would hurt

Roosevelt. Aside from an occasional insult tossed in Landon's direction, Father Coughlin, as we have seen, concentrated his fire on the President.

Despite the loudest efforts of Coughlin, Smith, and Lemke, the Union party suffered a crushing defeat in the election of 1936, receiving less than one million votes and failing to win the electoral vote of a single state. No one, not even Father Coughlin, had expected a Lemke victory, but most observers had anticipated a more substantial vote, since the National Union for Social Justice alone was supposed to have five million members. This group, combined with the followers of Townsend, Smith, and Lemke, was presumed capable of attracting well over a million votes. No election is ever fully explainable; human motivation is too complex for even the most careful researcher to chart. But the political historian must attempt a partial analysis of factors contributing to success or defeat at the polls.

In the 1936 presidential campaign, the one overriding consideration was the tremendous personal popularity of Roosevelt. For some inexplicable reason, Father Coughlin failed to grasp this fundamental fact. He played to his opponents' strength by resorting to wild accusations and vicious personal attacks against the President, which not only alienated Coughlin's own followers but also estranged numerous Townsendites who felt very kindly toward Roosevelt.[109] Thus it appears glaringly obvious, in retrospect at least, that 1936 was definitely not the year to conduct a solely negative campaign denouncing Roosevelt and all his works.

Another important consideration in Lemke's poor showing was the weakness of this anti-Roosevelt coalition. There was never any real coordination of effort between Coughlin, Smith, and Townsend. After pledging mutual fealty at the Townsend convention in July, each went his separate way in the campaign. Coughlin curtly dismissed any plans his two partners may have had for joint campaigning: "Why should they tag me around?"[110] Real cooperation was probably not possible; the three men represented diverse groups with vastly different aims; they were linked only by opposition to Franklin D. Roosevelt.

Coughlin's failure to influence more voters is puzzling because of his emotional hold on millions of radio listeners. A poll conducted by the American Institute of Public Opinion in June of 1936 indicated that 7 per cent of the American people would be inclined to support Coughlin's choice of a presidential candidate.[111] It would appear that many Americans loyally supported the priest's radio efforts, but voted for Roosevelt as their best hope of realizing even limited reforms. Coughlin claimed to have five million members in his National Union for Social Justice, but Lemke received, by the priest's own estimate, the support of only 10 per cent of the membership. The traditional reluctance of American voters to waste their votes on a hopeless cause, however worthy it might be, undoubtedly served to keep the Lemke vote down. Coughlin's Catholic priesthood, while an asset among some Catholics, was definitely a heavy liability with the American people as a whole.

Gerald L. K. Smith, the self-appointed successor to Huey Long as the leader of the Share-the-Wealth movement, had joined forces with Townsend at the time of the Bell Committee's harassment of the pension advocate in May of 1936.[112] Smith never appeared particularly interested in Lemke and admitted in July that he was more concerned about paving the way for his own candidacy in 1940.[113] A rabble-rousing orator, Smith struck the low note of the campaign in a Georgia speech when he shrieked, "We're going to drive that cripple out of the White House—and we're going to do it in 1936."[114] Despite his acknowledged ability to whip even the most passive of audiences into an emotional frenzy, Smith contributed few votes to the Union party in 1936. Lemke did not even appear on the ballot in Louisiana, the stronghold of the Share-the-Wealth movement, and received only 4,386 votes in the entire South.[115]

As for Townsend, there was no question but that he commanded the loyalty of several million would-be pensioners, but he was simply not a political organizer. A poll conducted by the American Institute of Public Opinion in June, 1936, indicated that Townsend's endorsement of a presidential candidate would favorably influence 10 per cent of the American people.[116] The elderly doctor personally campaigned for Lemke, but the Townsend clubs were not officially committed to support the Union party standard-bearer. Coughlin had scored an impressive personal triumph at the Townsend convention, but once the oratorical spell was broken, many of the pension plan advocates must have found it difficult to ignore the priest's obvious lack of enthusiasm for their program. Failure to place the Union party on the ballot in California, their strongest state, greatly diminished the Townsendite contribution to the Lemke vote total.

Another very important factor in the poor showing of the Union party was the negative reaction of liberals and progressives to the new party. Norman Thomas, perennial Socialist candidate for president, belittled the leader of the new party as "messiah of the mob." The Socialist chieftain was not much concerned about the Union party's political power in 1936, but was alarmed over the direction in which Coughlin and his supporters seemed to be heading.[117]

Some Progressives were sympathetic to the Union party cause but feared to split the liberal vote and risk a Landon victory. Floyd B. Olson, the radical Farmer-Labor governor of Minnesota, personified this attitude in a deathbed statement acknowledging "the utmost respect" for Coughlin and Lemke but warning that "for the liberals to split their votes is merely to play into the hands of the Wall Street gang."[118]

Another damaging blow to Lemke's prospects of attracting Progressive support was the public statement issued by the Progressive National Committee supporting Roosevelt for reelection. The declaration echoed Olson's view that any division among liberals would merely aid the reactionaries, and it urged Progressives to extend Roosevelt every assistance. The impressive roster of signatures included Robert and Philip LaFollette, George Norris, Frank R. Walsh, John L.

Lewis, Maury Maverick, Edward Costigan, Sidney Hillman, Thomas Amlie, Fiorello LaGuardia, Hugo Black, Elmer Benson, and Lewis Schwellenbach. Howard Y. Williams, a leading Farmer-Laborite, denounced the Union party as a tragic mistake which would only split the Progressive vote; he could see little grass-roots support for Lemke. But Henry C. Teigan, another prominent Farmer-Laborite, was very sympathetic with the Coughlin movement, feeling that the National Union for Social Justice platform was closer to the goals of the Farmer-Labor movement than that of any other organization. Teigan appeared to be deeply impressed with the fight that the radio priest had made for monetary reform and utility control.[119]

In view of Lemke's consistent championing of remedial farm legislation, it was expected that he would receive substantial support from the farmers, but this was not to be the case. The North Dakotan did receive the endorsement of the National Farmers' Union, a group which supposedly had about a quarter of a million members. But another farm organization, the Farmers Holiday Association, failed to agree on the issue of Lemke's endorsement. After a hopelessly stalemated meeting, five state presidents, under the direction of Representative Usher Burdick of North Dakota, Lemke's campaign manager, seceded to found a new organization, charging that the communists had controlled the meeting of the Farmers Holiday Association.[120] Lemke's failure to attract any sizable farm support is probably a tribute to the success of Roosevelt's Secretary of Agriculture Henry Wallace in convincing the farmers that the administration was really concerned about their problems. Another factor which cannot be documented, but which deserves consideration, was Lemke's close association with a Catholic priest, a situation which must have been very disconcerting to the predominantly Protestant farmers of the Midwest.

A final blow to any hopes Coughlin may have had of securing labor support was the enthusiastic backing Roosevelt received from Labor's Non-Partisan League in 1936. The group spent almost a million dollars on the Democratic President's behalf.[121]

Thus, far from rallying around Lemke, most progressives and liberals united behind Roosevelt as the most acceptable candidate in 1936. The Union party actually served to broaden the base of Roosevelt's support.

Another extremely important element in explaining the Union party's unimpressive showing at the polls was the total lack of any regular political organization. The establishment of a new party, with no patronage at its disposal, is at best a difficult task, but when a group attempts to organize and conduct a presidential campaign in four months, it is attempting the impossible. Father Coughlin must have known how difficult it would be even to get on the ballot such a short time before the election. His rash call for a new party in late June leads one to doubt that he ever entertained any serious hope of real success in 1936 but was merely paving the way for a more concerted effort in 1940. As any political scientist will attest, the election laws in the United States are highly unfavorable to the creation of new parties. But after much frantic petition-gathering, Coughlin succeeded in getting his party on the ballot in thirty-six states. Only in thirty states, however, was he allowed to use the name "Union party." In Michigan the Union party had to appear as the "Third party," in Pennsylvania as the "Royal Oak party," in Illinois as the "Union Progressive party," in New Jersey as the "National Union for Social Justice party," in Oregon as the "Independent Union party," and in South Dakota as the "Independent party." The Union party was severely handicapped by its inability to get on the ballot in the key states of New York, California, and Louisiana, where it probably had considerable strength. Coughlin possessed a well-organized following in New York, but according to state law a prospective Lemke voter would have had to write in the names of all forty-seven Lemke electors within three minutes, an impossible task. California, of course, was the keystone state of Dr. Townsend's pension movement; Louisiana was a significant loss because Smith's Share-the-Wealth movement was centered in the Bayou State and presumably would have cast a sizable number of votes for Lemke.

The Union party was also considerably weakened by the lack of local party slates. Coughlin was interested only in the national offices; he even discouraged independent Union party candidates for Congress wherever an acceptable candidate of a major party could be found worthy of National Union for Social Justice endorsement. With no city-hall or statehouse patronage at its disposal, the infant party existed in many areas in name only. It was totally dependent on the support of the national union, the Townsend clubs, and the Share-the-Wealth movement, all three of which failed to render wholehearted support.

Probably the weakest link in Coughlin's bid for political power was the rather incongruous candidate of the Union party, Representative William Lemke of North Dakota. Aside from his devotion to farm legislation, Lemke had little to commend himself to the American voter. He was clearly a sectional candidate, or more accurately, a special interest candidate. It is still not clear how Lemke came to be the candidate of the Union party, but he was a very weak choice. Virtually unknown outside the Midwest and a notoriously ineffective speaker, Lemke's political stature was not aided by the inane nickname of "Liberty Bill" which Coughlin bestowed upon him.[122] Few critics could resist saying that he was as cracked as the Liberty Bell. The North Dakotan was almost completely overshadowed by Coughlin and played a minor role in the campaign. Lemke spoke mostly to farm groups where he echoed his sponsor's attacks on international bankers. The Union party candidate's one positive proposal was a program calling for the creation, through conservation and irrigation, of a midland empire on the eastern slope of the Rockies "where the nation's youth will have an opportunity to build houses and enter industry."[123] Even this proposal did not have much impact; Roosevelt's efforts in the field of conservation had been highly successful. Lemke's true relationship with Father Coughlin is still not clear. There is little doubt that Coughlin dominated the party and the campaign in 1936, but it has been suggested that Lemke tolerated this in the hope that a real Farm-Labor Movement would evolve by 1940.[124] Whatever he really thought of his strange role and his chances of success, he publicly exuded optimism, predicting on the eve of the election that he would carry fifteen states and succeed in throwing the election into the House of Representatives.[125] Despite his failure to draw even a million votes as the Union party candidate for president, Lemke was easily reelected to Congress on the Republican ticket.

A brief analysis of the vote distribution is in order. As we have seen, Coughlin's fondest hope for Lemke was that he could draw enough votes away from Roosevelt to prevent the President from receiving a majority. The priest estimated that Lemke needed only 8 per cent of the total vote to throw the election into the House of Representatives, where Coughlin hoped a man better qualified than Roosevelt would be chosen. The radio priest was particularly hopeful of carrying the Dakotas, Minnesota, Wisconsin, Illinois, Ohio, Michigan, Massachusetts, Rhode Island, and Pennsylvania.[126] At one point *Social Justice* claimed 16 to 17 per cent of the vote for Lemke.[127] The Union party's meager total vote of 892,000, less than 2 per cent of the national vote, proved not only how inaccurate a vote prognosticator Coughlin was, but also how little influence the radio priest had.

Lemke achieved his greatest success in his native North Dakota, where he received 13 per cent of the vote. In only four other states—Massachusetts, Minnesota, Rhode Island, and Oregon—did he receive over 5 per cent of the total vote. Wisconsin, Michigan, and Ohio gave Lemke between 4 and 5 per cent. He ran his weakest race in the South, receiving only 4,386 votes; of these, 3,177 were from Texas alone. Coughlin's radio network had no Southern outlets and the priest apparently aroused little enthusiasm for his social justice crusade in this heavily Protestant area.

No Union party candidates were elected to Congress and all four Senatorial candidates were defeated.[128] *Social Justice* claimed a partial victory by assuming credit for the election of Senator Ernest Lundeen of Minnesota, who was supported in a much more significant fashion by Republicans and Farmer-Laborites, and sixty congressmen who had received National Union for Social Justice endorsement.[129] These congressmen did not run as national union or Union party candidates, but as Democrats or Republicans, and the majority were incumbents. Endorsement by the National Union for Social Justice undoubtedly played a significant role in some elections, but there is little doubt that major party affiliation was far more significant in determining the outcome of the elections. The blunt truth is that Father Coughlin, like many another reformer before him, discovered that attracting vast audiences is a far different matter from attracting votes. Another rather obvious point is that it is far easier to influence a primary than a final election. Only a small percentage of the electorate concern themselves with primaries, and a well-organized pressure group has a good opportunity to influence the choice of candidates.

The voting pattern of the Union party has been carefully analyzed by Samuel Lubell in his *The Future of American Politics*. Lubell discovered that Lemke received as much as 10 per cent of the vote in only thirty-nine counties outside of his native North Dakota. In twenty-one of these counties, Catholics comprised 50 per cent or more of the population, and in twenty-eight of them, Germans were the leading nationality. The four cities where Lemke received more than 5 per cent of the vote—Dubuque, St. Paul, Cincinnati, and Boston —were heavily German and Irish Catholic.[130] Professor James Shenton makes this point concerning the preponderance of Irish and Germans among Coughlin's supporters in his article in the September, 1958, *Political Science Quarterly*. Of seventy-eight letters Msgr. Ryan received denouncing him for attacking Coughlin, thirty-six were signed with Irish names and thirty-nine with German names. Lest one conclude that the majority of Irish and Germans supported the radio priest, the same author also drew attention to the fact that most of the letters in the Roosevelt Papers which criticized Coughlin were also signed by Germans and Irish.

In view of Coughlin's emphasis upon economic reform, Lubell makes the surprising observation that the key to understanding the Lemke vote was foreign policy rather than economics. To support this view, Lubell points to Minnesota, where Lemke ran poorest in the strongest Farmer-Labor counties despite the fact that his Union party platform was almost identical to the Farmer-Labor platform. The six . Minnesota counties where Lemke garnered more than 15 per cent of the vote were either predominantly Catholic or German.[131] While these are interesting statistics, they certainly do not prove that the bulk of Lemke's support resulted from antipathy to Roosevelt's foreign policy. It is far more probable that the majority of Lemke votes came from discontented Americans who agreed with Coughlin and Lemke that Roosevelt had failed to solve the nation's problems. The fact that these same voters later demonstrated isolationist tendencies is not a valid as an indication of a strong foreign policy influence in the 1936 election. It is true that Coughlin and his following were isolationist—nationalist, as they preferred to call it—but in 1936 foreign policy was definitely a secondary consideration with them.

After his humiliating repudiation at the polls, Father Coughlin had little choice but to live up to his pledge to leave the air if Lemke failed to receive nine million votes. In fairness, it should be noted that the radio priest fully accepted the verdict of the American people and spoke a sad but gracious farewell to his faithful radio audience on November 7. Agreeing with his gleeful newspaper critics that the National Union for Social Justice was completely discredited, he announced that the organization would cease to be active. Coughlin declared that in the future he would not even comment on the policies of Franklin D. Roosevelt. Quite understandably, the priest expressed his keen disappointment that only about 10 per cent of the National Union for Social Justice membership had remained loyal in the campaign, but attributed the large scale desertion to their feeling that Roosevelt was more capable of fulfilling their material needs than the leader of the national union. Coughlin emphasized that his decision to retire from broadcasting was his own and not a result of ecclesiastical censure; Bishop Gallagher, he insisted, had urged him to continue. Coughlin further maintained that his promise to leave the air if Lemke failed to receive nine million votes was not binding because it had been based on the assumption that the Union party ticket would appear on the ballot in all forty-eight states, but explained that he was withdrawing because "I love my country and my Church too much to become a stumbling block to those who have failed to understand."[132]

VI

THE CHRISTIAN FRONT AND WORLD WAR II

FATHER COUGHLIN's public career did not end on November 7, 1936. *Social Justice* continued its weekly criticism of all things Rooseveltian and on January 1, 1937, the Royal Oak pastor broadcast a special New Year's message. He explained that his return to radio was temporary and motivated primarily by a desire to wish his many friends a happy new year. At the same time, however, he paved the way for a possible resumption of weekly radio talks by announcing that he would return to the air if his supporters demonstrated their loyalty by raising the circulation of *Social Justice* from 600,000 to 1,500,000.[1] A subsequent issue of *Social Justice* lowered the magic number to 1,250,000.[2]

Coughlin suffered a staggering personal blow on January 20 when his close friend and loyal defender, Bishop Gallagher, died suddenly. Although *Social Justice* had obviously not reached the prescribed circulation goal of 1,250,000, the Detroit priest returned to the air Sunday, January 24, announcing that Bishop Gallagher's last request was that he resume broadcasting. The new series was carried by forty-three stations, but was not heard in the South or on the West Coast. The initial broadcast was an emotion-charged eulogy of the late bishop: "From this great bishop I gained my inspiration. By virtue of his encouragement I pursued the path that he had blazed for me."[3]

In the weeks that followed, Coughlin devoted much of his attention both on the radio and in the pages of *Social Justice* to the turbulent American labor scene. From his parish in Royal Oak the priest had a ringside seat from which to observe the bitter sit-down strike at General Motors and the militant tactics of the newly organized CIO. Coughlin sharply assailed all sides to the dispute, but was especially critical of the Irish-Catholic governor of Michigan, Frank Murphy, for his refusal to use the state militia to crush the strike, and of John L. Lewis, the CIO leader. The latter became a favorite Coughlin whipping boy in 1937. Lewis was described as a potential labor dictator upon whose shoulders lay the hopes of the Communist party in America. As the February 8 *Social Justice* expressed it: "John L. Lewis is Not a Communist But Communism in the U.S. Hinges on His Success."[4] As his own contribution to labor peace the Detroit priest reiterated his longstanding endorsement of a living wage coupled with government control of the dollar's purchasing value.[5]

In mid-February of 1937, Coughlin suddenly called upon all members of the dormant National Union for Social Justice to "awake." The national union was about to embark "upon a new phase of its existence untrammelled by local, state, congressional or national politics and political parties." The radio priest requested all loyal followers to "bind" themselves to him personally and follow carefully the instructions he would give over the air or in the pages of *Social Justice*. Thoroughly disillusioned with politics after the Union party debacle of 1936, Coughlin confessed his error in engaging in a direct political approach to reform: "Now we recognize it is impossible to fight politicians with politicians, because you can't clean dirt with dirt." The priest was even critical of the quality of his own National Union for Social Justice officers, accusing them of being more interested in the candidacy of some local politician than in the sixteen points of social justice. Coughlin also informed his readers that a meeting of the board of trustees had already been held in Detroit at which it was decided to withdraw the National Union for Social Justice charter from all states but Michigan. He explained that this move would make it very difficult for anyone to misuse the revived national union for his own political ends. It was typical of Coughlin's mode of operation that the faithful were not "consulted" but "informed" after the fact.[6]

The first project of the "reawakened" national union was the defeat of President Roosevelt's ill-fated court-packing scheme. Coughlin assailed Roosevelt's attempt to liberalize the Supreme Court as a step on the road to dictatorship. The Royal Oak orator maintained, with numerous other critics of the scheme, that constitutional amendments were the only answer to President Roosevelt's dilemma, namely, a conservative court blocking necessary reform legislation. Claiming he was forbidden by the Corrupt Practices Act from making a direct radio appeal on any matter affecting legislation, he used the pages of *Social Justice* to urge his supporters to wire Congress their protests against the court scheme.[7] There is no record of how many Coughlin-inspired protests descended upon Congress. So many diverse groups so strenuously opposed the bill that its undignified demise on July 22 cannot be attributed to Father Coughlin.

The court fight seemed only to whet Coughlin's appetite for combat. His radio speeches became progressively more critical of Roosevelt. A March 8 address gloomily forecast the end of the United States unless drastic monetary reforms were enacted: "We are very near a national crisis, the passing of a nation."[8] His April 11 broadcast far surpassed any previous efforts in its pessimistic prediction of a spine-chilling depression for 1938:

> America will soon taste the bitter tears of a worse depression than 1929. You will live to see your meager pocketbooks fail to meet the costs of foodstuffs.
>
> You will live to see before next April a depression setting in, in this country, that will make Mr. Hoover look like an archangel by comparison.

Even more caustic was his vitriolic denunciation of Franklin Roosevelt:

> Any jackass can spend money. Any crackpot with money at his disposal can build for himself a dictatorial crown. It takes no brains to be liberal with other people's money. It is time for the American public to perform a sit-down strike—not on industry, not on men of commerce, but on politicians. They are sitting down on you, waiting for the government executioner, waiting for the last chapter of the Bill of Rights to be burned at the stake like a witch, waiting for the Supreme Court to put its head on the chopping block.[9]

Not until the April 5 issue of *Social Justice* did Coughlin return to the subject of the new National Union for Social Justice. The priest was still rather vague about the actual operation of the organization, but he asked all members to reorganize in small groups. Each Social Justice club was to be affiliated directly with the national union in a very loose way: "In common with the National Union all Social Justice Clubs profess faith in the 16 principles of social justice, but each club will be responsible to no persons but to its own members in its own clubs." The purpose of these clubs was stated as follows:

> To learn social justice; to organize against sit-down legislatures and Congressmen; to battle Communism, Fascism and anti-Christianity wherever and whenever it is possible; to cure democracy before it withers and perishes; to protect our Supreme Court; to oppose the evils of modern capitalism without joining in the excesses of radical labor organizers and to secure an honest dollar and an honest living for all Americans.[10]

In June, Coughlin announced a new sixteen-point program of social justice which he said could form the basis of a complete social justice program at the community, county, and state levels. Ignoring previous references to "Social Justice

Clubs," the radio priest suggested the establishment of neighborhood "Social Justice Councils" to implement his new program. He warned all prospective members that no political activities would be tolerated. Coughlin reiterated his preference for small groups and expressed his willingness to advise all interested parties by mail.[11] The June 21 issue of *Social Justice* clarified the situation by making the obvious suggestion that the "clubs" become "councils." To add to the semantic confusion, it was announced that a group of Coughlinites had organized a "Workers Council for Social Justice" at the Ford Motor Company. This new group was actually a labor union dedicated to achieving Coughlin's new sixteen-point program. Significantly, all non-Christians were excluded. As *Social Justice* explained:

The new Christian Union has no quarrel with the Brahman, the Buddhist or the Jew.

The Workers Council for Social Justice believes that the Christian scheme of economics is better than either the Brahman, or the Buddhist, or the Jewish schemes of economics. Therefore, it will not compromise with nor accept the principles of these philosophies which are in conflict with Christianity, so the leaders say.[12]

This restriction of non-Christians was quite obviously aimed specifically at Jews, as neither Brahmans nor Buddhists were exactly numerous in the United States. This marked a radical departure from the original National Union for Social Justice policy of welcoming Jews and reflected a growing antipathy toward Jews on Coughlin's part.

The new union was clearly Coughlin's answer to the CIO's efforts to organize the auto workers. According to *Social Justice,* the Workers Council for Social Justice would attempt to persuade the Ford Motor Company to use its huge capital for its employees' benefit. Specifically recommended was the establishment of grocery, meat, and clothing centers which would sell these necessities at cost to Ford employees. None of these Utopian schemes were ever implemented, as the union failed to attract real support at Ford and the whole project died an ignominious death.

The new, confused structure of the national union was explained in *Social Justice* as follows:

> Henceforth, the National Union for Social Justice will be regarded as a hub of a wheel.
>
> The spokes are Social Justice Councils which will be thousands in number and to which belong Christians who believe in the divinity of Jesus Christ and who are willing to practice by word and by deed His principles of justice and charity.
>
> The rim of the wheel will be organizations known as Workers Councils for Social Justice.
>
> The National Union for Social Justice as such will have no responsibility whatsoever for these third organizations. The National Union for Social Justice will endorse the principles of these organizations when they are in harmony with those of the National Union for Social Justice. At no time will it endorse the local officers or the methods to be employed.[13]

Further proof of Coughlin's total disgust with politics at this time is clearly evident in his regular column in the June 21 *Social Justice*. Bitterly lashing out at all politicians, he proclaimed that his great mistake in 1936 was to believe that democracy could work. "History," the disillusioned priest went on to say, "has proven it to be impractical and unsound insofar as the politicians who seek not the welfare of the common good but only the welfare of their own pocketbook proved irrevocably that we the people are fools, if we trust them any longer."[14] Coughlin denounced the majority of American politicians of all faiths as procommunist and laid the nation's economic woes squarely at their doorstep. Even the international bankers were acknowledged to be less blameworthy than the politicians; this was a truly remarkable statement from a man who had made a radio career of castigating international bankers.

Apparently, Coughlin hoped that his new nonpolitical social action group could achieve the aims of social justice in a more direct practical manner than any new political party; but he never explained how this was to be done. He correctly forecast that his new movement would be labeled "Fascistic, un-American, and anti-Semitic," but he promised never to abandon his followers, no matter how vehement the opposition became: "I will never desert you even though it costs me my life to sustain that promise."[15]

Shortly thereafter he announced the appointment of Walter Baertschi, a wealthy Toledo Presbyterian, as National Coordinator of Social Justice Councils. Since no elected officers were to be permitted, Baertschi's chief responsibility was to appoint, in collaboration with Father Coughlin, moderators for each Social Justice Council. This dictatorial method was designed to avoid all "internal politics" in the National Union for Social Justice.[16] Two weeks later four other national coordinators were appointed to assist Baertschi. No membership figures were published, but the July 12 *Social Justice* announced that hundreds of Social Justice Councils had already been formed.[17] Future issues of *Social Justice* carried a special column of advice to the Social Justice Councils on the implementation of the social justice program, but nothing of vital importance occurred. For the most part, the councils appear to have faded in significance almost as soon as they were formed.

There was widespread speculation in the summer of 1937 that the newly appointed Archbishop of Detroit, Edward Mooney, would not look as kindly upon Coughlin's controversial radio broadcasts and diverse political activities as did his predecessor. Mooney attempted to dispel all hint of possible trouble by telling the press that he was "sure Father Coughlin does not want to be an issue, and I see no reason why he should be."[18] There was little occasion for any verbal fireworks during the summer; Coughlin followed his usual practice of taking a long summer vacation from broadcasting.

Coughlin's public clash with Mooney came with dramatic

suddenness early in October, before the radio priest had even resumed broadcasting. Coughlin referred to the "personal stupidity" of Franklin Roosevelt in the course of a press interview on October 4, in which he criticized Roosevelt's appointment of Hugo Black, a former member of the KKK, to the Supreme Court. On October 7 Mooney issued a public statement completely dissociating the Detroit Archdiocese from Coughlin's statement and expressing regret that the Detroit priest had not availed himself of "the prudent counsel of a friendly critic." The archbishop also chastised Coughlin for insisting that no Catholic could belong to the CIO, which the radio priest alleged was a Communist organization. Coughlin, in his usual blatant manner, had declared the CIO as incompatible with Catholicism as Mohammedanism. Mooney dissented vigorously:

> Catholicism and Mohammedanism are incompatible on the basis of clearly stated fundamental principles of both. Catholicism and Communism are incompatible on the same basis.
>
> But no Catholic authority has ever asserted that the C.I.O. is incompatible with Catholicism on the basis of its publicly stated principles—though it is undoubtedly true that there are Communists in the C.I.O. who are making every endeavor to gain control of the organization for Communist purposes, and it is the conscientious duty of Catholics in the C.I.O. to relentlessly oppose these efforts.[19]

Coughlin must have been stunned by such a public rebuke from his religious superior. This was a totally new experience for a priest who had always enjoyed the cordial support of his bishop. The Royal Oak pastor at once prepared an answer to Mooney and submitted it for his approval before releasing it to the press. Mooney refused permission: "I advised Father Coughlin against publishing it because it seemed to me to go beyond the specific points in my statement." Coughlin himself was the epitome of clerical correctness in acceding to his bishop's wishes, but exploded a bombshell of his own by canceling his radio broadcasts for the coming 1937-38 season. The details are obscure even at this writing, but it is clear that Coughlin made this decision himself rather than submit to Mooney's censorship. As the priest's attorney, Prewitt Semmes, none too tactfully expressed it in a press release of October 9: "It was quite apparent that Father Coughlin would be permitted only to talk platitudes that mean nothing, that he could not say what he thinks, but only what the Archbishop thinks."[20]

Any doubt as to the intensity of the loyalty Coughlin commanded from his followers was soon dispelled as letters poured in to Royal Oak and the Detroit Chancery Office urging that the priest return to the air.[21] As could be expected, *Social Justice* immediately swung into action to defend its founder. The October 25 issue contained the complete text of the late Bishop Gallagher's 1935 radio defense of Coughlin as well as an additional personal statement in which Gallagher all but canonized the radio priest.[22] On October 19 Walter Baertschi, one of the national coordinators of the Social Justice Councils, announced that he was launching a crusade to restore Coughlin to the airwaves. The Toledo businessman insisted that he was acting on his own in response to the requests of hundreds of Coughlin's friends.[23] Shortly thereafter it was announced that *Social Justice* had been sold to Baertschi and that he would serve as president of the Social Justice Publishing Company until Coughlin was able to resume control. No mention of money was made but a thousand shares of no-par stock were transferred from the Radio League of the Little Flower to Baertschi.[24]

The November 8 *Social Justice* contained Baertschi's call to battle. The Toledo Presbyterian urged the immediate formation of a Committee of Five Million to protest directly to Pope Pius XI to have Coughlin restored to the air. Baertschi solemnly pledged himself to support Coughlin's ideals and to return the paper to the priest when "his voice is freed from restrictions; when his pen, likewise, is free to write as it did in the past."[25]

Almost at once *Social Justice*, in its militant zeal to restore its founder to his former status, clashed openly with Archbishop Mooney. The latter, assuming that *Social Justice* was a Catholic paper, requested that the paper clarify the Coughlin controversy by printing verbatim, without comment of any kind, Father Coughlin's press interview of October 4 and the archbishop's statement of October 7. It was clearly insinuated that Mooney felt that *Social Justice* was not objectively presenting the facts of the case to its readers: "This action of the Archbishop is taken with a view to supplying the correcting influence of full information and thus safeguarding your Catholic readers against misleading and disturbing inferences which the Archbishop fears they might, without such full information, draw from your article."26

Prewitt Semmes, attorney for *Social Justice*, not only refused the archbishop's request but also informed the chancery office that *Social Justice* was not, and never had been, a Catholic paper. Semmes stated that *Social Justice* would eventually publish the desired statements but would freely comment on the archbishop's "implied endorsement of the C.I.O." Semmes went on to rebuke Mooney for his pro-CIO stand, saying that the publisher of *Social Justice* found it "inconceivable" that Catholicism and the CIO were not incompatible.27

Meanwhile *Social Justice* continued to blame Archbishop Mooney for Coughlin's radio silence. Representative of typical *Social Justice* tactics was a feature story of November 8 under the banner, "Did Archbishop Mooney Silence Father Coughlin?" The unsigned article, a frequently used *Social Justice* device, accused Mooney of wishing "to wash his hands of the Father Coughlin 'decision.'" *Social Justice* further stated that the archbishop forced Father Coughlin off the air because the prelate's public criticism of the Royal Oak pastor led people to believe that Coughlin not only did not speak for the Church but was expounding views contrary to those of the Church. "Nothing was left for Father Coughlin to do but to bow to his superior's judgment, or else appear before a microphone as a 'black sheep' in the eyes of millions of Catholics and non-

Catholics in open contradiction to his lawful superior." As further proof of Mooney's perfidy, *Social Justice* noted that the archbishop had previously refused permission for Coughlin to publish a collection of *Social Justice* articles entitled, "Can Christians Join the C.I.O.?"[28]

Despite the archbishop's obvious disapproval, Baertschi's nationwide campaign to restore Coughlin to the air gathered increasing momentum. The Cleveland Social Justice Councils announced that they were seeking a hundred thousand signatures on a petition to be sent to the Pope; fifteen hundred Coughlinites attended a rally in Erie, Pennsylvania; New York friends of the priest organized in every county of the Empire State to solicit personal letters to Church authorities on Coughlin's behalf. Baertschi personally addressed large Coughlin rallies in Chicago and Detroit.[29]

Vivid confirmation that the protests were having a meaningful impact was an official statement issued by Archbishop Ameleto Cicognani, the Apostolic Delegate to the United States, on November 20, 1937. Cicognani said the Vatican had instructed him to say in reply to the many inquiries then being received that the "corrections made by the Archbishop of Detroit to the remarks of Father Coughlin were just and timely." The statement contained a strong but indirect rebuke to Coughlin for not restraining his enthusiastic followers:

> Every bishop has not only the right but the duty to supervise Catholic teaching in his diocese. Any priest who feels aggrieved by the action of the bishop has the right of orderly recourse to the Holy See, but in loyalty to the Church, he also has the duty of using his influence to keep the matter from becoming the occasion of public agitation and thus possibly creating confusion in the minds of many Catholics.[30]

Coughlin obviously understood the implied rebuke, for two days later he issued a dramatic appeal to his followers to cease agitating in his behalf:

> As a loyal priest of the Catholic Church I urge all my friends and I have stated many times privately, that I de-

plore the public agitation which has been caused by the cancellation of my radio broadcasts.

In the spirit of loyalty to my church I urge all my friends and followers to stop the holding of mass meetings or the sending of letters or telegrams to his Excellency the Archbishop of Detroit, or to the Holy See, with the design of securing the resumption of these radio broadcasts.[31]

On the very day of Coughlin's appeal for an end to the clamor, Walter Baertschi told the *Toledo Blade* in a telephone interview that he would pay no heed to the Vatican's statement or to Coughlin's request, but would continue the fight for the restoration of the radio priest.[32] The next issue of *Social Justice* (November 29) carried Baertschi's emotional appeal on page 1:

I know that Father Coughlin is an obedient priest. He cannot give his consent to our rallies, but in two years of association with him I know how his great heart loves social justice. As chairman of the Committee of Five Million I cannot let the people down. No fewer than 40,000 persons this week have begged me to carry on this fight for social justice and the restoration of our great leader to the radio. We cannot stop; We Must Carry On![33]

In the same defiant tone, *Social Justice* answered the rebuke of the Apostolic Delegate by stating that the Vatican had never heard Coughlin's side of the story. Furthermore, *Social Justice* scornfully insisted that the Apostolic Delegate was not speaking for the Pope anyway, but that Cicognani's statement was really drafted by the executive committee of American Catholic bishops, then meeting in Washington. Meanwhile, Baertschi and his associates continued to hold mass meetings demanding Coughlin's return.[34]

At the height of the uproar over his supposed "silencing," Coughlin suddenly announced that he was returning to the air. Since neither Father Coughlin nor the Detroit chancery office are willing to comment on the matter, a certain air of mystery still surrounds the whole episode. Since Mooney was on record as stating that Coughlin's decision to leave the air was entirely the priest's own choice, it is quite possible that the radio priest simply decided to submit to the archbishop's censorship and return to the air. This was certainly the impression the Detroit prelate gave. When questioned by reporters, Mooney declared that Coughlin's return "represents an exercise of liberty of action which he has always enjoyed in this matter." The archbishop even went so far as to refer to Coughlin's "recognized power as an exponent of Catholic teaching."[35] Coughlin himself declined comment, saying he would explain all on his first broadcast, but the *New York Times* noted that the Detroit priest had recently met with the Apostolic Delegate and speculated that this meeting may have cleared the way for Coughlin's return to the airwaves.[36]

As could be expected, *Social Justice* greeted the news of Coughlin's return with rapturous enthusiasm. The paper admitted that it "battled fiercely—if not always wisely" in Coughlin's behalf. The olive branch was extended to Archbishop Mooney, who, it was suggested, would learn "to love the pastor of the Shrine of the Little Flower."[37]

Coughlin himself returned to the pages of *Social Justice* in the December 20 issue as Editorial Counsel with Walter Baertschi remaining as President of Social Justice Publishing Company. In his first regular column, the radio priest took the paper to task for straying from the path of social justice. He was openly critical of "intemperate followers" who actually hindered his cause. He singled out for special criticism the paper's insinuation that the Apostolic Delegate did not speak for the Pope. Coughlin acknowledged that good intentions had motivated these errors but emphasized that *Social Justice* must spurn quarrels of any type and concentrate its efforts on a positive program of social justice. For his part, Baertschi acknowledged that the paper had made mistakes, but said this merely proved their dependence on Coughlin's prudent guidance.[38]

Coughlin triumphantly returned to the air on January 9,

1938, with an oft-repeated plea for capital and labor to work together for social justice. He reiterated that he had voluntarily left the air and that he had always had Mooney's permission to speak out on public affairs. The radio priest declared he now regarded the whole affair as a "closed incident" and preferred to get on with his fight for social justice. Sixty-three stations carried the broadcast, but conspicuous by its absence from the list was powerful WOR of New York, which announced a new policy prohibiting "controversial subjects on religious broadcasts on a commercial basis." The WOR management explained that it had previously made an exception for Father Coughlin, who had begun broadcasting before the ruling, but when he did not resume broadcasting in the fall they took advantage of the opportunity to terminate their agreement.[39]

Coughlin continued to hammer away at the money interests, insisting that true monetary reform was still the nation's only economic salvation. In March, Coughlin clashed openly with Roosevelt again. The occasion was the President's ill-fated reorganization bill. For reasons still not fully clear, the anti-Roosevelt forces were able to persuade a very high proportion of the American people that this much-needed tightening of the governmental structure was a major step on the path to a Roosevelt dictatorship. The bill envisioned a major reshuffling of government agencies by the President in the interest of more efficient government. Coughlin told his still impressive radio following that the real solution to America's problems was not the President's bill but the establishment of the Corporate State. His almost total contempt, which had grown steadily since his own political debacle in 1936, for established American political institutions was never more clearly expressed. No longer were congressmen to be elected by districts. Under Coughlin's scheme they were to be elected according to a complicated formula giving representation to various segments of society such as steel workers, auto workers, grain farmers, capitalists, etc. Senators were to be divided equally between capital and labor; each state was to have one senator representing labor and one representing capital. All political parties were to be eliminated. The President of the United States would no longer be chosen by the people but by the House of Representatives. This corporate arrangement was to prevail at every level of government—local, state, and national —and would presumably achieve the ever elusive goal of social justice for all.[40]

Having summarily disposed of over one hundred and fifty years of American democratic political traditions with a vague proposal for an authoritarian corporate state, Coughlin then accused Roosevelt of dictatorial ambitions. Not content with this, the Detroit priest even went to the ridiculous extreme of charging the President with planning to seize all Catholic schools in the United States. This was too much for Archbishop Mooney, who differed with his troublesome subordinate publicly: "I see nothing in the bill to expand present functions of Federal education agencies and therefore to arouse fears in regard to Catholic interests."[41] But few Coughlinites were as levelheaded as the Detroit bishop. At Coughlin's urging, thousands of telegrams descended upon Washington warning wavering congressmen of the dire political consequences in store for those who supported the President's bill. *The New York Times* reported that Western Union and the Postal Telegraph were both flooded with calls minutes after Coughlin made one of his radio appeals.[42] After a special thirty-minute antireorganization bill broadcast on March 31, *The New York Times* reported that ten thousand wires were dispatched from Detroit alone.[43] A later *Times* article reported that eighty thousand of Coughlin's followers had loyally followed his request to bombard their congressmen with wires protesting the bill.[44] After a narrow Senate victory, the bill met an unexpected defeat in the House on April 8 by an eight-vote margin, 204–196, with 108 Democrats deserting the perplexed Roosevelt. *Social Justice* somewhat inconsistently hailed the defeat as a great victory for democracy.[45]

Despite this convincing manifestation of loyalty, the Coughlin forces were in a state of chaotic disarray in 1938. It was announced in January that Coughlin himself would no longer supervise the affairs of the Social Justice Councils as he had promised, but was shifting this responsibility to Walter Baertschi and a board of directors. The priest would thereby be free to devote all his time and energy to his radio broadcasts and *Social Justice*. As convincing evidence that a real division of responsibility was envisioned, it was disclosed that Baertschi was constructing a headquarters for the Social Justice Councils in Toledo.[46] Then, inexplicably, just seven weeks later, Baertschi announced the dissolution of the Social Justice Councils, explaining that there had been too much dissension and insubordination to warrant their continuance. He was especially critical of the misuse of Father Coughlin's name in various fund-raising ventures. Many units, it seemed, failed to send their financial receipts to Royal Oak.[47] Nothing more was ever said about the ill-fated Social Justice Councils or the labor councils. They reveal some of the confusion in the Coughlin ranks at that time as to how best to proceed in the fight against the monied interests and the communists.

In the May 23 *Social Justice*, Coughlin urged the formation of groups of twenty-five or less to study the principles of social justice under his guidance through the pages of *Social Justice*. He reiterated his opposition to reorganizing the national union on its old basis, despite the numerous requests he had received. The priest declared that he had no intention of forming a new political party in 1940, but he did request that his followers "prepare themselves for action in 1940." In fact, he denied having founded the Union party in 1936. Coughlin insisted that the national union had simply supported the Union party's candidates. Even now, the priest was prepared to support Roosevelt in 1940 if the President changed his monetary policies to conform to the needs of social justice.[48]

But organizations were Coughlin's perennial weakness and he could not long resist the temptation to try again. Thus, in June, *Social Justice* announced the formation of the Million League. Instead of councils, the units were to be known as platoons, an unhappy choice of words which was to provide timely ammunition to those Coughlin critics who accused him of dictatorial ambitions. No specific program was immediately outlined for the new organization, although Coughlin issued a personal plea that it serve the poor of all races and creeds. But prospective members were told that "at the proper time Social Justice Platoons can be merged into a great thinking army that can swing our teetering nation back to sanity and right thinking."[49] Taken at face value, these words have an ominous tone, hinting at a possible secret movement to take over the government, but no one who was at all familiar with Coughlin's uninhibited oratory and *Social Justice*'s peculiar brand of journalism could take the radio priest's new movement seriously. There had been too many Cassandra-like prophesies and militant organizations emanating out of Royal Oak for any levelheaded observer to consider Coughlin a genuine threat to American democracy.

In July *Social Justice* carried a full-page appeal for the immediate formation of a Christian Front of which the Social Justice Platoons would be integral parts. There is still so much confusion about this matter that it is probably best to repeat this statement in its entirety:

> The term "Popular Front" was coined by European Communists as an appealing smoke-screen behind which to conceal their subversive destructionism.
> The moniker "Democratic Front" is the latest catchpole by which the Browderites hope to ensnare deluded Americans in a Red web. Never in the history of language has a word been so misused as "democracy" by Communists in this country. The fact that they have the effrontery to use the word despite what has happened under Communism in Russia, Spain and Mexico is some indication of their contempt for the intelligence of American citizens.
> If there must be "fronts," let us have a Christian Front!
> Not a "front" to throttle, enslave and destroy America, but one to PRESERVE America as one of the last frontiers of human liberty!

Outside of practical Christianity in the United States, all is darkness, confusion and despair. On one side stand the unrelenting rocks of greedy industrial capitalism. On the other, billowing swells of mistreated workers are being gradually rolled up into a Communist sea.

Without APPLIED CHRISTIANITY there can be no charity on one side, no peace on the other.

Then—let us have a Christian Front!

A Christian Front made up of Catholics and Protestants who still BELIEVE that America, as it is NOW, is capable of containing both capital and labor under conditions of progress and mutual co-operation.

A Christian Front that will FORCE industrial capitalism to yield to labor a fairer share of the nation's wealth.

A Christian Front of such solidity and energy as will curb the Molochs of international finance and will restore to the Congress of the United States its Constitutional right to issue and regulate the money of this Nation.

A Christian Front that will NEVER compromise with Communism, Fascism, Nazism or any other movement tending to destroy representative government.

A Christian Front that will not temporize for a moment with the hypocrisy of subversive agents who attempt by mealy-mouthed insincerity to show "there is nothing irreconcilable between Christianity and Communism."

A Christian Front which is not afraid of the word "fascist" because it knows the word "fascist" is merely bandied about as part of Communism's offense mechanism.

A Christian Front which will not fear to be called "anti-Semitic," because it KNOWS the term "anti-Semitic" is only another pet phrase of castigation in Communism's glossary of attack.

A Christian Front that will be FOR America AT Washington—not AGAINST America FROM Moscow!

* * * *

Every Social Justice Platoon now formed and in operation is an integral part of the Christian Front.

If you have not yet organized your friends and neighbors into a Platoon for the purpose of advancing the cause of social justice in America, do so at once.

There are now close to 2,500 Social Justice Platoons of 25 persons functioning in the United States as units of the "MILLION LEAGUE."

The time for you to take your part in this great drive is TODAY.

Show that you will do this by filling in and returning the Co-Operation Coupon below.[50]

Thus, it is rather clear that the Christian Front was intended more as a general alliance of all Christians against communism rather than as a specific organization of any kind. This was clearly the meaning of Bishop John F. Noll of Fort Wayne, Indiana, who publicly endorsed such a movement in *Our Sunday Visitor,* the popular Catholic weekly which he edited. *Social Justice* enthusiastically cited the bishop's support of such a Christian Front, so it is reasonable to assume that they were in general agreement as to its meaning.[51]

Coughlin continued to hammer away at the Roosevelt administration throughout the spring and summer of 1938. Roosevelt was held personally responsible for the severe recession which swept the nation in the winter of 1937-38. As early as January, *Social Justice* was gloomily editorializing: "Has our president led us to the end of the democratic-capitalistic road."[52] By July Coughlin was again linking President Roosevelt with the Communists. In a severely critical *Social Justice* column entitled "Mr. Roosevelt and Liberalism," the priest attacked almost all of Roosevelt's policies. Then, noting that even the Soviet Union was preparing a "liberal" constitution, he warned, "It is well to ponder this when you hear an American talking of liberalism, especially an American who has not repudiated publicly his following of Communists."[53] The President's vivacious, widely-traveled wife, Eleanor Roosevelt, was the victim of a full-scale *Social Justice* smear. Using tactics all too reminiscent of the McCarthy era, the magazine ran Mrs. Roosevelt's picture, tinted in pink, on the cover of its July 11 issue, under the caption "The First Lady Likes Pink."[54] A savagely critical article by Msgr. Edward Lodge Curran, a close associate of Coughlin who became a regular columnist for *Social Justice* in 1938, continued the attack on page 3. For good measure, *Social Justice* also gave the President's eldest son James the same sarcastic treatment in its July 18 issue.[55]

In August Coughlin astonished everyone by endorsing the candidacy of John O'Connor for Congress. O'Connor, who had once threatened to thrash the priest publicly, was now engaged in a battle for political survival in the Roosevelt purge of 1938. Despite Coughlin's strange, unsolicited endorsement, the conservative Chairman of the Rules Committee was the only victim of the President's personal vendetta against uncooperative Democratic congressmen.[56]

Although Coughlin devoted little air time to the subject in 1938, foreign policy came to occupy an increasing amount of space in the pages of *Social Justice*. The paper was right in tune with the extreme isolationism of the period; Senator Borah and Senator Nye were its folk heroes. Roosevelt's January request for increased military appropriations was branded "a war measure."[57] Japanese aggression against China was excused on the grounds that the Japanese were only imitating the British in their pursuit of empire. Coughlin did devote his broadcast of February 6 to attacking the idea of United States intervention in Asia. The title "Shall America Fight for British in Asia?" is eloquent proof of Coughlin's typical Irish-American scorn for all things British. The priest was quite willing to accept the Japanese slogan of "Asia for Asiatics" at face value. A cartoon in *Social Justice* depicted United States troops fighting under the Standard Oil Company banner in China with the caption: "The American Flag in China?"[58]

The two great diplomatic crises of 1938, the Austrian Anschluss and the Sudetenland Crisis, were treated in the usual confusing *Social Justice* style. An article by Joseph P.

Wright cited the broken pledges of Hitler and Mussolini as the reason for Austria's downfall. But there was no real criticism of the German Fuehrer's action, and Mussolini was cited as the magazine's "Man of the Week" in the May 23 issue.[59] The tragic demise of Czechoslovakia was also treated in a very erratic fashion. An unsigned article in the September 19 *Social Justice* was highly critical of the Czech abuse of the German population of the Sudetenland, which the author thought justified Hitler's bellicose actions. When the appeasement policies of British Prime Minister Neville Chamberlain at Munich averted immediate war, Coughlin extravagantly praised the British leader as "one of the most outstanding statesmen in the history of the British Empire." The priest had no fault to find with the Fuehrer; his venom was reserved instead for two of Chamberlain's most outspoken critics, Anthony Eden and Winston Churchill. But in October, *Social Justice* engaged once again in journalistic acrobatics and carried an editorial sympathizing with the Czechs and remarking on their fair treatment of the Germans within their borders.[60]

Far more important than any of Coughlin's foreign policy pronouncements, however, was the priest's sudden espousal of anti-Semitism in July of 1938 with the publication in *Social Justice* of *The Protocols of Zion*. Originally published in Russia in 1905, the *Protocols* purports to be an account of a Jewish conspiracy to seize control of the world. Thoroughly discredited by reputable scholars, the *Protocols* had previously appeared in Henry Ford's *Dearborn Independent* and in the hate literature of the KKK in the 1920's. It is true that Coughlin had been accused of anti-Semitism before, but there was always some reasonable doubt as to the truth of these accusations. With the publication of the *Protocols*, Coughlin squarely aligned himself with the leading Jew-baiters of the day. Naturally, he never admitted openly, or perhaps even to himself, that he was anti-Semitic. He was fond of rationalizing his position by talking about good Jews and bad Jews, much in the fashion of present-day racists who rationalize their anti-

Negro prejudices by making such distinctions between the Negroes who know their place and the troublemakers who wish to be treated as white people. Unfortunately, Coughlin's anti-Semitism was shared by countless Americans of all creeds, although it certainly was all too easy for uneducated Catholics to take the harsh language directed against the Jews in the Roman Missal literally and apply it, not to the ancient Jews who crucified Christ, but to their Jewish neighbors down the street. The problem is too complex for adequate treatment here, but anti-Semitism was at a peak in the United States in the depression-ridden 1930's when the Jews provided a ready target for those who sought convenient scapegoats for the economic ills of the world.

It is illuminating to examine Coughlin's introductory statement to the first chapter of the *Protocols*. He noted that many sources had cast doubt on the authenticity of the *Protocols* but maintained that it did not matter whether they were true or not, they corresponded with "very definite happenings which are occurring in our midst." He then proceeded to challenge the "righteous Jewish leaders to campaign openly, in season and out of season, against these Communistic attempts to overturn a civilization":

> The Book of "The Protocols of the Meetings of the Learned Elders of Zion" is preeminently a Communistic program to destroy Christian civilization: The best rebuttal which the modern leaders of Zion can offer to the authenticity of the Protocols is to institute a vigorous campaign against Communism. Jews as a whole oppose Nazism and Fascism.[61]

Coughlin continued to print excerpts from the *Protocols* throughout July, August, September, October, and November. In the August 8 issue of *Social Justice,* he stated his reasons for publishing the *Protocols*:

> (1) to advertise the contents of the Protocols so that all peoples will know that the tyranny, oppression and needless

poverty in the world are not of God's devising but are the results of planning, for the most part, by men who hate and detest the Christian principles of brotherhood and the Christian economics of plenitude; (2) to encourage the mass of Jews to join with us in opposing the Jew money changers as well as the Gentile money changers; (3) to invite the Jews as a whole to become militant, together with the Gentiles, against the spread of Communism with as much vigor as they oppose Fascism or any other foreign "ism."[62]

The Detroit priest accused the Jews of regarding Russia as a haven because it was the only country in which anti-Semitism was outlawed, but warned them that Stalin was in the process of turning against them and would "out-Hitler Hitler in persecuting the sons of Abraham." Quoting freely from *The Mystical Body of Christ in the Modern World*, a controversial book written by Father Dennis Fahey, an Irish priest, Coughlin strongly implied his agreement with Fahey's charge that the Jewish banking house of Kuhn, Loeb & Co. had financed the Russian Revolution and that the Jews had controlled Russia since that time.[63]

Despite the numerous charges of anti-Semitism leveled against him for publishing the *Protocols*, Coughlin stoutly maintained in the September 19 *Social Justice* that if anti-Semitism ever appeared in America he would be the first to fight it. The following week the priest exhibited a rare display of journalistic objectivity by publishing an article by Philip Slomovitz, Editor of the *Detroit Jewish Chronicle*, which thoroughly exposed the *Protocols* as being nothing more than an anti-Semitic fraud. *Social Justice* quickly countered with an article by one of its regular staffers, Ben Marcin,[64] entitled, "The Truth About the *Protocols*." Commenting on Slomovitz's scholarly attempt to disprove the authenticity of the *Protocols*, Marcin declared "that neither Father Coughlin, nor the oppressed millions of the world's population, nor myself, are interested in their authenticity. We are interested in their factuality and particularly in the factuality of the inordinate control of the world's economy under the Jewish system of modern capitalism."[65]

Coughlin himself wrote an even more absurd commentary on the *Protocols* in the November 21 *Social Justice*, in which he seriously maintained that prophecies of the *Protocols* were rapidly being fulfilled:

> The *Protocols of the Wise Men of Zion* cannot be proven to have been written by the "Wise Men of Zion," but the factuality of the content of the *Protocols* is about us at every turn.
>
> Is it not true that the synagogue of Satan, under the leadership of anti-Christ, has hindered and hampered the activity of the Mystical Body of Christ?
>
> Is it not true that some unseen force has taken Christ out of government, business, industry and, to a large degree, education?
>
> Is it not true that a force, over which we Christians seem to have no control, has gained control of journalism, motion pictures, theatres and radio?
>
> Is it not true that Communism has made progress in the world—Communism which is anti-Christ, anti-God, anti-liberty, anti-Christian and only pro-Semite as long as the Semites do not practice their own ancient religion?
>
> Is it not true that some unseen force has woven the threads of international banking to the detriment of civilization; that a godless force is dominating industry, has monopolized control of many industrial activities, has used governments as their servants, and has been instrumental in flinging one nation against another nation's throat?
>
> Is it not true that even the so-called freedom of the press and of the radio is questionable when we view the propaganda which filters through the ether to the detriment of peace and prosperity?
>
> Is it not true that gold, the international medium of exchange, has been concentrated in the hands of a few private individuals while nations languished, poverty-stricken, with want in the midst of plenty?

Is it not true that there is an intensification of armament building; that discord and hostility are being sown throughout the world; that we are being conditioned to expect the outbreak of a universal war?[66]

In November, at the very time when *Social Justice* was at the peak of its anti-Semitism, Coughlin assumed the presidency of Social Justice Publishing Company. Presumably he had the permission of Archbishop Mooney to resume total control of his paper. Why he had this permission in November of 1938 and did not enjoy it in 1937 is a perplexing question; *Social Justice* in 1938 was more of an embarrassment to the Catholic Church than it had ever been before.

Coughlin launched a new broadcasting season on November 6, 1938. This time forty-six stations carried the radio priest in his familiar Sunday afternoon time slot. No network would accept his broadcasts, nor would the leading stations in New York, Chicago, and Philadelphia. The Detroit priest was not heard west of Kansas or south of Maryland. He inferred that his difficulty in securing air time was the result of Jewish control of CBS, NBC, Mutual, and WOR.[67]

Father Coughlin's first two broadcasts were general in nature, with Coughlin merely reiterating his passionate belief in social justice and his vigorous opposition to communism. But, on November 20, 1938, thousands of Americans must have been jolted out of their chairs as he delivered the most fantastic speech of his controversial broadcasting career. Under the guise of sympathetically tracing the cause of the vicious persecution of the Jews in Nazi Germany, which had reached horrendous proportions in November of 1938, the Detroit priest actually proceeded to explain the Nazi action as a defense mechanism against communism. He expressed full agreement with the Nazi theory that the Jews were responsible for the Russian Revolution and occupied twenty-four of the twenty-five top posts in the 1917 Lenin government. For documentation of this, Coughlin presented the official Nazi list of Soviet officeholders, which he said he would be glad to send free of charge to all those interested. The radio priest again accused Kuhn, Loeb & Co. of New York City of being one of the principal financiers of the Communist Revolution, citing as his source a British "White Paper" of 1919. Interspersed throughout the address were references to the persecution of Christians in Russia, Mexico, and Spain which he alleged were far more serious than the German persecution of the Jews and which received far less publicity. Coughlin implied that the persecuted German-Jews were not deserving of sympathy unless Jews everywhere properly sympathized with persecuted Christians, a strange thought for a Christian clergyman to be publicly espousing. Even while making this absurd attack on the Jews, Coughlin had the gall to cloak himself in the mantle of charity:

> Believe me, my friends, it is in all charity that I speak these words as I seek to discover the causes that produced the effect known as Nazis—Nazism which was evolved to act as a defense mechanism against the incursions of Communism.
> Let us not forget the object of this discussion. My purpose is to contribute a worthwhile suggestion to eradicate from this world its mania for persecution.[68]

After Coughlin's bizarre talk, WMCA, in New York City, announced that "unfortunately, Father Coughlin has uttered certain mistakes of fact." The station presented its own expert, Professor Johan Smertenko, Director of the Nonsectarian Anti-Nazi League, to refute Coughlin's anti-Semitic accusations. It was later revealed that WMCA had received an advance copy of Coughlin's talk. Smertenko had corrected it and had returned it to Coughlin with a suggested bibliography on the Communist Revolution. Coughlin adamantly refused to change the text and Archbishop Mooney had declined to intervene.[69] WMCA then decreed that all future Coughlin speeches must be submitted to the station forty-eight hours in advance since, as the station described it, his last speech was "calculated to incite religious and racial strife in America." The New York station said it would make an exception the first week and give Coughlin until noon Sunday to submit a copy of his next talk.

The Royal Oak orator balked at this and announced through one of his assistants, Father Cyril Hasting, that he would not be able to comply with WMCA's conditions because the speeches were not prepared early enough to allow time for WMCA to read them after they had been passed by the diocesan censor.[70]

Thus, it is clear that Coughlin's radio talks were being preread by Church authorities. What is not clear is why the censors failed to tone them down. As was noted earlier, Archbishop Mooney publicly criticized Coughlin in October of 1937 for using the word "stupid" in reference to the President of the United States, but now, when the radio priest was inciting race hatred, on a vast scale, there was no public criticism or direct attempt to restrain him. Perhaps the archbishop was merely extending Coughlin the fullest measure of free speech, or another explanation is that Mooney hesitated to take any action that might produce another protest movement on the scale of that of 1937. Whatever the reasons, his failure to act caused many Americans to believe that Coughlin spoke for the Catholic Church.

Having quickly secured WHBI, Newark, to cover the New York area in lieu of WMCA, Coughlin returned to the air November 27 with a stirring defense of his November 20 broadcast. With his usual flair for the dramatic, the priest played a recording of carefully selected portions of his previous talk to demonstrate that he was not anti-Semitic. He then reiterated his charges that American Jewish bankers had helped finance the Communist Revolution in Russia. As proof he cited an article from the September, 1920, issue of *The American Hebrew* magazine which he stated proved Jewish participation in the revolution. He again cited Father Fahey's book, *The Mystical Body of Christ in the Modern World*, in which Fahey stated that the United States Secret Service had prepared a report on Jewish financiers of the Russian Revolution. Coughlin then proceeded to list some of the names contained in this alleged report, including leading members of Kuhn, Loeb & Co. As for WMCA's expert, Professor Johan

Smertenko, Coughlin dismissed him as a professional anti-Nazi who was using an expurgated edition of the British "White Paper" which did not contain the United States Secret Service report.[71] Reaction to the second broadcast came fast and furiously. Alexander F. Kerensky, Leon Trotsky, the U.S. Secret Service, Kuhn, Loeb & Co., and *The American Hebrew* magazine all vigorously contradicted Coughlin. The U.S. Secret Service issued a statement denying Coughlin's charge that it had prepared a report linking United States Jews to the financing of the Russian Revolution. Kuhn, Loeb & Co. categorically denied affiliation with any Russian government: "The firm of Kuhn, Loeb & Co. has never had any financial relations, or other relations with any government in Russia, whether Czarist, Kerensky, or Communist." The editors of *The American Hebrew* magazine produced a copy of the September, 1920, issue to prove that the radio priest had misquoted it. Leon Trotsky, the exiled Soviet leader, ridiculed Coughlin's charges that Jews had engineered the Russian Revolution.

Alexander F. Kerensky, who headed the first Russian revolutionary government, dismissed Coughlin's criticism of the Jews as a "mass of distortions and misinformation." The exiled revolutionary expressed genuine surprise that "any intelligent person can be so misinformed as Father Coughlin appears to be." Kerensky declared that there was not a single Jew in the first Soviet government which he headed, and that financial credits were first extended to it by the United States Government, not by Jewish bankers. Far from favoring Jews, Kerensky maintained, the Bolsheviks actually persecuted them. He curtly disposed of Coughlin's argument that the Germans were struggling to save the world from communism by citing the dramatic First World War episode when the German government shipped the exiled Russian Communist leader, Nikolai Lenin, into Russia in a sealed box car for the express purpose of fomenting revolution: "The Germans have no moral or political right to the claim that they are the defenders of civilization against bolshevism. They helped it to power."[72]

At the same time WMCA issued a public statement explaining its refusal to continue carrying the Coughlin broadcasts. The station charged that the Detroit priest's speech of November 20 "was calculated to stir up religious and racial hatred and dissension." Thus, it felt obliged to refuse to allow the use of its facilities to the Royal Oak orator unless he allowed the station some control over his future talks. When Coughlin refused, the station felt its first obligation was to the public and broke its contract with the controversial priest.[73] WMCA's stand was immediately applauded by *The New York Times* in a November 29 editorial: "Responsible persons everywhere will approve the action of those radio stations that refused to broadcast a speech plainly calculated to stir up religious prejudice and strife."[74] Supporting Coughlin to the hilt was *The Brooklyn Tablet,* the Jew-baiting weekly of the Archdiocese of Brooklyn, which, under the editorship of Patrick Scanlon, had long been Coughlin's staunchest backer in the ranks of the Catholic press. The *Tablet* editorial openly took the Jews to task:

> The feeling is abroad that in the present crisis in Germany, the Jews in America have overreached themselves. They have coralled everyone from the President down to plead their case. Yet they have shown no sympathy for the persecuted in other lands. WMCA itself had not a broadcaster ready to check "mistakes of facts" when speakers over its facilities pleaded for help for Loyalist Spain and other like causes. . . .
>
> This was the whole point of Father Coughlin's address. That it went home and that it carried a weighty truth is proven better by the action of WMCA than by any word of Father Coughlin.[75]

A far more respected journal of Catholic opinion, *America,* took a strangely insensitive view of the matter. Totally ignoring the fact that Coughlin's talk had obviously incited hatred against the Jews, *America* insisted that the real issue was the right of stations to censor "a nationally known speaker, respected by millions of his fellow citizens."[76] In contrast, the more liberal Catholic weekly, *Commonweal*, was sharply critical of Coughlin and noted the enthusiastic reception his speech had received in Nazi Germany. *Commonweal* denounced the *Protocols* as false and discredited, and scornfully referred to *Social Justice* as "that Hearstian adventure in journalism curiously called Social Justice."[77]

Riding Coughlin very hard as usual was the *Detroit Free Press*, which referred to the priest's Sunday broadcasts as his "weekly attack on the Jews." Coughlin became so enraged at this sort of treatment that he initiated a $2,000,000 libel suit against the paper. As had been the case with similar legal actions in the past, the suit was later dropped.[78]

Meanwhile, the New York followers of Father Coughlin were again rallying to the defense of their embattled leader. Six thousand of the faithful attended a rally at Manhattan Center sponsored by an organization calling itself the Committee for the Defense of Constitutional Rights. The chairman, Judge Herbert O'Brien of Brooklyn, an ardent Coughlinite, drew resounding cheers for the radio priest when he declared that Coughlin had thrice saved America by his effective opposition to the World Court, to court-packing, and to the reorganization bill. A resolution was adopted asking the FCC to revoke WMCA's license for having refused Coughlin air time. Allen Zoll, representing the Committee of American Patriots, Inc., announced plans for the picketing of WMCA and issued a veritable declaration of war against the station: "I think we ought to put WMCA out of business. Let's make a horrible example out of that station so that no other station in America will have the nerve."[79] The following Sunday two thousand pickets demonstrated in front of WMCA, many of them carrying anti-Semitic signs.[80] Every Sunday for the next several months, Coughlinites and assorted anti-Semites turned out in force to picket WMCA.[81]

By this time many Catholics were deeply concerned about the false image Coughlin was presenting of their Church as an anti-Semitic organization. Cardinal Mundelein of Chicago, in rapidly failing health, prepared a public statement emphatically declaring that the Detroit priest did not speak for the Catholic Church: "As an American citizen, Father Coughlin has the right to express his personal views on current events, but he is not authorized to speak for the Catholic Church nor does he represent the doctrine or sentiments of the Church." Too ill to deliver the message personally, Mundelein had Auxiliary Bishop Bernard J. Sheil read it for him over the NBC network on December 11, 1938.[82] Another Catholic champion of fair play for the Jews was Frank Hogan, the President of the American Bar Association, who broadcast a very moving attack on anti-Semitism. Hogan cleverly quoted Pope Pius XI on the subject, a source no loyal Catholic would openly disparage:

> Abraham is called our patriarch, our ancestor. Anti-Semitism is not compatible with the reality of this text; it is a movement Christians cannot share. No, it is not possible for Christians to take part in anti-Semitism. We are Semites, spiritually.

As further evidence that Coughlin's talks were not in harmony with Catholic thinking, Hogan referred to the following statement in the *Michigan Catholic,* the official newspaper of Coughlin's own diocese: "Totally out of harmony with the Holy Father's leadership are Catholics who indulge in speeches or writings which in fact tend to arouse feelings against the Jews as a race."[83] *Commonweal* devoted a good portion of its December 30 issue to refuting Coughlin. Monsignor John A. Ryan contributed an article entitled "Anti-Semitism in the Air," in which he ridiculed the Detroit priest's interpretation of history and urged all Catholics to shun participation in this anti-Semitic campaign. George Shuster, former editor of *Commonweal,* and then President of Hunter College, attempted to salvage some respect for Catholic scholarship and journalism, matters of deep personal concern to him, by presenting a brief scholarly history of German communism. Shuster noted as a typical Coughlin distortion of fact the priest's labeling Friedrich Ebert a Jewish communist leader when in reality he was a member of an old Baden Catholic family and a dedicated foe of communism.[84]

In the midst of all the uproar over Coughlin's anti-Semitic speeches, *Social Justice* added to the confusion by launching a short-lived McCarthy-type exposé of Soviet penetration of the Roosevelt administration. The November 28 issue carried the following warning to the administration:

> This National Weekly has long had in its possession information that ace operatives high in the council of the O.G.P.U. (Russian Secret Police) have wormed their way into the Washington bureaucracies—often in preference to native born Christian Americans.
>
> We repeat that *Social Justice* has long refrained from giving circulation to any such disparaging information embarrassing to the Administration, in the full hope and expectation that Washington officialdom intended to clean house. News of the house cleaning IS LONG OVERDUE.[85]

The exposé began in the December 19 issue with a bizarre story identifying Leon G. Turrou, a top agent of the FBI, as a Soviet agent.[86] The following week Coughlin printed a full-page retraction under his own signature stating that further investigation revealed that the "evidence" was not accurate. There was no apology to Mr. Turrou or to *Social Justice* readers, just a pat on the back for *Social Justice* for its fairness in retracting the story.[87] The Turrou fiasco marked the end of *Social Justice*'s pseudorevelations concerning the infiltration of Communist agents in the Roosevelt administration.

The year 1939 was to be made infamous by the beginning of the most catastrophic war in history. As the new year opened, Father Coughlin shifted most of his attention to blocking the revision of the Neutrality Act of 1937. The law as it then stood completely prohibited the shipment of arms to belligerents. As the general European diplomatic situation grew steadily worse, the Roosevelt Administration began to give serious consideration to repealing the "arms embargo" provision of the Neutrality Act. This, it was argued, would give the United States a more flexible foreign policy and enable the government to render assistance to innocent victims of military aggression. Well aware of the strong isolationist sentiments of a great percentage of the American people, President Roosevelt gingerly introduced the subject in his annual message to Congress, January 4, 1939:

> At the very least, we can and should avoid any action, which will encourage, assist, or build up an aggressor. We have learned that when we deliberately try to legislate neutrality, our neutrality laws may operate unevenly and unfairly—may actually give aid to an aggressor and deny it to the victim. The instinct of self-preservation should warn us that we ought not to let that happen any more.[88]

Roosevelt's words evoked a bitter outburst of emotional criticism from isolationists of diverse political views. The liberal *New Republic* and the conservative *Chicago Tribune* were as one voice in denouncing the proposed change. For his part, Roosevelt pursued a very cautious tack and accepted the offer of Senator Key Pittman to allow the Senate Foreign Relations Committee, of which he was chairman, to draft the proposed revision and steer it through the troubled congressional waters. Pittman announced on January 11 that hearings on the bill would begin around the end of January, but just eight days later the Nevada senator declared that the hearings were postponed indefinitely due to the press of other committee business. He backed down so abruptly because of the desperate efforts of pro-Loyalist Americans to modify the law to permit arms to reach the Spanish Government before Franco won a final decisive victory. Left-wing groups, alarmed at the desperate position of the Spanish government, marshaled all their forces in sponsoring a "Lift the Embargo Week." Catholic groups immediately counterattacked with a "Keep the Embargo Week." Roosevelt had seriously considered lifting the embargo on arms to Spain as recently as November, but now a Franco victory appeared certain and the administration was extremely anxious to prevent the whole discussion of neutrality revision from being mired in a divisive argument over the Spanish question.

A long-time supporter of Franco, Father Coughlin leaped into the fray in his radio broadcast of January 15, charging that the repeal of the embargo against Spain would be a victory for the communists. He once again urged all his followers to telegraph their views to their congressmen as quickly as possible. *The New York Times* reported that the telegraph offices were flooded with wires shortly after the priest left the air. The same source estimated that over a hundred thousand wires had been received in Washington as of January 16.[89] Caught in the crossfire, the unhappy Senate Foreign Relations Committee courageously decided that discretion was the better part of valor and voted to postpone the whole business indefinitely.[90]

On January 29, Coughlin conveniently blended isolationism and anti-Semitism by declaring himself to be unalterably opposed to any war to aid the Jews in Germany or elsewhere in the world. The priest linked all agitation for the repeal of the arms embargo to Jews seeking aid for their European brothers.[91] He was also quick to defend Hitler's unprincipled rape of Czechoslovakia in March of 1939, saying that most American critics had exploited the issue as a convenient excuse to attack Germany.[92]

Social Justice also proved itself a willing apologist for the fascist regimes of Germany and Italy. The March 27 issue defended Mussolini's persecution of the Jews on the grounds that "most Jews were anti-Fascist." The April 3 *Social Justice* heralded the Rome-Berlin Axis as a "firm rampart against Communism," and carried Hitler's picture on the back cover. The accompanying story admitted that Hitler had persecuted Catholics, Protestants, and Jews, but suggested that no one was perfect, and absurdly invoked the biblical quotation: "He who is without sin, let him cast the first stone." Coughlin himself threw the first stone in the following issue, April 10, when he lashed into the "pagan Nazis" for arresting priests and seminarians in Frankfurt on trumped-up charges. It is interesting to observe how quick he was to attack an injustice involving fellow Catholics while remaining coldly insensitive to the horrors being perpetrated against the Jews.[93] In contrast to the favorable April 3 treatment accorded Herr Hitler was *Social Justice*'s April 24 publication of President Roosevelt's picture on its cover under the caption "President Roosevelt Wants War For U.S."[94] According to *Social Justice*'s peculiar interpretation of events, Roosevelt and his cabinet were pushing hard for war with Germany even though England and France were working for peace. This, of course, contradicted several previous and future *Social Justice* stories which insisted that Great Britain was selfishly dragging the United States into the war to save her empire, but inconsistency was the one thing the discriminating reader could always count on *Social Justice* to provide.

Throughout the spring and summer of 1939 there were clashes on the streets of New York between Coughlin supporters and his enemies. The most notable incident from the standpoint of sheer numbers occurred on April 8 when a crowd of several thousand people mobbed ten newsboys selling *Social Justice*.[95] It was also common for the Coughlinite pickets at WMCA to be involved in violence with their more vocal critics.[96] A bizarre development in the WMCA affair was the arrest in July of the pickets' leader and organizer, Allen Zoll, on a charge of extortion. Donald Flam, President of WMCA, charged that Zoll asked him for $7,500 to call off the pickets and had already taken $200 in marked bills as a down payment. Zoll claimed that he had taken the money as salary for his job as sales consultant to WMCA in which capacity he was to get rid of the troublesome pickets who had been annoying the station since December 18, 1938.[97] Zoll was later acquitted of the charges due to insufficient evidence.

Street brawls involving Christian Fronters and Jews became frequent in New York City, and there were numerous complaints that the predominantly Irish-Catholic police force was showing partiality to the Coughlinites. When James Wechsler echoed this charge in a *Nation* article entitled "The Coughlin Terror," the colorful mayor of New York, Fiorello H. La Guardia, was quick to issue an indignant denial. The mayor eliminated most of the trouble in September when he issued an order limiting the number of pickets at WMCA to four.[98] Coughlin, it must be admitted, was in no way directly responsible for the violent actions of his New York supporters, but he did help to create an atmosphere of hate and must bear his share of responsibility for the ugly consequences. To his credit, the Royal Oak pastor called off a proposed anti-Red march his New York followers had planned for mid-August and thus avoided a possibly bloody riot since the anti-Coughlin forces were already planning a simultaneous anti-Fascist rally.[99] Earlier, Coughlin had announced that he had received three letters threatening him with assassination if he didn't cease all public pronouncements by Labor Day.[100]

The steady flow of controversial statements in his broadcasts and in the pages of *Social Justice* continued to evoke a lively response from Coughlin's numerous critics. Perhaps the best Catholic critique of this period was penned by John Cogley, then editor of the *Chicago Catholic Worker* but better known as an editor of *Commonweal* in future years. In an open letter to Father Coughlin, Cogley pleaded with the radio priest to control his followers:

> In a sense you are the most powerful Catholic voice in the United States today. . . . You are a unique priest. You are heartily disliked. You are genuinely beloved. You are a definite, undeniable force on what novelists like to call the American scene. Your opinions sway millions; you dismay millions more. . . .
>
> You were a pioneer, and nobody who is devoted to the cause of social justice can forget that it was you who first made the word encyclical a part of America's working vocabulary. . . .
>
> But there is an unmistakable group of your faithful

friends, violent supporters of you and your program, that have come popularly to be called "Coughlinites." They get into people's hair. They get into mine. At times they probably get into yours. . . . They are probably good simple people who don't have much sense, and it should not reflect on you that they have rallied 'neath your banner. . . . This "fringe" has become notorious for its burning anti-Semitism, and they have persisted in canonizing you as the patron of prejudice. They have become psychotic on the question of Jews. They are using your controversial Russian revolutionist figures to justify a senseless, unChristian attitude toward Mrs. Cohen, the delicatessen lady around the corner, and Meyer, the insurance collector. They have confused your anti-Communism campaign with an anti-Semitism campaign. . . .

These Christians, many of them Catholics who are known as "Coughlinites," have the thing all balled up. Something should be done to set them right. Somebody should talk to them. They would listen if you did. . . . What you could say would help to make up for the pain and insult many innocent, godly Jews have received from your confused followers.[101]

Not so gentle in its criticism was an editorial in *The Christian Century* denouncing Coughlin as "thoroughly Hitlerish in outlook, in method and the effect he produces."[102] The priest was also thoroughly castigated at a public rally held in New York under the sponsorship of the American Jewish Alliance. An audience estimated at a thousand heard the Reverend Guy Emery Shipler, editor of *The Churchman*, a Protestant Episcopal publication, accuse Coughlin of "dropping a torch into a world filled with high explosives." Rabbi Benjamin Plotkin, head of the American Jewish Alliance, minced no words in labeling Coughlin "an enemy of democracy," "a fascist," "a Nazi."[103] Elliott Roosevelt joined the chorus of critics by attacking the priest on his weekly radio series on the Mutual Network. He denounced Coughlin's "anti-Semitic oratory" and suggested even radio censorship might not be too high a price for the country to pay to be rid of such hate-mongering. The President's eldest son invited Coughlin to appear on his program and defend his position.[104] A spokesman for Father Coughlin read his reply to Elliott Roosevelt on Coughlin's broadcast of Sunday, July 16. The statement again denied that Father Coughlin was anti-Semitic and dared Mutual to give him radio time since the priest alleged there was a communist conspiracy to silence him. The Coughlin statement also accused the communists of calling anyone who criticized them anti-Semitic.[105] Both Mutual and Elliott Roosevelt made a bona fide offer of free radio time, but the priest declined with thanks, saying he preferred to answer Elliott Roosevelt on his regular Sunday broadcast.[106]

A more potent criticism of Coughlin was published in 1939 by the General Jewish Council—a book entitled, *Father Coughlin, His "Facts" and Arguments.* In view of the emotion-charged atmosphere of the times, with Jews suffering severe persecution in Germany, the book was unfortunately, albeit understandably, as extreme in its rebuttal as Coughlin was in his original charges.[107]

Social Justice quickly sprang to Coughlin's defense with a series of articles under the byline of Ben Marcin entitled, "An Answer to Father Coughlin's Critics." Later published in book form, the articles restated all of Coughlin's familiar arguments linking Jews to communism.[108] Marcin quoted at some length the laudatory remarks the late Bishop Gallagher made concerning Coughlin, and implied that since Archbishop Mooney had not "repudiated" them he must approve of the Royal Oak pastor's work. Coughlin was quick to correct this implication. It is entirely possible that he did so at Mooney's insistence. Whatever his motive, the radio priest made it very clear that he alone was responsible for his actions:

> That I have made many mistakes no one appreciates more keenly than I do. I do not wish either to saddle my mistakes upon the Archbishop nor do I wish to present him

as condoning any ill-advised policy or error which, unconsciously, I have adopted, or I may adopt.

Certainly, neither Bishop Gallagher in the past, nor Archbishop Mooney at present, can be on record as having approved or approving everything I have said or will say, what I have done or will do.[109]

Another damaging blow to whatever was left of Coughlin's reputation was the testimony before the Dies Committee of Fritz Kuhn, the German Bund Leader, that the Bund was openly anti-Semitic and that he had invited Coughlin and his followers to Bund meetings because the organization "cooperates with everybody who has the same aims and purposes we have." Kuhn revealed that only about 60 per cent of the Bund's membership was German, Italians and Irish comprising the better part of the remaining 40 per cent.[110]

Coughlin's personal reply to all charges of anti-Semitism or pro-Nazism was given over the air on June 5:

When, either in speech or writing, have I advocated Nazism? It is true that I have regarded it as a defense mechanism against Communism. It is true—this following statement is supported by incontestable facts—that many Jews were among those responsible for furthering Communism in Germany and bringing that country to such a despondent state that Nazism became a reality.[111]

Another interesting apologia appeared in the August 12 issue of *Liberty* magazine. Coughlin granted an interview to Edward Doherty of *Liberty* and talked freely about his alleged anti-Semitism to the sympathetic journalist:

The average Jew, the kind we admire and respect, has been placed in jeopardy by his guilty leaders. He pays for their Godlessness, their persecution of Christians, their attempts to poison the whole world with Communism.

My purpose is to help eradicate from the world its mania for persecution, to help align all good men, Catholic and Protestant, Jew and Gentile, Christian and non-Christian, in

a battle to stamp out the ferocity, the barbarism and the hate of this bloody era. I want the good Jews with me, and I'm called a Jew baiter, an anti-Semite. . . .
I am anti-Communist and anti-Nazi. I am an American. No true American can favor either Communism or Nazism. . . .
We must admit, though, that pro-Communist sentiment is growing in America. Newspaper and radio propaganda is responsible along with the shallow thinking of those exposed to that propaganda. In order to whip up sentiment for Communism our people are being flooded with accounts of Nazi atrocities. You almost never hear anything or read anything about Communist persecutions.[112]

The Detroit priest noted that only Germany, Italy, and Spain had avoided the control of international bankers. The United States was contrasted unfavorably with Germany and Italy who, Coughlin argued, were at least feeding their people. Having said this, the priest sardonically quipped: "There, I've actually said a good word for the totalitarian countries, so, naturally, I'll be called both a Fascist and a Nazi."[113]

After months of neglect, the radio priest revived the idea of the Christian Front in July of 1939. Coughlin broadcast an appeal on July 30 for all Christians to band together against Communism, but he gave no real information as to the structure of the organization. The July 31 *Social Justice* contained glowing praise for the Christian Front movement, and claimed it was rapidly spreading from Brooklyn to other eastern cities and the Midwest. The paper, in very militant language, announced that the Christian Front was to operate as a "defense mechanism against Red activities and as a protector of Christianity and Americanism." *Social Justice* said the group hoped to achieve a membership of five million by 1940.[114]

Coughlin insisted that he himself was in no direct way connected with the Christian Front. Elaborating upon his July 30 broadcast in a special message in *Social Justice* he unequivocally stated his intention to remain aloof from all organizations:

My Position Towards Organizations

Permit me to clarify my position in connection with the broadcast of Sunday, July 30th, relative to the Christian Front.

First and foremost, let all those who are interested in either organizing the Christian Front or joining it understand that I am neither the organizer nor the sponsor of the Christian Front; and moreover, that it is not becoming for me to identify myself with this organization or any other organization.

From time to time, fine, zealous persons have approached me to associate myself with various organizations. To protect any usefulness that I may have as a public speaker, I resolved, following the experience of the National Union in 1936, to hold absolutely aloof from all organizations. I must not depart from this policy even in the case of the Christian Front.

However, if Christians as individuals or as groups desire to establish a Christian Front with the objective in mind of incorporating the spirit and the doctrines of Christianity into our social life, that is commendable. Nevertheless, as a clergyman, I do not find it compatible to identify myself with any movement in any way whatsoever. I prefer to remain entirely outside all organizations.

As a clergyman, I do not find it irregular to support labor unions in general, even though labor unions, in some instances, have been responsible through some of their members and leaders for seizure of property and contempt of law. However, I do not belong to any of them; I do not attempt, except as an outsider, to sustain or direct them.

Thus, as I support labor unions, so can I support a Christian Front whose advertised principles and whose officers propose to defend Christianity against the unjust aggressions of anti-Christian forces, even though some members of the Christian Front will be deserving, by reason of their ill-advised actions, of just criticism.

Therefore, gentlemen of the Christian Front, and those of you who are contemplating establishing units of it, please understand my position. I must hold myself disengaged from your organization; I must act in no other capacity toward you than as a friend and counsellor, whose privilege it is to address you in your homes each Sunday. But I am determined to be independent of your group, and therefore must refuse to undertake to advise you how to organize, whom to select as your officers and what to do in specific instances.

To depart from this program would destroy any usefulness I may have; for I would be assuming both an authority and a position altogether impractical.

While I earnestly encourage the establishment of a Christian Front along the general lines which I indicated in my radio address, Sunday, July 30th, I hope I have clarified my position towards it and have satisfied you as to its reasonableness.

Therefore, while I encourage you to carry on in the spirit of Christ and in the spirit of America, I am sure that I can be of more service to the cause by refraining from participating in it either as an active member, an active officer, or an active organizer, and by continuing to be a voice that is friendly to your cause and to every other good cause without participating in their activities.

What I have said relative to myself also holds good for SOCIAL JUSTICE magazine.[115]

Undeterred by previous failures, Coughlin issued another appeal in December for the formation of Social Justice Study Clubs of about a dozen or so members. He repeated his belief that the poor organizational structure of the national union was the principal cause of its downfall. The appeal contained no mention of the fate of the Social Justice Study Clubs of 1937-38.[116]

Throughout the uneasy summer of 1939, which saw President Roosevelt fail in a dramatic bid to repeal the arms embargo just weeks before the outbreak of the Second World War, Coughlin remained an ardent isolationist Anglophobe. Even the Nazi-Soviet Pact of August 23 failed to change Coughlin's isolationist views. His oft-repeated contention that Nazism served as a defense mechanism against communism was shattered with a stroke of the pen in Moscow, but no acknowledgment of error was ever forthcoming. In his radio address of August 27, he merely reiterated his plea for America to remain neutral and appeared to be far more critical of America's foreign policy than Germany's: "America must hold herself free from foreign entanglements. Have we not learned our lesson that we have no business in recognizing Russia, in preferring Russia to Germany." He did acknowledge that "this means that henceforth we must treat Communism and Nazism alike," but insisted that the United States should make no alliance with England, France, Belgium, and the Netherlands until they purged themselves of the evils of "modern capitalism and nationalism."[117]

When Germany invaded Poland on September 1, 1939, President Roosevelt finally threw the full weight of his personal prestige into the battle to repeal the arms embargo in order to make it possible for the peaceful democracies of Europe to buy desperately needed arms in the United States. The President called a special session of Congress to consider the issue and in a dramatic opening address pleaded with Congress to repeal the arms embargo and return to the established traditions of international law. It was a shrewd speech, in which Roosevelt emphasized again and again his desire for American neutrality and completely avoided any reference to the administration's desire to aid England and France.[118]

Coughlin once again threw himself wholeheartedly into the battle, determined that the ban on the sale of arms should remain firmly rooted in the neutrality law. On his September 10 broadcast he implored his audience to write or wire their congressmen demanding, "No cash or carry, no foreign entanglements, and no blood business."[119] As usual, thousands of the faithful responded. *The New York Times* reported that the Senate mail volume increased from ten thousand to a hundred thousand pieces of mail a day, an increase at least partly attributable to Coughlin's plea. The heavy mail was very much one-sided in favor of retaining the embargo, the ratio at times ranging as high as 1,000 to 1.[120] Two weeks later the radio priest answered Roosevelt's call for a return to international law by declaring that international law had long since ceased to exist. The arms trade, the Detroit priest shouted, was nothing more than "merchandising in murder." On September 28 Coughlin addressed a cheering crowd of eighteen thousand at a peace rally in Cleveland. Archbishop Francis J. Beckman of Dubuque sent a personal representative to the meeting with a warm letter endorsing Coughlin which was read to the delegates by Msgr. Edward Lodge Curran, a frequent contributor to *Social Justice.* Curran also delivered a strong isolationist pitch, in the course of which he mentioned that he had the permission of his own religious superior, Bishop Thomas Malloy of Brooklyn, to speak out on these public issues.[121]

On October 1 the Royal Oak orator delivered his most impassioned plea for retaining the embargo, predicting that repeal would put the United States in the war within one year and would benefit only the communists. With much emotion and little logic, the priest declared "This is Stalin's war; this is the Communists' war and this will be anti-Christ's victory unless there is immediate peace."[122] Hitler's maniacal scheme for control of Europe is never even alluded to. Coughlin was apparently so obsessed with his fear of communism that he just could not focus intelligently on anything else. He failed to comprehend that there could be other major evils in the world. Occasionally, it is true, he would briefly criticize fascism, but he never once showed any concern over the possibility of a Hitler-dominated Europe. On the contrary, he naively called upon England and France to accept Hitler's peace offers and end the war. The implication is strong that he believed Hitler was fighting a just war against the stubborn, imperialistic British and French.[123] Continuing to dwell on the communist theme, Coughlin maintained that the repeal of the arms embargo would be the first step toward communism and renewed his charges that the Roosevelt administration had "coddled" the communists.[124] On his regular Sunday broadcast of October 29, Archbishop Francis Beckman of Dubuque joined Coughlin in a moving plea for total neutrality. Beckman repeated Coughlin's charge that only the communists would gain by the repeal of the arms embargo or any form of American involvement. The Dubuque prelate saw the war as a communist plot "to destroy Christian Civilization." Hitler's role in all this was never mentioned, much less clarified. The archbishop said he was compelled to speak out for two reasons: "(1) I could stand no longer to see the Catholic Church in America used for private and political ends, (2) I am firmly convinced of the fact that the present European war is a most unjust and un-Christian conflict—an economic war based on greed which will only benefit international Communism."[125]

The proponents of neutrality revision were so concerned about the Detroit priest's influence among American Catholics that they secured radio time for Msgr. John A. Ryan, an old Coughlin nemesis, to answer the radio priest. Ryan, speaking under the auspices of the Non-Partisan Committee for Peace through the Revision of the Neutrality Law, eloquently attacked Coughlin's moral obtuseness: "The person who asserts that we should be impartial and indifferent with regard to the conflict between the Hitler government and the Allies repudiates not only Christ's gospel of brotherly love, but the principles of national morality. In the present crisis our country is morally obliged to do all that it can reasonably do to defeat Hitler and Hitlerism."[126]

Despite the frenzied pleas of Coughlin and other isolationists, the arms embargo was repealed on November 3 with a stipulation that all trade in arms be on a cash-and-carry basis. The Royal Oak orator accurately prophesied that the cash-and-carry clause would be eliminated as soon as the Allies had exhausted their cash reserves. Coughlin not only denounced the neutrality bill as the first step toward war, but declared that the United States had actually entered the war against Germany.[127]

In the heat of the arms embargo fight, the National Association of Broadcasters drafted a new code of broadcasting standards aimed specifically at barring Father Coughlin from the airwaves. The new code prohibited all "controversial" speakers from buying radio time unless they appeared on some form of panel with others taking divergent views. The association did not define "controversial," but any reasonable definition of the term would have barred all news commentators of the day, such as Gabriel Heatter, Raymond Gram Swing, Walter Winchell, and others. Naturally, the code did not refer to Coughlin by name, but it was obvious that it was contrived primarily to bar him from the air. One manifestation of this was the telegram dispatched by Mr. Edward Kirby, the Secretary of the Code Compliance Committee of the National Association of Broadcasters, to all radio stations:

> For the consideration of the Code Committee, please advise headquarters immediately if you are now carrying Father Coughlin's broadcasts, date of present contract's expiration, whether renewal has been offered or accepted. If broadcasts found to violate NAB Code, what are provisions for cancellation?

One irate broadcaster who refused to be dictated to was the Reverend W. A. Burk, S.J., Director of WEW, St. Louis, which was owned and operated by St. Louis University, a Jesuit institution. Father Burk curtly refused to comply with the NAB's implied order to cancel the Detroit priest. In the course of his lengthy letter of protest to the NAB, the St. Louis Jesuit declared his support for Coughlin's "patriotic work" in fighting the communists and said there would be "nothing less than a revolution among the Catholics and Protestants" of St. Louis if WEW dropped Coughlin. Father Burk revealed that on one occasion an erroneous story circulated in St. Louis that Coughlin was to be canceled and WEW received sixteen thousand letters in two weeks, only twenty of which criticized the Detroit orator. Kirby's somewhat feeble response denied that the code was aimed at Coughlin and defended the regulations as preventing people of great financial means from controlling public opinion by buying all available radio time to express their own views.[128] The ironic fact was that Coughlin's broadcasts were paid for by thousands of small donors, and all major networks had refused him time. Kirby had the effrontery to add that nothing prevented Coughlin from speaking on free time; the code only outlawed the selling of time for "controversial" programs. This was small consolation to Coughlin, who was having increasing difficulty in purchasing air time. Even Elliott Roosevelt, who had gone on record a few months earlier as favoring censorship of Father Coughlin, was alarmed at the implication of the broadcasting bar; he offered to sell the priest time on his Texas network.[129] Most stations appeared willing to honor their contracts with Coughlin, but WIRE of Indianapolis dropped Coughlin at once and was followed shortly thereafter by stations in Milwaukee and Scranton.[130]

Already badly shaken by the NAB action, Coughlin suffered an even more damaging blow in January of 1940. Seventeen young members of a Brooklyn Christian Front Sports Club were arrested by federal authorities and charged with conspiring to overthrow the government of the United States. Seized with the youths were twelve rifles and eighteen homemade bombs. The New York press had a field day denouncing the Christian Front and its alleged leader, Father Coughlin. At last it was thought the radio priest had overreached himself and the Christian Front was openly exposed as a menace to democracy.

Questioned in Detroit by reporters, Coughlin quickly disavowed all connection with the seventeen alleged conspirators. He denied any affiliation with a specific Christian Front organization, but admitted advocating a Christian Front against the communists. The priest suggested that the arrested men probably were associated with the German Bund of the communists: "For some time they have been praising me, holding meetings in my name, and pretending to collect money for my support. I have roundly disavowed them."[131] It is true that Coughlin had spurned the Christian Mobilizers and had returned funds they raised for him. It is possible that he spoke out on this occasion without having complete information at his disposal. But whatever the reason, his statement appeared to many to be a cowardly attempt to shirk responsibility for the actions of his followers. *The New York Times* lost little time in documenting Coughlin's association with the Christian Front, utilizing *Social Justice* itself as its principal source.[132] A committee of twelve prominent educators, including Dr. Guy Emery Shipler, editor of *The Churchman*, and Professor Harold C. Urey of Columbia, wired Attorney General Frank Murphy demanding that the Justice Department investigate Father Coughlin as the real leader of the Christian Front.[133]

Coughlin completely reversed his position on his January 21 broadcast when he proudly and defiantly told his listeners, "I take my stand beside the Christian Fronters." The Detroit priest charged that the press, not the Justice Department, had placed the Christian Front and the whole anticommunist movement on trial. Thus it was his clear duty to come forward "as a friend of the accused. It matters not whether they be guilty or innocent; be they ardent followers of the principles of Christianity or the betrayers of them, my place is by their side until they are released or convicted. There I take my stand." Coughlin left no doubt that he stood squarely on his past record without equivocation of any kind and would continue his crusade to save America from the communists:

> While I do not belong to any unit of the Christian Front, nevertheless, I do not disassociate myself from that movement. I reaffirm every word which I have said in advocating its formation; I re-encourage the Christians of America to carry on in this crisis for the preservation of Christianity

and Americanism, more vigorously than ever despite this thinly veiled campaign launched by certain publicists and their controllers to vilify both the name and the principles of this pro-American, pro-Christian, anti-Communist and anti-Nazi group.

The priest also questioned the Justice Department's failure to apprehend the two thousand or more communists whom he claimed were employed by the government in Washington.[134]

As might be expected, Coughlin's critics had a field day with the episode. *The New Republic* referred to the plot as "The Brooklyn Beer Hall Putsch" and was largely critical of the Catholic hierarchy for not restraining the Royal Oak pastor. An article in the same journal declared that Coughlin's "dissemination of hatred and fear to millions of minds was of more importance than the violence of 17 misguided young men in Brooklyn."[135] *Commonweal* assailed Father Coughlin, *The Brooklyn Tablet,* and *Social Justice,* and charged all three with responsibility for the unhappy plight of the seventeen Brooklyn youths.[136] *The Nation* editorialized against what it called "The Coughlin Terror" and appeared to consider the Brooklyn episode a serious plot against the government.[137] A more moderate approach was that of *The Christian Century,* which, while critical of Coughlin, admitted that the nation needed a Christian front, but not an irresponsible one.[138] *Equality,* described by *The New York Times* as a nonsectarian monthly dedicated to opposing racial and religious intolerance, openly appealed to Archbishop Mooney, Francis Cardinal Spellman, Bishop Malloy of Brooklyn, John Cardinal Glennon of St. Louis, William Cardinal O'Connell of Boston, Dennis Cardinal Dougherty of Philadelphia, and Archbishop Murray of St. Paul to take action against Coughlin:

> The facts about Father Coughlin and the Christian Front are clear, they are incontrovertible, they are as damning as can be. *Equality* appeals to the hierarchy of the Catholic Church to take cognizance of these facts and to act upon

them. We appeal to the Catholic leaders of America to end their silence, to disavow the Christian Front and to rebuke Father Coughlin.[139]

Several groups and individuals petitioned the Justice Department to investigate Father Coughlin. Among these were the Jewish Peoples Committee who charged the radio priest with unlawful use of the mails, false statements, and inciting his followers to hatred, bigotry, and anti-Semitism.[140] The Justice Department acknowledged that it had received numerous complaints against Coughlin but denied that any action was being taken by the government.[141] Cognizant of the many rumors circulating about the imminence of government action against him, the priest defiantly challenged the government to move against him and accused the Roosevelt administration of attempting to silence all opponents of war.[142]

As the bizarre Brooklyn sedition trial dragged on, Father Coughlin and *Social Justice* continued to champion the cause of total isolationism for the United States. The April 15 *Social Justice* reprinted all the usual revisionist charges, so popular in the 1920's and 1930's, that America's intervention in the First World War was primarily motivated by a desire to save British imperialism.[143] On his May 12 broadcast Coughlin deprecated the current allied war effort and declared that capitalism was the only issue at stake.[144] On May 30 he joined Archbishop Beckman in a strong neutrality appeal on the campus of Loras College. The Detroit priest told an overflow crowd that the administration wanted to involve the United States in the war to defend international capitalism. He and Archbishop Beckman both emphasized that the European war was not a holy war, but merely a clash of conflicting economic interests.[145]

The June 17 *Social Justice* reverted to anti-Semitism with a vengeance. Page 1 blared: "Social Justice Will Take 500 Christian Refugees." The accompanying story declared that the Social Justice Publishing Company would sponsor five hundred Christian children because "the persecution suffered by the Jews in Germany is not to be compared to the persecution now being suffered by the Christians and Gentiles."[146] This last statement reveals Coughlin's blind, unreasoning anti-Semitism more vividly than his previous public pronouncements.

The same issue of *Social Justice* praised Hitler for solving Germany's economic problems and chided Roosevelt for failing to cure America's.[147] William Allen White, Chairman of the Committee to Defend America by Aiding the Allies, did not fare as well as the Fuehrer. *Social Justice* called White "a sanctimonious stuffed shirt" and his committee a collection of "Quislings" and "Judas Iscariots."[148]

Father Coughlin scored a tremendous moral victory on June 24 when all fourteen defendants in the Brooklyn sedition trial were freed by a jury which deliberated for a grueling 47 hours and 37 minutes.[149] (Three of the original seventeen were freed earlier due to lack of evidence.) Nine of the fourteen were acquitted, and mistrials were declared in the other five cases. In a sense it was Coughlinism itself that was on trial and that was vindicated. The defense attorney for the seventeen, Leo Healey, in his final appeal to the jury actually charged that the whole affair was "a plot to get Father Coughlin and the Christian Front."[150]

The Royal Oak priest was understandably elated at the outcome of the trial: "The result of all this will be that the Christian Front movement will emerge more victorious and potent than ever." Coughlin also claimed that the episode had backfired on its instigators and had actually increased anti-Semitism rather than curbed it.[151]

As the presidential election of 1940 approached, *Social Justice*, conceding Roosevelt the Democratic nomination, centered its interest on the Republican choice. Even before he received the Republican nomination, Wendell Willkie was *Social Justice*'s choice to save the nation from four more years of Roosevelt. The July 1 back cover of *Social Justice* boomed a Willkie-Lindbergh ticket complete with pictures. The

Roosevelt administration was castigated in typical *Social Justice* fashion:

> Another term of Roosevelts, Ickeses, Perkinses, Morgenthaus, Pittmans, and the 50,000 un-American appointees they have foisted upon us, will put a price tag on this nation of a "dime a dozen." If Mr. Roosevelt is re-elected —and we hope he is nominated—we will be buying gas masks for Christmas presents.[152]

After Willkie had received the Republican nomination at Philadelphia, *Social Justice* demonstrated once again its mania for the inconsistent by expressing grave doubts about his political beliefs. What disturbed *Social Justice* was the enthusiastic reception the Indianan's nomination received in the British press. *Social Justice* smelled a rat at once and suggested that the American people had been deprived of any real choice.[153] However, the August 26 issue found much that was good in Willkie's acceptance speech and urged its readers to support him. The next issue analyzed the very same speech and declared it proof that both parties were the same. "Old-fashioned Americans know not for whom to vote. They have no candidate."[154]

But if *Social Justice* was having doubts about Mr. Willkie, the Republican candidate had none about the desirability of Coughlinite support. The Indiana Republican spurned all such dubious assistance with a clearly worded statement that he would rather lose the election than accept the aid of any group "opposed to certain people because of their race or religion."[155] Coughlin was quick to reply that he had not endorsed Willkie or anyone else. In an action that remains unexplained to the present day, he insisted that he was not responsible for what appeared in *Social Justice* and had not written an article for it in over six months. It is true that he relinquished the presidency of *Social Justice* to E. Perrin Schwarz in September of 1939, but this did not appear to change anything but titles.[156] The Royal Oak priest again vigorously denied that he was anti-Semitic:

I am not against Jews as Jews. Many are my friends. On November 20, 1938, I said I wanted good Jews to support us in our fight against both communism and nazism, and I repeated that statement on subsequent occasions. Naturally, I am against Communistic Jews, or for that matter, Communistic Irishmen or any others who oppose our ideals and our institutions.[157]

Social Justice, for its part, accused the Jews of pressuring Willkie into repudiating Father Coughlin. Candidate Willkie was charged with stirring up anti-Semitism by bringing up the issue.[158]

Social Justice continued mercilessly to criticize the foreign and domestic policies of the Roosevelt administration. The Burke-Wadsworth peacetime-conscription law was heatedly denounced as a "communist" bill "to place every adult between the ages of 18 and 64 in the militia" where *Social Justice* alleged they "could be hurled behind the barbed wire entanglements of internment camps at the mere nod of a Hitlerized President and his American Gestapo."[159]

The high point of *Social Justice*'s anti-Roosevelt hysteria was an incredible editorial in the October 21 issue, demanding the President's impeachment:

Roosevelt Should Be Impeached

On previous occasions Congressmen have called for the impeachment of the President.

On those occasions most citizens disagreed with the Congressmen.

At length, however, an event has transpired which now marks Franklin D. Roosevelt as a dangerous citizen of the Republic—dangerous insofar as he has transcended the bounds of his Executive position.

In plain language, without the knowledge or consent of Congress, he has denuded this country of thirty-six flying fortresses, either selling or giving them to Great Britain.

By this action Franklin D. Roosevelt had torpedoed our

national defense, loving Great Britain more than the United States.

He has consorted with the enemies of civilization—through the continued recognition of Soviet Russia.

He has deceived the citizens of the United States—telling the newspaper reporters, who are the people's eyes and ears at Washington, that he did not know the whereabouts of these flying fortresses.

He has transcended the bounds of his Executive position—spurning the authority of Congress.

He has invited the enmity of powerful foreign nations—on whose natural resources we depend for essential tin and rubber.

Because he has encouraged the British government to reopen the Burma Road, and encouraged Britain to declare war on the German government, when Britain was unable to care for the English people—he stands revealed as the world's chief war-monger.

All these events, culminating with the transfer of these 36 flying fortresses without the consent of Congress, demand that he be impeached.

For these words this National Magazine invites the lightning flashes of Administration reprisal.

What of it?

In the spirit and the words of Patrick Henry we repeat: *"Give us liberty, or give us death."*

The day for pussyfooting is past.

The Gethsemane days of tribulation and persecution may be at hand.

Let the citizens of America recognize what this Executive has done to the country.

Let them rise in protest—now if ever—against this power-mad dictator who would place upon his own brow the crown of World Messiah.[160]

Coughlin's already declining fortunes suffered a tremendous blow right in the midst of the presidential campaign when he found himself unable to renew his broadcasting contracts with his regular stations and was forced to cancel his 1940-41 season. It appears that the larger stations seized upon the new NAB Code as a convenient excuse to bar the troublesome radio priest. Only some smaller stations, with limited audiences, were willing to sell time to Coughlin. A financial report of the Radio League of the Little Flower, which went public in 1942, shows a marked decline in revenue in 1940 over the previous years. Only $82,263 was raised compared to $102,254 in 1939 and $574,416 in 1938. But it is doubtful if his precarious financial position was the principal reason for the 1940 cancellation. Coughlin frequently operated on a week-to-week basis and conceivably could have raised additional funds if he still had access to a sizeable radio audience.[161]

Stung to the quick by his expulsion from radio, the radio priest bitterly lamented that his belief in a policy of:

> no foreign entanglements, in peace, in constitutional government and in America for Americans is temporarily outmoded. Not until there is an opportunity for the pendulum to swing to the right will I resume my place before the microphone.
>
> It may be in 10 months. It may be in 10 years. It will not be until we cease being war-minded.
>
> I want it understood that I am not retiring from broadcasting permanently. I have been retired, temporarily, by those who control circumstances beyond my reach.[162]

Despite its earlier doubts and trepidations, *Social Justice* finally went all out for Wendell Willkie as the only hope of avoiding American involvement in war. The November 4 cover beseeched the faithful to "Vote for Willkie to Avert War and Stop Dictatorship."[163] When Roosevelt triumphed in his bid for an unprecedented third term, *Social Justice* bewailed that the American people had lost the election unless Roosevelt was "willing to liquidate his international ideas and adopt the principle of America for Americans."[164]

Always critical of all American aid to Britain, *Social Justice* was virtually hysterical in its opposition to Roosevelt's controversial lend-lease proposal of January, 1941. The plan, which did not pretend to be neutral, involved massive assistance to Great Britain to enable the British to continue in their desperate struggle against Germany. *Social Justice* attacked the lend-lease plan as an invidious plot to destroy private enterprise and establish a "Marxian economy" in the United States:

> The lend-lease bill is not substantially concerned with lending or leasing or giving materials to Britain. It is concerned, however, with scuttling the last vestige of democracy in the world—American democracy. . . . The lend-lease bill will substitute Karl Marx for George Washington.[165]

Later in 1941 when lend-lease aid was also extended to Russia, *Social Justice* was outraged. Citing Pius XI's encyclical on *Atheistic Communism* as its source, *Social Justice* absolutely insisted that no Catholic could render any aid whatsoever to communist Russia. The *Michigan Catholic* took public exception to this view in an editorial of October 30, 1941, and was promptly insulted by *Social Justice* in a scathing rebuke:

> Our regret is that America did not think of giving spiritual aid to Russia until Russia became the ally of the New Deal and the British Government in a war being fought not for spiritual ideals but for the retention of imperialism and international capitalism.[166]

Monsignor Maurice A. Sheehy, formerly vice-rector of Catholic University, then a Navy chaplain, also incurred *Social Justice's* wrath for his outspoken approval of aid to Russia.[167]

In March of 1941 the United States Army banned *Social Justice* from all military posts. No official explanation was given. The editors of *Social Justice* responded with a bitter anti-Roosevelt tirade:

> Will *Social Justice* join in this world's greatest sell-out of a mesmerized people—mesmerized by British gold and Jewish propaganda?

Not as long as a printing press can be found to spread the truth as we can see it. We will not oppose Mr. Roosevelt physically. But by the eternal God, we will not acclaim his radicalism, his crackpotism, and his un-Americanism.

Social Justice is honored in having been singled out to become the leading victim of dictatorial censorship.[168]

In April *Social Justice* endorsed the American Firster Movement and stated that Coughlin would have been an active spokesman of the group had he been free to do so, another strong hint that Archbishop Mooney had severely restricted his activities.[169] This would have involved a reunion with one of Coughlin's old Union party cohorts of 1936, Gerald L. K. Smith. The uneasy partnership was so strained in 1936 that it is difficult to envision a successful collaboration in 1940. It was not long before the America Firsters had *Social Justice's* endorsement, a mixed blessing, and openly repudiated all connection with the Coughlinites.[170]

Anti-Semitism again reared its ugly head in a bizarre fashion in the September 29, 1941, *Social Justice*. Commenting on the great number of pro-war Jews in the U.S. government, the *Social Justice* writer savagely declared: "The Jew should retire from the field of politics and government. He has no more business in that sphere than has a pig in a china shop."[171]

In the final months before Pearl Harbor, *Social Justice* became more violently anti-Roosevelt and anti-international. A page 1 headline story in August accused Roosevelt of forcing Japan into a war she didn't desire.[172] Roosevelt's "Shoot on Sight" order to American convoys was castigated with the headline, "U.S. War Makers Invite an Incident."[173] A November issue accused Roosevelt of being more ruthless than Hitler "by establishing a more savage form of Nazism in America than was ever proposed for Central Europe."[174] The idealistic Atlantic Charter left *Social Justice* totally unmoved by any emotion except rage:

Stalin's idea to create world revolution and Hitler's so-called threat to seek world domination are not half as dangerous combined as is the proposal of the current British and American administrations to seize all raw materials in the world. Many people are beginning to wonder who they should fear most—the Roosevelt-Churchill combination or the Hitler-Mussolini combination.[175]

Even the sudden Japanese attack on Pearl Harbor on that memorable first Sunday of December failed to lure Father Coughlin out of silence. A spokesman announced that the priest would have no comment to make on the subject.[176] *Social Justice* greeted the war news with a strange editorial which explained the war as "a super world war fought between Christ and anti-Christ." Not a spark of genuine patriotism or criticism of Japan can be found in the editorial, which gloomily predicted that all democratic liberties were now lost, and that the U.S. Government would become totalitarian in order to fight the totalitarian regimes of Germany and Japan.[177] Future issues bitterly criticized the Roosevelt administration for the Pearl Harbor calamity, with special ridicule reserved for Secretary of the Navy Frank Knox, whom the magazine held personally responsible for the disaster. Not until January 12 did *Social Justice* get around to describing the Japanese attack as "dastardly," and this comment was in an article criticizing the Roosevelt administration.[178] Even the emotional patriotic slogan "Remember Pearl Harbor" was twisted against the administration: "Indeed we will remember Pearl Harbor. And we will not forget that someone blundered, tragically blundered."[179]

The December 22 issue contained one editorial comment that was almost patriotic: the writer urged the government to develop better planes, ships, and pilots than the Japanese.[180] But there was no discernible change in the paper's basic slant; it continued its anti-British, anti-Semitic, antiwar, and anti-Roosevelt policies. One grudging exception to this was the purchase of $25,000 worth of war bonds by the Social Justice

Publishing Company. The paper explained that "there is no other way we can put our shoulder to the financial wheel."[181] Roosevelt's January 6 State of the Union address was ridiculed for referring to the righteousness of the allied cause;[182] *Social Justice* was still more concerned over the alleged irregularities of the Treaty of Versailles than over the bombing of Pearl Harbor, the rape of Poland, the bombing of Rotterdam, or Japanese aggression in China. The January 19 issue was replete with vicious criticism of Roosevelt as a "muddling" war leader:

> The inefficiency, rank carelessness and possible criminal negligence associated with Pearl Harbor stands eclipsed by what is transpiring at Washington.
>
> Our nation's Capital is the scene of a national tragedy which is appalling. It is best characterized by the single word—"muddling."
>
> Full responsibility for this muddling is laid directly on the doorsteps of the White House and in the chambers of Mr. Roosevelt's official family and political first cousins.[183]

Social Justice's choice for Commander-in-Chief was General Douglas MacArthur.[184]

Anglophobia in *Social Justice* continued during 1942. Churchill was roundly criticized at every turn, the British nation as a whole was accused of aggression, and to cap off its journalistic folly *Social Justice* referred to the landing of U.S. troops in Northern Ireland with front-page headlines screaming "U.S. Invades Ireland." The incredible cover story went on to imply that the American troops posed a threat to the freedom of the Irish Free States.[185]

Even in war, *Social Justice* did not give up its attempt to smear the red communist label over Franklin Roosevelt and his close associates. The February 23 issue contained a fantastic diatribe entitled "Have the Reds Got Us?":

> Too many of us do not realize that the Marxists' greatest victory, to date, has been won not in Europe nor in Asia but at the city of Washington, D.C.

There our preparedness has been sabotaged.

There our morale has been beaten into the mud.

There our spirit has been crushed.

There the enemy is preparing for the final blow.

We contend that Moscow and Tokyo are operating under a secret alliance.

We contend that the German retreat and the Soviet winter victory are a twin hoax designed to deceive us.

We have come to the conclusion that the Communists in America are working hand-in-glove with Moscow, Tokyo and Berlin—else the national apathy, the national unpreparedness and the national dissipation of men, munitions, armaments and money over the face of the earth are inexplicable.

Was Pearl Harbor an accident?

Was the scuttling of the Normandie an accident?

Was the diabolical program of governmental muddling an accident?

Or was all this planned that way—planned from within; planned by men who prated of democracy while blueprinting chaos; planned by radicals who love Moscow and hate Washington; planned by international wolves dressed up in the sheep's clothing of patriotism; planned by the Father of Lies whose offspring are grooved in his identical mentality?

This is no time to spread the poison of fear.

This is the time to rip the red bandage of practiced deceit from our eyes.

Why is there an impending shortage of oil? Because it was planned?

Why is there a shortage of tin? Because it was planned?

Why is there a shortage of steel? Because it was planned?

Why is there a shortage of rubber? Because it was planned?

Why is there a lack of unity between labor and industry? Because it was planned?

Why is there a lack of national defense in airplanes, submarines, destroyers? Because it was planned? Why is there a lack of national spirit? Because it was planned?

Were all these things planned by Satanic saboteurs—even down to the details of assassinating public confidence through the appropriation of funds for striptease dancers, obsolete Congressmen and public officials—in the face of a national emergency that cries for national sacrifice?

While the heroic MacArthur and his immortal band are left forelorn to die or surrender on the peninsula of Bataan, have we civilians been foresaken to die or surrender in our homeland?

Unbelievable as it is, there appears to be a plot hatched in Moscow, blessed in Berlin, grinned at in Tokyo and executed in Washington to defeat the United States of America from within.

The sooner Americans rise in their wrath and demand the expulsion of Communists and Communist-lovers from Washington—yea, demand their incarceration in concentration camps—the sooner victory will be ours—but not until then.[186]

Even more absurd was the March 16, 1942, *Social Justice* which featured a story accusing the Jews of starting the Second World War. As proof, *Social Justice* cited an August 6, 1933, radio address made by Samuel Untermeyer, an American Jew, urging all Jews to engage in an economic boycott of Hitler's Germany. *Social Justice* twisted this 1933 talk into a Jewish declaration of war against Germany. Page 1 headlines ran: "Who Started 'Sacred' War?" *Social Justice* answered its own question on page 3:

Soon nine years will have elapsed since a worldwide "sacred war" was declared on Germany not by the United States, not by Great Britain, not by France, not by any nation, but by the race of Jews. . . . Americans were under the impression that this was a war to save democracy; a war to guarantee the lastingness of the four liberties. Mr. Untermeyer has been truthful and told us the real objectives of the war.

Answering the frequent charge that Father Coughlin was pro-Nazi and un-American, *Social Justice* declared:

If pro-Americanism consists in boycotting a suffering 40-million German people upon whose neck there rested the yoke of the Nazi Party; if pro-Americanism consists in casting the entire civilized world into a seething cauldron of bloody war for the protection of 600,000 racialists or religionists—as you care to call them; if pro-Americanism is identified with secret economic conferences at Amsterdam and dictatorial decrees emanating from Prague which nullifies the peaceful progress of our country—then Americanism, under that interpretation, is not worth while fighting for.[187]

Not long after this attack on the war effort, the government took action against Father Coughlin. Attorney General Francis Biddle, determined to avoid the harsh governmental censorship of the First World War, had been extremely reluctant to place any restrictions on free speech. But the pressures of public opinion and the irritation of Roosevelt became too great for Biddle to ignore. Biddle writes in his memoirs that Roosevelt would send him examples of abusive literature with the comment, "What about this?" or "What are you doing to stop this?" Despite his own reluctance, Biddle began to crack down on homegrown Fascists and other antiwar agitators. Father Coughlin's turn finally came in April when Biddle wrote Postmaster General Frank Walker and asked him to invoke the Espionage Act of 1917 to "suspend or revoke" the second-class mailing privilege of *Social Justice* on the grounds that copies of the paper "presumably reached persons in the armed forces and those subject to induction and enlistment." The First World War measure expressly outlawed all efforts to interfere with the military forces of the United States. Walker, a Catholic himself, took immediate action and notified the publisher of *Social Justice* that a hearing would be held in two weeks to determine whether the paper could retain its mailing privileges.

Meanwhile the postmaster at Royal Oak was ordered not to handle *Social Justice* until further notice. Coughlin himself was not named in the official notice because officially he was not directly responsible for editing or publishing *Social Justice*. Biddle also ordered the federal grand jury already investigating sedition to check the ownership of *Social Justice*. Never a man to be ignored, or to ask others to fight his battles for him, Coughlin wrote to Biddle and offered to waive immunity, answer all questions, and take full responsibility for any violations of the law. But hauling Father Coughlin before a grand jury was the last thing the Attorney General Biddle wanted to do. He believed, probably correctly, that Coughlin eagerly sought a martyr's role and was determined to deny him an opportunity to pose as the courageous champion of free speech. Biddle feared that indicting Coughlin would drive Catholics to his defense and severely hamper the war effort. As Biddle expressed it: "The point was to win the war—not to indict a priest for sedition."[188]

Uncertain of his course of action, Biddle tactfully sought the aid of Leo T. Crowley, a distinguished Catholic layman, then serving as chairman of the board of the Federal Deposit Insurance Corporation. Crowley agreed to fly to Detroit to ask Archbishop Mooney to silence Coughlin and thus prevent the demoralizing effects of a highly publicized sedition trial. Archbishop Mooney cooperated fully. Coughlin was called before him on May 1 and ordered to cease all public pronouncements for the duration of the war under penalty of defrockment. The fiction of his divorce from *Social Justice* was fully exposed, since part of the agreement was that *Social Justice* never be published again. Coughlin, realizing he must choose between the priesthood or a secular career, accepted these terms.[189]

Franklin Roosevelt knew nothing of the Biddle-Crowley

strategy until after the matter had been settled, but was "delighted" with this suave handling of a very troublesome nuisance. Mooney confirmed the deal with a brief letter to Roosevelt but, unfortunately, it is not in the Roosevelt Papers and could very possibly have been destroyed. Biddle states that no real guarantee was given that Coughlin would not be tried, but that it was clearly implied, as "the whole point of the arrangement was to avoid a trial."[190]

Meanwhile the postal authorities continued their action against *Social Justice*. It was announced on May 4 that Postmaster General Walker had revoked the paper's second-class license since the magazine's editor and publisher had failed to show cause why *Social Justice* should not be banned for violation of the sedition law. No *Social Justice* officials were present at the hearing, but a letter was read from E. Perrin Schwarz, President and Editor of *Social Justice*, promising that *Social Justice* would not be published and surrendering its second-class mailing privileges. Coughlin sent a telegram to Walker endorsing Schwarz's action. Calvin Hassell, Assistant Solicitor of the United States, presented evidence consisting of quotations from *Social Justice* which he alleged proved that every issue since Pearl Harbor had been seditious.[191] Thus ended eight years of scurrilous journalism.

Obviously relieved to see the end of what, for him, must have been a particularly vexing experience, Archbishop Mooney issued the following statement to the press:

> I am gratified to learn that the question between the Post-office Department and *Social Justice* magazine, involving a priest of this diocese, has been disposed of as reported in today's paper.
>
> Regardless, however, of how the matter might have been disposed of, I had a definite and explicit commitment from Father Coughlin on May 1 that, from that date forward, his severance of all connection, whether direct or indirect, with the magazine would be absolute and complete.
>
> My understanding with him is sufficiently broad and firm

to exclude effectively the recurrence of any such unpleasant situation.[192]

The question that has puzzled most commentators on the Coughlin affair is the failure of Mooney to act against the contentious radio priest much sooner. Mooney was clearly never in sympathy with Coughlin's ideas and considered the radio priest a vexatious nuisance. But the archbishop was apparently badly shaken by the reaction to his 1937 attempt to discipline Coughlin and decided to pursue a very cautious tack with his troublesome subordinate. The details, of course, are still not public knowledge, but Mooney was fearful that any precipitate action on his part would create even greater scandal than Coughlin was already causing. He was especially concerned about the New York Coughlinites and their threats to wreak vengeance upon the Jews if *Social Justice* were silenced. Unsure of a prudent course of action, Mooney consulted with the Vatican and also sought the advice of his fellow American bishops about the Coughlin problem. He was relieved that the government acted when it did; thus all animosity was directed against the government, not the Catholic Church.[193]

Coughlin dropped almost completely from public view in the years that followed. He was allowed to keep control of his parish and the Shrine of the Little Flower and apparently remained in good standing with his Church superiors. The National Union for Social Justice was officially dissolved on August 17, 1944, when Coughlin and a secretary filed the necessary papers at Lansing, Michigan.[194]

In December of 1962 Coughlin broke twenty years of silence and gave an exclusive interview to Harold Schachern of the *Detroit News*. The priest vigorously defended his anti-Roosevelt views of the 1930's, but stated that he now thought U.S. presidents should not be criticized. Twenty years had also failed to change Coughlin's views concerning the Second World War: "It wasn't because I was for Germany, but here you had the extreme left and the extreme right of totalitarianism, both the same, and I felt we should let them fight it out among themselves." The radio priest candidly admitted that he had found the adjustment from the life of a nationally known radio orator to that of a parish priest very difficult.[195]

Shortly afterward Father Coughlin granted an interview to Bernard Eismann of CBS News. On this occasion the priest appeared almost apologetic concerning his controversial past: "Well I suppose I committed an egregious error which I am the first to admit when I permitted myself to attack persons. I could never bring myself to philosophize the morality of that now. It was a young man's mistake." Asked if he were finally permitted to talk openly of his past activities, Coughlin cautiously replied, "Oh, I'm not necessarily free. . . . I'm not expressing myself on things philosophical."[196]

Today, at seventy-three, Coughlin is still pastor of the Royal Oak parish he founded in 1926.

VII
FATHER COUGHLIN IN RETROSPECT

FATHER COUGHLIN is a puzzling phenomenon. Discovering almost accidentally that he had tremendous appeal as a radio orator, the priest spoke out vigorously against the capitalistic system he held responsible for the great depression and the immeasurable human misery it created. Bitterly assailing the Hoover administration for failing to alleviate the widespread suffering, Coughlin became an early admirer of Franklin D. Roosevelt. Even before the Chicago convention, the Detroit priest came to regard the Hyde Park patrician as the economic savior of the nation. Roosevelt, for his part, was happy to receive support from so popular a Catholic priest and carefully cultivated the relationship in its early stages. At this time the radio priest was already a national figure in his own right through his radio popularity. Coughlin looked to Roosevelt for great things. Roosevelt looked to Coughlin for Catholic votes. While it is true that the priest expected to influence some New Deal policies and was intensely proud of his personal relationship with the President of the United States, it is not accurate to say that he used the relationship in a desperate bid for national recognition.

After Roosevelt's inauguration, Coughlin gradually found himself dissatisfied with Roosevelt's halfway reform measures, but counseled patience, professing to believe that the President would like to act more decisively if only Congress and the

239

public would support him against the vested interests of capitalism. The radio priest mistakenly believed that money was the key to the intricate economic problems of the depression. Neither an economist nor a monetary theorist, Coughlin was obsessed with the notion that a few unprincipled international bankers had deliberately plotted the worldwide depression. He never tired of castigating the Morgans, the Kuhn-Loebs, and the Rothschilds as the symbols of all that was evil in the world. While it is certainly true that this oversimplified approach was made to order for Coughlin's radio harangues, there is no tangible evidence that he was insincere. Actually, as the Pecora investigations demonstrated, the financial community had been guilty of irresponsible and unethical conduct on a vast scale. Coughlin's basic error lay in not realizing that financial reform was only a part of the answer to restoring prosperity to America.

Originally, the priest was content to endorse Roosevelt's revaluation of the dollar and enthusiastically defended the President against his conservative critics, including Al Smith. Deciding that revaluation alone was not enough, Coughlin joined the silver movement in the fall of 1934. The priest added nothing new to the silver argument, apparently accepting the old Populist doctrine that the more money in circulation, of whatever variety, the more prosperous the nation would be.

As for Coughlin's much-publicized silver speculations, it must be admitted that this was the height of folly on his part. The priest's rather feeble explanation that his secretary invested the funds of his Radio League entirely on her own initiative is too absurd to be taken seriously. At the same time, there is no reason to believe that Coughlin was ever interested in personal financial gain. The most significant aspect of the silver list episode was the change it marked in the radio priest's relationship with Roosevelt. No longer feeling the need of Coughlin's support nor fearing his hostility, the President, without warning, sanctioned Morgenthau's discrediting of the priest along with other silver speculators. Roosevelt acted under tremendous pressure from the silver lobby in Congress, but if he had still valued Coughlin's support, he could have deleted his name from the list.

It has been clearly demonstrated that Roosevelt was pragmatic in his relationship with Coughlin from the beginning. In his almost childlike eagerness to be liked and to feel important, the priest fell victim to Roosevelt's persuasive charm. Coughlin obviously took great pride in their association, referring to the President frequently as "the Boss," as if he himself were a member of the administration. While the evidence is not conclusive, there is every suspicion that the administration used Coughlin in the Detroit banking crisis in March of 1933, but kept the relationship as nebulous as possible to sidestep whatever unfavorable reaction might develop.

More astonished than angered by the silver list episode, the priest attempted to maintain the fiction that Roosevelt personally had played no part in it. But he grew increasingly impatient, throughout the fall of 1934, at the administration's failure to achieve sweeping economic reform. Basic New Deal measures such as AAA and NRA came in for bitter criticism. Finally, in November of 1934, Coughlin announced the formation of the National Union for Social Justice, a nationwide lobby of the people, with the objective of establishing a new and more equitable economic order based on a sixteen-point program which included the nationalization of the monetary system and of private utilities. Ostensibly the national union was not an anti-Roosevelt organization but was aimed at counteracting other pressure groups. Coughlin repeatedly emphasized that the National Union for Social Justice was not a political party but a lobby of the people. At one point, he claimed a membership as high as eight million, but the usual estimate was four to five million. Not particularly effective as a lobby, with the possible exceptions of the World Court and bonus issues, the National Union for Social Justice did demonstrate significant political strength in the 1936 primaries.

Whatever success the organization enjoyed was clearly a personal victory for Coughlin. He dominated the movement completely.

The radio priest broke openly with Roosevelt in November of 1935, apparently losing patience with the President's failure to nationalize the currency. There was no one dramatic incident to highlight the split; rather, it was a result of Coughlin's growing awareness that Roosevelt never really intended to enact the reforms envisioned by the priest.

Arthur Schlesinger and others have suggested that Coughlin was not truly sincere in his criticism of the New Deal, but created controversies in order to keep his radio audience interested. At present there is no evidence to support such a charge. It is at least equally possible that Coughlin was truly dismayed at Roosevelt's moderate course and simply gave vent to his exasperation. The Royal Oak pastor was receiving a vast amount of mail from ordinary Americans who were losing the desperate battle for economic survival in the grim years of the depression. This voluminous catalogue of human misery could easily have embittered a man of Coughlin's emotional nature. There is no reason to question his genuine sympathy for the poor, and it is abundantly clear from the record that the priest was an impassioned orator who frequently said things in the heat of the moment that he later regretted.

A close examination of Coughlin's monetary and economic theories reveals that his most serious error was to consider nationalization of currency a panacea for economic recovery. Nationalization may have been a desirable reform, but it is doubtful that this alone would have cured the economic slump in the United States in 1933. Many respected historians and economists agree with Coughlin that some form of inflation was necessary in 1933, but that too proved to be less than a cure-all. Silver also failed to solve any economic problems and benefited only a small group of silver owners and speculators rather than raising prices and increasing foreign trade. Coughlin's constant haranguing of international bankers may have been demagogic, but the concentration of wealth in the hands of a few irresponsible financial tycoons was a serious problem in the United States in the 1930's.

One of the radio priest's fatal weaknesses was his own ignorance of economics, a condition he himself would never admit. He vaguely advocated something called social justice, involving a large measure of government control, but denounced the various New Deal agencies for doing this very thing. Making allowances for his confused statements, it would appear that what Coughlin really advocated was reform capitalism, or a mild form of socialism. But he never acknowledged this and castigated socialists as vehemently as he did communists, usually grouping them together indiscriminately.

After his disastrous setback at the polls in 1936, Coughlin aimlessly floundered in search of an issue. He became even more severely critical of Franklin Roosevelt, savagely denouncing the President's attempt to pack the Supreme Court. He also made increasing use of the communism issue, centering his fire on John L. Lewis and the CIO. Adding to the priest's woes was the death in January, 1937, of his beloved friend and supporter, Bishop Gallagher, thus removing his only guarantee of freedom from ecclesiastical censure. To make matters worse, Gallagher's successor, Archbishop Mooney, was not at all sympathetic to the radio priest and did not hesitate to rebuke him publicly in October of 1937 when Coughlin called President Roosevelt "stupid" for appointing Hugo Black, a former Ku Klux Klan member, to the Supreme Court.

Despairing of American democracy as too decayed to operate effectively, Coughlin in April, 1938, announced his own drastic solution—the Corporate State. This proposal does give some slight credence to the oft-expressed fear that Coughlin planned some form of fascism for the United States.

Overshadowing all else, however, was Coughlin's espousal of anti-Semitism in the summer of 1938 in *Social Justice*, and more dramatically over the radio in November of the same year. The priest had previously demonstrated anti-Jewish feelings, but in November he openly revealed pronounced anti-Semitic sentiments. The Jews became the convenient scapegoats for all problems, foreign and domestic. This theme was repeated over and over again with little variation until Coughlin's suppression in 1942.

From 1937 onward Coughlin strongly emphasized a militant nationalistic isolationism with anti-British overtones and hysterical anticommunism. Germany was defended more as the foe of Great Britain and communism than for her own merits. The Christian Front was organized in 1938 to enlist all "Christians" of good will in a great crusade against communism. In reality the Christian Front was little more than a name despite the antics of a few misguided fanatics in cities like New York, Boston, and Philadelphia. Despite countless rumors and insinuations, there is no evidence to connect Father Coughlin with the German-American Bund or the German government. Certainly it can be demonstrated that Coughlin parroted the official Nazi line on numerous occasions, but this simply proves that he was naive and gullible enough to be taken in by Goebbels and Company. John Carlson in his controversial account of subversive activities of the era, *Undercover*, links Coughlin with the leading Nazi sympathizers of the day but presents no real proof of affiliation. It is true that Coughlin was hailed as a true friend of Germany and that *Social Justice* was enthusiastically read in the Bund training camps. The Dies Committee prudently ignored the Coughlin Movement, but the public hearings of the committee's investigation of Fritz Kuhn and the German-American Bund revealed no link between Coughlin and the Bund. The radio priest was admired and considered useful, but he was never a member in any sense.

As for Coughlin's isolationism, it was shared by millions of Americans of all faiths, nationalities, and geographical areas, but most were not so hysterical about it and were willing to support the war effort out of loyalty. Anglophobia was also common in America; in fact the priest would have been almost unique among his Irish-American compatriots if he had been anything but anti-British.

Any attempt to measure Coughlin's actual influence must

be qualified. Clearly, he did not at any time exert significant influence upon New Deal policies. Two dramatic examples of Coughlin's power, however, were the World Court and soldiers' bonus controversies. The priest successfully fought Roosevelt on these issues, but both were conditional triumphs. In the case of the World Court defeat, Coughlin was merely an extremely effective spokesman for a militantly isolationist opposition; he had strong assistance from the Hearst newspaper chain. The soldiers' bonus was an even more nebulous victory. The measure received powerful backing from well-organized veterans' groups and might very well have passed without Coughlin's efforts. Nevertheless, the priest did bring considerable pressure to bear on Congress and was partly responsible for its ultimate passage. The radio priest failed completely in his efforts to force currency nationalization on the administration, and he also suffered a humiliating defeat on the Frazier-Lemke bill. His greatest influence lay in creating, with others, a climate of opinion in the United States that helped Roosevelt obtain the necessary support for his essentially moderate New Deal reform measures. Many conservatives and moderates, in their terror of the Coughlins and Longs, became more amenable to Roosevelt's middle-of-the-road program.

Conclusive evidence of Coughlin's relatively small political influence was the crushing defeat of the Union party in 1936. The whole affair was so naive politically that it bordered on the ludicrous. After repeatedly denying any political aspirations, Coughlin organized a new political party almost on the eve of the 1936 presidential election. Forming an uneasy alliance with Gerald L. K. Smith and Dr. Francis Townsend, the priest conducted a vicious anti-Roosevelt campaign, concentrating on the absurd charge that the Democratic President was under communist domination. While the Union Party's anemic showing brought little prestige to Coughlin, it is nonetheless true that most of Lemke's 900,000 votes could be traced to the priest's influence rather than to the efforts of Lemke, Smith, or Townsend.

Despite the widespread confusion which surrounded the role of the Catholic Church with respect to Coughlin, there is convincing documentation that the Detroit priest was speaking only for himself, and not for the Catholic Church as such. Because of the sympathetic attitude of his close friend and religious superior, Bishop Gallagher, the priest until 1937 was allowed free rein in his political activities; they were neither encouraged nor sanctioned by the Vatican or the American hierarchy. As for Archbishop Mooney, there can be no doubt that he thoroughly disapproved of his troublesome charge, but feared the consequences of decisive action against Coughlin.

It is generally assumed that Father Coughlin was a leading American fascist of the 1930's. But as Shenton's incisive article in the Autumn, 1960, *Wisconsin Magazine of History* so ably demonstrates, "fascist" was the scare word of the 1930's much as "communist" was in the 1950's. Thus, Raymond Gram Swing, Forrest Davis, and others applied this label to Father Coughlin. But no generally accepted definition of fascist fits the Royal Oak pastor. Nor does the image his critics have created. Except for his occasional references to a corporate state, there is little reason to charge Coughlin with fascist sympathies. Only an extremely loose interpretation would find clear similarity between his proposals and fascism. The priest was a frustrated, disgruntled demagogue lashing out at the world around him, but he was no fascist. In fact, to catalogue him left, right, or center is impossible; the man is simply too erratic to be so neatly classified as a particular species of political animal. True, interesting comparisons can be made. His movement is sometimes thought of as a successor to the Populists: he championed inflation, was anti-British and anti-Semitic, and drew large support from the so-called Populist Midwest. But it is not at all necessary to be in the Populist tradition to espouse these ideas.

To complicate matters, it is now becoming intellectually fashionable to denounce Populism as a brand of homegrown American fascism, making it possible to link Coughlin with fascism and McCarthyism via the Populist route. Victor Ferkiss makes this point in his thought-provoking article in the June, 1957, *Western Political Quarterly*. He is ably supported by the provocative essay in *The Radical Right* by Peter Viereck, who sees Father Coughlin as "the missing link" between the Populism of the late nineteenth century and the McCarthyites and John Birchers of our own day. This theory holds that the new right has appropriated the extreme nationalism and militant anticommunism of the old American fascists. These theories. stimulating as they may be, remain unproved.

Any serious political ambitions Father Coughlin may have had were doomed from the start. There was simply no chance of a Catholic priest's gaining the support of a meaningful political coalition of American fringe groups. Some of these organizations, such as the Black Legion in Coughlin's home state of Michigan, were openly anti-Catholic, and the Huey Long-Gerald L. K. Smith crowd was too militantly Protestant ever to support a Catholic priest. The hard core of Coughlin's support seems to have come principally from working-class Irish and Germans in the East and Midwest. His followers were a desperate, uneducated, naive group who easily fell under the spell of his persuasive oratory. Coughlin was never a serious threat to American democracy, but the mere fact that he could win the support of so many Americans for such incredible notions should alarm any American who believes that our democratic system is worth saving. There is no sure guarantee that the demagogic challenge of a future Coughlin would be offset by the tremendous popularity of a responsible political leader such as Franklin Roosevelt.

APPENDIX I

THE PLATFORM OF THE UNION PARTY

1. America shall be self-contained and self-sustained—no foreign entanglements, be they political, economic, financial or military.

2. Congress and Congress alone shall coin, issue and regulate all the money and credit in the United States through a central bank of issue.

3. Immediately following the establishment of the central bank of issue, Congress shall provide for the retirement of all tax-exempt, interest-bearing bonds and certificates of indebtedness of the Federal Government, and shall refinance all the present agricultural mortgage indebtedness for the farmer and all the home mortgage indebtedness for the city owner by the use of its money and credit which it now gives to the control of private bankers.

4. Congress shall legislate that there will be an assurance of a living annual wage for all laborers capable of working and willing to work.

5. Congress shall legislate that there will be an assurance of production at a profit for the farmer.

6. Congress shall legislate that there will be assurance of reasonable and decent security for the aged, who, through no fault of their own, have been victimized and exploited by an unjust economic system which has so concentrated wealth in the hands of a few that it has impoverished great masses of our people.

7. Congress shall legislate that American agricultural, industrial and commercial markets will be protected from manipulation of foreign monies and from all raw material and processed goods produced abroad at less than a living wage.

8. Congress shall establish an adequate and perfect defense for our country from foreign aggression either by air, by land, or by sea, but with the understanding that our naval, air and military forces must not be used under any consideration in foreign fields or in foreign waters whether alone or in conjunction with any foreign power. If there must be conscription, there shall be a conscription of wealth as well as a conscription of men.

9. Congress shall so legislate that all federal offices and positions of every nature shall be distributed through civil service qualifications and not through a system of party spoils and corrupt patronage.

10. Congress shall restore representative government to the people of the United States to preserve the sovereignty of the individual States of the United States by the ruthless eradication of bureaucracies.

11. Congress shall organize and institute federal works for the conservation of public lands, waters and forests, thereby creating billions of dollars of wealth, millions of jobs at the prevailing wage, and thousands of homes.

12. Congress shall protect small industry and private enterprise by controlling and decentralizing the economic domination of monopolies to the end that these small industries and enterprises may not only survive and prosper but that they may be multiplied.

13. Congress shall protect private property from confiscation through unnecessary taxation with the understanding that the human rights of the masses take precedence over the financial rights of the classes.

14. Congress shall set a limitation upon the net income of any individual in any one year and a limitation of the amount that such an individual may receive as a gift or as an inheritance, which limitation shall be executed through taxation.

15. Congress shall re-establish conditions so that the youths of the nation as they emerge from schools and colleges, will have the opportunity to earn a decent living while in the process of perfecting themselves in a trade or profession.

APPENDIX II

THE UNION PARTY VOTE IN 1936

State	Name on Ballot	Votes
Alabama	Union	551
Arizona	Union	3,307
Arkansas		
California		
Colorado	Union	9,962
Connecticut	Union	21,805
Delaware	Union	442
Florida	Union	1
Georgia	Union	136
Idaho	Union	7,678
Illinois	Union Progressive	89,439
Indiana	Union	19,407
Iowa	Union	29,687
Kansas	Write in	494
Kentucky	Union	12,501
Louisiana		
Maine	Union	7,581
Maryland		
Massachusetts	Union	118,639
Michigan	The Third Party	75,795
Minnesota	Union	74,296
Mississippi		
Missouri	Union	14,630
Montana	Union	5,539
Nebraska	Union	12,847
Nevada		
New Hampshire	Union	4,819
New Jersey	National Union for Social Justice	9,405
New Mexico	Union	924
New York		
North Carolina	Union	2
North Dakota	Union	36,708
Ohio	Union	132,212

State	Name on Ballot	Votes
Oklahoma		
Oregon	Independent Union	21,831
Pennsylvania	Royal Oak	67,467
Rhode Island	Union	19,569
South Carolina		
South Dakota	Independent	10,338
Tennessee	Union	296
Texas	Union	3,177
Utah	Union	1,121
Vermont		
Virginia	Union	223
Washington	Union	17,463
West Virginia		
Wisconsin	Union	60,297
Wyoming	Union	1,653

BIBLIOGRAPHICAL NOTE

UNFORTUNATELY there are no Coughlin Papers available for historical research. It is not even known for certain that they exist. Neither Father Coughlin nor the Detroit Archdiocese would cooperate in any fashion. The Roosevelt Papers shed much light on Coughlin's relationship with President Roosevelt. The Ryan Papers are helpful on the Ryan-Coughlin controversy and the Walker Papers contain a very important letter of Archbishop Mooney's revealing the embarrassing dilemma Coughlin posed for Catholic authorities.

The most indispensable sources for this study were *Social Justice*, various editions of Coughlin's speeches, and *The New York Times*. An interview with E. Perrin Schwarz, former editor of *Social Justice*, was most helpful; correspondence with Mrs. Eleanor Roosevelt, Msgr. Maurice Sheehy, and Raymond Moley provided answers to important questions.

There are a few useful books concerning Father Coughlin. The official biography by Louis Ward, *Father Charles E. Coughlin: An Authorized Biography* (Detroit, 1933) is quite helpful for the early years; so is a hagiographical biography by Ruth Mugglebee, *Father Coughlin of the Shrine of the Little Flower* (Boston, 1933). Interesting, but far from reliable, is John Spivak's *Shrine of the Silver Dollar* (New York, 1940). Also severely critical is William Kernan's *The Ghost of Royal Oak* (New York, 1940). Especially useful for the New Deal period are Arthur Schlesinger's *The Age of Roosevelt* (3 vols.) (Boston, 1957, 1959, 1960), James M. Burns' *Roosevelt: The Lion and the Fox* (New York, 1956), and Rexford G. Tugwell's *The Democratic Roosevelt* (Garden City, New York, 1957). The many personal reminiscences of New Dealers were also of invaluable aid.

There are numerous articles on Father Coughlin in the periodicals of the day. The most significant usually appeared in *The Nation*, *The New Republic, Commonweal, America,* and *The Christian Century*. Worthy of special note are Professor James Shenton's two scholarly articles, "The Coughlin Movement and the New Deal," *Political Science Quarterly*, LXXIII (September, 1958), 352-73, and "Fascism and Father Coughlin," *Wisconsin Magazine of History*, XLIV (Autumn, 1960), 6-11.

NOTES TO CHAPTERS

I. FROM SUBURBAN PASTOR TO RADIO PRIEST

1. Raymond Gram Swing, "Father Coughlin: The Wonder of Self Discovery," *Nation*, January 2, 1935, pp. 9-11.
2. Louis Ward, *Father Charles E. Coughlin* (Detroit, 1933), pp. 14-16.
3. *Ibid.*
4. Interview with E. Perrin Schwarz, July 21, 1959.
5. Ward, *op. cit.*, pp. 16-23; Swing, *loc. cit.*
6. Ruth Mugglebee, *Father Coughlin of the Shrine of the Little Flower* (Boston, 1933), pp. 161-71; Ward, *op. cit.*, p. 27.
7. Ward, *op. cit.*, pp. 28-29.
8. *Ibid.*, pp. 55-69.
9. Charles E. Coughlin, *By the Sweat of Thy Brow* (Detroit, 1931), p. 7.
10. *Ibid.*, p. 26.
11. Ward, *op. cit.*, pp. 75-76.
12. Ward insists that someone tapped Coughlin's phone. *Ibid.*, pp. 83-85.
13. *Ibid.*, pp. 83-86.
14. Mugglebee, *op. cit.*, pp. 215-18.
15. *New York Times*, March 21, 1934.
16. *Ibid.*, March 22, 1934.
17. Swing, *loc. cit.*
18. Ward, *op. cit.*, p. 93.
19. *Ibid.*, pp. 97-98.
20. *Ibid.*, pp. 97-98.
21. *Father Coughlin's Radio Discourses 1931-32* (Royal Oak, Michigan), p. 19.
22. *Ibid.*, pp. 20-21.
23. *Ibid.*, pp. 127-29.
24. Swing, *loc. cit.*
25. *Father Coughlin's Radio Discourses, 1931-32*, pp. 149-50.
26. *Ibid.*, pp. 149-53.
27. Roosevelt Papers (hereafter referred to as R.P.), Testimony of Father Charles E. Coughlin Before House Ways and Means Committee, April 12, 1932.
28. *New York Times*, April 13, 1932.

29. *Ibid.*, June 10, 1932.
30. *Ibid.*, August 10, 1932.
31. R.P., G. Hall Roosevelt to Franklin D. Roosevelt, May 5, 1931.
32. *Ibid.*, March 7, 1932.
33. Frank Freidel, *Franklin D. Roosevelt: The Triumph.* (Boston, 1956), p. 285.
34. R.P., telegram, Fr. C. E. Coughlin to F.D.R., July 2, 1932.
35. R.P., Fr. C. E. Coughlin to F.D.R., August 12, 1932.
36. Mugglebee, *op. cit.*, pp. 241-43.
37. R.P., Fr. C. E. Coughlin to F.D.R., August 12, 1932.
38. R.P., F.D.R. to Coughlin, August 21, 1932.
39. *Ibid.*, September 16, 1932.
40. *Ibid.*
41. R.P., Guernsey F. Gross to Fr. C. E. Coughlin, September 20, 1932.
42. Rev. C. E. Coughlin, *Eight Discourses on the Gold Standard and Other Kindred Subjects* (Royal Oak, 1933) .
43. "Demagogy in the Pulpit," *Literary Digest*, May 7, 1932, pp. 113-18; *Boston Pilot*, April 18, 1932.
44. *New York Times*, May 10, 1932.
45. *Buffalo Echo*, May 5, 1932.
46. Rexford Guy Tugwell, *The Democratic Roosevelt* (Garden City, New York, 1957) , p. 350.
47. Mrs. Eleanor Roosevelt to author, March 16, 1960.

II. "PARTNERSHIP" WITH ROOSEVELT

1. *New York Times*, January 18, 1933.
2. Roosevelt Papers (hereafter referred to as R.P.) , telegram, Father Coughlin to Franklin D. Roosevelt, March 4, 1933.
3. *New York Times*, March 23, 1933.
4. Mrs. Eleanor Roosevelt to author, March 16, 1960; R. Moley to author, March 17, 1960.
5. Interview with E. Perrin Schwarz, July 29, 1959.
6. Police Commissioner James Watkins, himself a stockholder in the First National, who made several radio broadcasts attacking the government reorganization of Detroit finances. Louis Ward, *Father Charles E. Coughlin* (Detroit, 1933) pp. 85-86.
7. R.P., Memo for M. McIntyre, March 23, 1933.
8. *Ibid.*
9. *New York Times*, March 28, 1933.

10. R.P., Memo, McIntyre to Howe, March 27, 1933.
11. Letter, Raymond Moley to author.
12. *Detroit Free Press*, March 27, 1933.
13. R.P., Tel., E. D. Stair to F.D.R., March 27, 1933.
14. R.P., Tel., Fr. Coughlin to McIntyre, March 27, 1933.
15. R.P., Tel., W. J. Parrish to F.D.R., March 27, 1933.
16. R.P., F. L. Lowmaster to Harold Ickes, April 1, 1933.
17. R.P., McIntyre to Ickes, April 5, 1933.
18. R.P., P.W.K. to F.D.R., March 29, 1932.
19. R.P., P.W.R. to F.D.R., March 30, 1933.
20. R.P., Louis J. Hartmann to F.D.R., March 30, 1933.
21. R.P., Fred N. Cook to McIntyre, April 6, 1933.
22. *New York Times*, August 24, 1933.
23. *Ibid.*
24. *Ibid.*, August 25, 1933.
25. *Ibid.*, August 26, 1933.
26. R.P., Father Coughlin to Jesse Jones, June 30, 1933.
27. R.P., Father Coughlin to William Julian, June 30, 1933.
28. R.P., Father Coughlin to McIntyre, June 30, 1933.
29. R.P., L.F. to M. LeHand, March 23, 1934.
30. R.P., Pfc. E. Schubert to Stephen Early, April 14, 1942.
31. R.P., Early to McIntyre, April 20, 1942.
32. Ward, *op. cit.*, p. 107.
33. Father Coughlin was usually on the air from October to April.
34. Rev. C. E. Coughlin, *Eight Discourses on the Gold Standard* (Royal Oak, Michigan, 1933), p. 12.
35. *Ibid.*, pp. 1-36.
36. *Ibid.*, p. 44.
37. Rev. C. E. Coughlin, *Driving Out the Money Changers* (Detroit, 1933), pp. 5-13.
38. *Ibid.*, pp. 23-32.
39. *Ibid.*, pp. 13-22.
40. *Ibid.*, pp. 72-93.
41. R.P., Roosevelt to Father Coughlin, July 11, 1933.
42. Arthur Schlesinger, Jr., *The Coming of the New Deal* (New York, 1959), p. 42.
43. Telegram, Father Coughlin to Roosevelt, July 21, 1933.
44. R.P., F.D.R. to McIntyre, August 7, 1933; McIntyre to Father Coughlin, August, 1933; telegram, S. Early to Father Coughlin, September 22, 1933.
45. R.P., Father Coughlin to Roosevelt, August 5, 1933.
46. *New York Times*, September 6, 1933.
47. R.P., Telegram, Father Coughlin to McIntyre, September 22, 1933.

48. R.P., Father Coughlin to Roosevelt, September 23, 1933.

49. R.P., Father Coughlin to McIntyre, August 12, 1933.

50. R.P., Father Coughlin to Roosevelt, September 24, 1933.

51. R.P., Father Coughlin to McIntyre, November 14, 1933.

52. R.P., W.L.S., Comptroller, Royal Oak Post Office, to Farley, March 17, 1935.

53. Rev. C. E. Coughlin, *The New Deal in Money* (Royal Oak, Michigan, 1933), pp. 22-34, 35-52.

54. Schlesinger, *op. cit.*, pp. 248-52.

55. *New York Times*, November 6, 1933.

56. A rather heterogeneous group of private citizens which supported monetary inflation as a solution to the depression. Influential members included Frank A. Vanderlip, Assistant Secretary of the Treasury under McKinley, who was then a prominent New York banker, Robert Wood of Sears Roebuck, Frank Gannett of the Gannett Papers, and James H. Rand of Remington Rand. Economic advisors were Professor Irving Fisher of Yale, well-known for his long crusade for the "commodity dollar," and Professor Charles Warren of Cornell, principal architect of Roosevelt's gold purchase plan. See Schlesinger, *op. cit.*, pp. 198-99.

57. *New York Times*, November 28, 1933.

58. R.P., Memo for McIntyre, November 24, 1933.

59. Alfred E. Smith, "Sound Money," *New Outlook*, Dec., 1933.

60. R.P., Telegram, Father Coughlin to Roosevelt, November 24, 1933.

61. *New York Times*, November 27, 1933.

62. *Ibid.*, November 29, 1933.

63. *Ibid.*, November 29, 1933.

64. *Ibid.*

65. *Ibid.*, November 30, 1933.

66. *Ibid.*

67. *Ibid.*

68. *Ibid.*, December 1, 1933.

69. *Ibid.*, December 4, 1933.

70. *Ibid.*, December 5, 1933.

71. *Ibid.*, December 3, 1933.

72. "Dangers of Demagogy," *Commonweal*, December 8, 1933, p. 144.

73. James M. Gillis, "Father Coughlin, Al Smith and the Popular Mind," *Catholic World*, March 1934, pp. 641-51.

74. *New York Times*, November 29, 1933.

75. John M. Carlisle, "Priest of a Parish of the Airways," *New York Times Magazine*, October 29, 1933, pp. 9, 19.

76. "Three Priests Preach the Gospel of Social Justice," *Literary Digest*, December 23, 1933, p. 21.

77. *New York Times*, January 1, 1934.

78. Rev. Charles E. Coughlin, *Eight Lectures on Labor, Capital and Social Justice* (Detroit, 1935), pp. 7-19. Hereafter cited as: *Eight Lectures*.

79. *Ibid.*

80. *New York Times*, January 5, 1934.

81. *Ibid.*, January 12, 1934.

82. *Ibid.*, January 15, 1934.

83. *Ibid.*

84. *Ibid.*, January 17, 1934.

85. For specific examples see Arthur Schlesinger, Jr., *The Crisis of the Old Order* (Boston, 1957), pp. 459-61.

86. *New York Times*, January 19, 1934.

87. *Ibid.*, February 5, 1934.

88. *Ibid.*

89. *Ibid.*, February 19, 1934.

90. *Ibid.*; Coughlin, *Eight Lectures*, pp. 65-82.

91. *New York Times*, February 26, 1934; Coughlin, *Eight Lectures*, pp. 83-99.

92. Real wealth, as used by Coughlin, meant the natural resources of the United States as well as the value of productive labor.

93. *New York Times*, March 5, 1934.

94. Coughlin, *Eight Lectures*, pp. 100-14.

95. *New York Times*, April 9, 1934.

96. *Ibid.*, April 16, 1934.

97. *Ibid.*

98. *Ibid.*, April 29, 1934.

99. "Gentile Silver," *Nation*, May 9, 1934, p. 522.

100. E.C.H. to Mrs. Roosevelt, November 19, 1933; Stephen Early to E.C.H., January 12, 1934.

101. R.P., S.S. to Roosevelt, November 13, 1933; M.M. to S.S., November 20, 1933.

102. A term employed by some New Deal historians to describe the first two years of the Roosevelt administration, 1933-35, when the emphasis was on relief rather than reform.

103. See Schlesinger, *op. cit.*, p. 252.

III. THE NATIONAL UNION FOR SOCIAL JUSTICE

1. Roosevelt Papers (hereafter referred to as R.P.), Father C. E. Coughlin to F.J.A., September, 1934.

2. James Farley, *Jim Farley's Story* (New York, 1948), p. 52; Harold Ickes, *First Thousand Days* (New York, 1953), p. 472.

3. R.P., Memo, F.D.R. to Asst. Sec. of Navy, Hyde Park, September 10, 1934.

4. *New York Times*, October 12, 1934.

5. *Ibid.*, October 29, 1934.

6. *Ibid.*, November 5, 1934; Charles E. Coughlin, *A Series of Lectures on Social Justice*, (Detroit, 1935), pp. 1-6.

7. Coughlin, *A Series of Lectures*, pp. 7-8.

8. *Ibid.*, p. 16.

9. *Ibid.*, pp. 16-17.

10. *Ibid.*, pp. 17-18.

11. Raymond Gram Swing, "The Wonder of Self-Discovery," *Nation*, December 26, 1934, pp. 731-33. H. M. Berg of Detroit in a letter to *The Nation* (March 20, 1935) referred to attending a session of Father Coughlin's Tuesday evening public forum where the priest explained that democracy was provided for in point I which advocated "liberty of conscience."

12. Coughlin, *A Series of Lectures*, p. 23.

13. *Ibid.*

14. *Ibid.*, pp. 25-28.

15. *Ibid.*, pp. 43-45.

16. Raymond G. Swing, "The Phase of Action," *Nation*, January 2, 1935, pp. 9-11.

17. Coughlin, *A Series of Lectures*, pp. 52-54.

18. *New York Times*, March 25, 1934.

19. *Proceedings AFL*, Vol. 53, 1933, p. 512.

20. Coughlin, *A Series of Lectures*, p. 54.

21. *Ibid.*

22. *Ibid.*, p. 57.

23. *Ibid.*, p. 65.

24. *Ibid.*, pp. 67-68.

25. Coughlin informed his audience that he made the attack on the cardinal only after consultation with Bishop Gallagher. E. Perrin Schwarz told the author that Bishop Gallagher actually assisted in the drafting of the talk.

26. Coughlin, *A Series of Lectures*, pp. 70-71; *New York Times*, December 10, 1934.

27. Coughlin, *A Series of Lectures*, p. 81; *New York Times*, December 17, 1934.

28. Coughlin, *A Series of Lectures*, pp. 88-96; *New York Times*, December 24, 1934.

29. Coughlin, *A Series of Lectures*, pp. 98-99.

30. *Ibid.*, pp. 109-10.

31. *Ibid.*, p. 111.

32. *Ibid.*, p. 117.

33. *Ibid.*, p. 122.
34. *Ibid.*, p. 125.
35. *Ibid.*, p. 123.
36. *New York Times,* January 29, 1935.
37. *Ibid.*, January 30, 1935.
38. Julius W. Pratt, *A History of United States Foreign Policy* (Englewood, New Jersey, 1955), p. 533; T. A. Bailey, *A Diplomatic History of the American People* (New York, 1958), p. 632.
39. *New York Times,* January 30, 1935.
40. Coughlin, *A Series of Lectures,* pp. 144-45.
41. *Ibid.*, pp. 137-38.
42. *Ibid.*, p. 141.
43. *Ibid.*, pp. 142-43.
44. *Ibid.*, p. 152.
45. *Ibid.*, pp. 142-43.
46. *Ibid.*, pp. 147-51.
47. *Ibid.*
48. *Ibid.*, pp. 152-59.
49. *Ibid.*, pp. 166-78, *New York Times,* February 18, 1935.
50. Coughlin, *A Series of Lectures,* pp. 184-92.
51. *Ibid.*, pp. 193-96.
52. *Ibid.*
53. *New York Times,* March 4, 1935.
54. *Ibid.*, March 5, 1935; Hugh S. Johnson, "Pied Pipers," *Vital Speeches,* March 11, 1935.
55. *New York Times,* March 6, 1935.
56 "The Pied Piper of Hamlin," *Business Week,* March 9, 1935, p. 44.
57. "Clergy and Politics," *Commonweal,* March 22, 1935, pp. 579-80.
58. *New York Times,* March 12, 1935; Coughlin, *A Series of Lectures,* pp. 219-31.
59. *Ibid.*
60. *Ibid.*, March 13, 1935.
61. *New York Times,* March 12, 13, 1935.
62. *Ibid.*, March 19, 1935.
63. *Ibid.*, April 23, 1935.
64. Harold L. Ickes, *The Secret Diary of Harold L. Ickes: The First 1000 Days* (New York, 1953), pp. 352-53.
65. James Farley, *Jim Farley's Story* (New York, 1948), p. 52.
66. *Ibid.*
67. *Newsweek,* March 16, 1935, pp. 3-5.
68. T. Harry Williams to author, April 14, 1961.
69. *New York Times,* March 9, 12, 1935.

70. *Ibid.*, March 13, 1935.

71. Raymond Gram Swing, "Buildup of Long and Coughlin," *Nation*, March 20, 1935, pp. 325-26.

72. "Churches and American Fascism," *Christian Century,* March 13, 1935, pp. 327-29.

73. *Times* (London), March 29, 1935.

74. Hamilton Basso, "Radio Priest in Person," *New Republic,* June 5, 1935, pp. 96-98.

75. "Father Coughlin's Program," *New Republic,* April 24, 1935, pp. 299-300.

76. *New York Times,* April 8, 1935.

77. *Ibid.*, April 13, 1935.

78. "A Christian Minister," *Business Week,* May 18, 1935, p. 36.

79. Rev. Daniel Colony, "Dictator Coughlin: Fascism Under The Cross," *Forum*, April, 1935, pp. 196-201.

80. *New York Times,* April 22, 1935.

81. Rev. Edward Dargin, "Father Coughlin and Canon Law," *Ecclesiastical Review*, July, 1935, pp. 29-35; *New York Times*, June 23, 1935.

82. *New York Times,* June 23, 1935.

83. Rt. Rev. William F. Murphy, "Priests In Politics," *Ecclesiastical Review*, September, 1935, pp. 269-88; *New York Times*, August 23, 1935.

84. *New York Times,* June 23, 1935.

85. R.P., C.L.H. to Roosevelt, March 3, 1935.

86. R.P., L. O'Neil to Roosevelt, March 3, 1935.

87. R.P., A.C.L. to Roosevelt, March 5, 1935; R.A.L. to Roosevelt, March 3, 1935.

88. R.P., Elzey Roberts to Roosevelt, March 16, 1935.

89. *Ibid.*, March 21, 1935.

90. Daniel J. Tobin to James A. Farley, April 3, 1935.

91. James Farley, *Jim Farley's Story* (New York, 1948), p. 52.

92. R.P., Roosevelt to R. S. Baker, March 20, 1935.

93. Arthur Schlesinger, Jr., *The Politics of Upheaval* (Boston, 1960), pp. 1-11.

94. Walter Davenport, "The Shepherd of Discontent," *Colliers,* May 4, 1935, pp. 12-13, 50ff.

95. *New York Times,* March 31, 1935.

96. *Ibid.*, April 25, 1935.

97. *Ibid.*

98. *Ibid.*, "Coughlin Movement Launched," *Literary Digest,* May 4, 1935, pp. 4-5.

99. *New York Times,* April 27, 1935.

100. *Ibid.*, April 28, 1935.

101. *Ibid.*, April 28, 19, 1935.
102. *Ibid.*, April 29, 1935.
103. *Ibid.*, May 6, 7, 1935.
104. *Ibid.*, May 15, 1935.
105. *Ibid.*, May 18, 1935.
106. *Ibid.*, May 22, 1935.
107. *Ibid.*, May 23, 1935.
108. *Ibid.*, May 27, 1935.
109. *Ibid.*, May 9, 1935.
110. Schlesinger, *op. cit.*, pp. 299-300.
111. *New York Times*, May 22, 1935.
112. *Ibid.*, May 23, 1935.
113. Rev. Wilfred Parsons, "Father Coughlin and the Banks," *America*, May 25, 1935, pp. 150-52; *New York Times*, May 23, 1935.
114. *New York Times*, May 23, 1935.
115. *Ibid.*, May 24, 1935.
116. *Ibid.*, "Father Coughlin's Ideas on Money," *America*, June 1, 1935, pp. 174-76.
117. *New York Times*, May 24, 1935.
118. *Ibid.*, May 27, 1935.
119. *Ibid.*, June 3, 10, 1935.
120. *Ibid.*, July 1, 1935; "Coughlin Versus AFL," *Business Week*, July 13, 1935, p. 15.
121. *New York Times*, September 2, 1935.
122. *Ibid.*, July 3, 27, 1935.
123. *Congressional Record*, 74th Congress, 1 Sess., pp. 11, 841-43, 11,906.
124. *New York Times*, July 30, 1935.
125. *Ibid.*, August 13, 1935.
126. *Ibid.*, September 11, 12, 1935.
127. *Ibid.*, October 17, 1935.
128. *Ibid.*, November 4, 1935.
129. *Ibid.*, November 18, 1935.

IV. THE UNION PARTY

1. *New York Times*, November 25, 1935.
2. *Ibid.*, December 2, 1935.
3. *Ibid.*, November 25, 1935.
4. *Ibid.*, December 10, 1935.
5. *Ibid.*, December 16, 1935.

6. *Ibid.*, December 23, 1935.
7. *Ibid.*, December 30, 1935.
8. *Ibid.*, January 6, 1936.
9. *Ibid.*, January 5, 1936.
10. *Ibid.*, January 9, 1936.
11. *Ibid.*, February 3, 1936.
12. *Ibid.*, February 3, 10, 1936.
13. Roosevelt Papers (hereafter referred to as R.P.), Memo for Files from M. H. McIntyre, January 28, 1936.
14. *New York Times*, February 17, 1936.
15. *Ibid.* This was the only manner in which a bill could be forced out of committee, and a majority of members had to sign such a petition for it to be effective. Since there were 435 Congressmen, 218 signatures were required.
16. *Ibid.*, February 17, 1936.
17. *Ibid.*, February 18, 1936.
18. *Ibid.*
19. *Ibid.*
20. *Ibid.*
21. *Ibid.*, February 19, 1936.
22. *Ibid.*
23. *Ibid.*
24. *Newsweek*, February 29, 1936, pp. 12-14; *New York Times*, February 23, 1936.
25. *New York Times*, February 19, 1936.
26. *Ibid.*, February 27, 1936.
27. *Social Justice*, March 13, 1936.
28. *Ibid.*
29. Interview with E. Perrin Schwarz, July 21, 1959.
30. *Social Justice*, March 13, 1936.
31. *Ibid.*, March 20, 27, 1936.
32. *Ibid.*, March 27, 1936.
33. *Ibid.*, April 3, 1936.
34. *New York Times*, April 21, 1936.
35. *Social Justice*, March 20, 1936.
36. *Ibid.*, April 17, 1936.
37. *Ibid.*
38. *Ibid.*, March 27, 1936.
39. *Ibid.*, April 17, 1936.
40. *Ibid.*
41. *Ibid.*, April 24, 1936.
42. *Ibid.*, May 8, 1936.
43. *Ibid.*

44. *Social Justice,* May 1, 1936, May 15, 1936; *New York Times,* May 11, 1936.
45. *New York Times,* May 14, 1936.
46. *Social Justice,* May 22, 1936.
47. *New York Times,* May 14, 1936.
48. *Cleveland Press,* May 13, 1936, as reprinted in *Social Justice,* May 22, 1936.
49. *Social Justice,* May 15, 1936.
50. *New York Times,* May 14, 1936, *Social Justice,* May 22, 1936.
51. *Social Justice,* May 22, 1936.
52. *Ibid.,* May 29, 1936.
53. *New York Times,* May 23, 1936.
53. *Ibid.*
54. *Social Justice,* May 29, 1936.
55. *New York Times,* May 29, 1936.
56. *New York Sun,* May 27, 1936, as reported in *New York Times,* May 28, 1936.
57. *Social Justice,* June 5, 1936.
58. *Ibid.*
59. *Ibid.,* June 12, 1936.
60. *New York Times,* June 17, 21, 1936.
61. *Ibid.,* June 17, 1936.
62. *Ibid.,* June 19, 1936.
63. *Social Justice,* June 22, 1936.
64. *Ibid.*
65. *Ibid.*

V. LEMKE FOR PRESIDENT

1. *Social Justice,* July 6, 1936.
2. *New York Times,* June 24, 1936.
3. *Ibid.*
4. *Social Justice,* June 29, 1936.
5. *Ibid.*
6. *New York Times,* June 21, 1936.
7. *Ibid.*
8. *New York Herald Tribune,* June 21, 1936, reprinted in *Social Justice,* June 29, 1936.
9. *New York Times,* June 21, 1936.

266   FATHER COUGHLIN AND THE NEW DEAL

10. *Philadelphia Evening Bulletin,* June 21, 1936, reprinted in *Social Justice,* June 29, 1936.
11. "Al Smith to the Right of Them, Coughlin to the Left of Them," *New Republic,* July 1, 1936.
12. T.R.B., "Washington Notes," *New Republic,* July 8, 1936, pp. 265-66.
13. Paul W. Ward, "Lemke: Crackpot For President," *Nation,* July 11, 1936, pp. 34-36.
14. The full text of the Union party platform is included in Appendix I.
15. *Social Justice,* July 6, 1936.
16. *Ibid.*
17. *Ibid.,* July 13, 1936; *New York Times,* July 5, 1936.
18. *New York Times,* July 6, 11, 1936.
19. *Ibid.,* July 7, 1936.
20. *Ibid.,* July 11, 1936.
21. *Ibid.,* July 17, 19, 1936; *Social Justice,* July 27, 1936.
22. *Social Justice,* July 27, 1936.
23. *New York Times,* July 19, 1936.
24. *Ibid.,* July 16, 1936.
25. *Ibid.,* July 19, 20, 1936.
26. *Ibid.,* July 29, 1936.
27. *Ibid.,* July 25, 1936.
28. *Ibid.,* July 24, 1936.
29. *Social Justice,* July 27, 1936.
30. *New York Times,* July 26, 1936.
31. *Ibid.,* July 27, 1936.
32. *Ibid.,* July 21, 1936.
33. *Ibid.,* July 26, 1936.
34. *Ibid.,* July 27, 28, 1936.
35. *Ibid.,* July 28, 1936.
36. *Ibid.,* August 2, 1936.
37. *Ibid.,* August 3, 1936.
38. *Commonweal,* August 28, 1936, p. 415.
39. *New York Times,* August 13, 14, 15, 16, 17, 18, 1936; *Social Justice,* August 24, 31, 1936; *Commonweal,* August 28, 1936, p. 415; *New Republic,* August 26, 1936, pp. 72-74; *Nation,* August 22, 1936, pp. 201-04.
40. *Social Justice,* August 31, 1936; *New York Times,* August 16, 1936.
41. *New York Times,* August 14, 1936; Jonathan Mitchell, "Father Coughlin's Children," *New Republic,* August 26, 1936, pp. 72-74.
42. *New York Times,* August 10, 1936; *Social Justice,* August 17, 1936.

43. *New York Times*, September 3, 1936.
44. *Newsweek*, September 12, 1936, pp. 36-37.
45. *New York Times*, September 4, 1936.
46. "Vatican Voices," *Time*, September 14, 1936, pp. 61-63.
47. *New York Times*, September 6, 1936.
48. "Vatican Voices," *Time*, September 14, 1936.
49. *New York Times*, September 7, 1936; *Social Justice*, September 14, 1936.
50. *New York Times*, September 10, 1936.
51. *Ibid.*, September 13, 1936; *Social Justice*, September 21, 1936.
52. *New York Times*, September 15, 1936.
53. *Ibid.*, September 13, 1936.
54. *Ibid.*, September 17, 1936.
55. *Social Justice*, September 28, 1936.
56. *New York Times*, September 20, 1936.
57. *Ibid.*, September 17, 1936.
58. *Ibid.*, September 23, 26, 1936.
59. *Ibid.*, September 26, 1936.
60. *Ibid.*, September 15, 1936.
61. *Social Justice*, October 5, 1936.
62. *New York Times*, September 16, 17, 18, 24, 1936.
63. *Ibid.*, September 30, October 1, 6, 7, 12, 13, 18, 1936; James M. Curley, *I'd Do It Again!* (Englewood Cliffs, N.J., 1957), pp. 296-98.
64. *New York Times*, October 1, 2, 1936.
65. *Ibid.*, October 9, 1936.
66. *Ibid.*, October 28, 1936.
67. *New Masses*, October 20, 1936, p. 96.
68. *New York Times*, October 4, 1936; *Social Justice*, October 12, 1936.
69. *New York Times*, October 9, 1936.
70. *Ibid.*
71. *Social Justice*, October 19, 1936.
72. *Commonweal*, November 6, 1936, pp. 44-45.
73. Msgr. John A. Ryan Papers (hereafter cited as Ryan Papers), F.H.A. to Ryan, November 26, 1936.
74. Ryan Papers, Mrs. C.F. to Ryan (no date).
75. Ryan Papers, Mrs. A.B. to Ryan, November 8, 1936.
76. *Commonweal*, November 6, 1936, pp. 44-45.
77. *New York Times*, October 16, 1936.
78. "Ryan-Coughlin Controversy," *Commonweal*, October 23, 1936, pp. 597-98.
79. Roosevelt Papers (hereafter referred to as R.P.), Mrs. E.W. to F.D.R., July 21, 1936.

80. R.P., Mrs. J.R. to F.D.R., July 26, 1936.

81. R.P., W.M. to F.D.R.., August 5, 1936. In a memo to Early of August 12, 1936, Farley agreed to try to use Murray, but nothing developed from this.

82. *New York Times*, August 14, 1936.

83. *Ibid.*, November 1, 1936.

84. *Ibid.*, October 25, 1936.

85. R.P., B.N. to Early, August 16, 1936.

86. *New York Times*, September 18, 1936.

87. *Ibid.*, September 26, 1936.

88. R.P., J.F.N. to J.M., October 26, 1936, c/o McClure Syndicate, Fort Wayne, Indiana.

89. R.P., B.M. to F.D.R., July 21, 1936.

90. R.P., Rev. Maurice S. Sheehy to Roosevelt, July 18, 1936.

91. Msgr. Maurice S. Sheehy to author, December 12, 1959.

92. Rev. Maurice S. Sheehy to M. LeHand, April 10, 1937.

93. *New York Times*, October 14, 1936; *Social Justice*, October 26, 1936.

94. *New York Times*, October 17, 1936; *Social Justice*, October 26, 1936.

95. *New York Times*, October 18, 1936.

96. *Ibid.*

97. *Ibid.*, October 25, 1936; *Social Justice*, November 2, 1936.

98. *New York Times*, October 27, 1936.

99. *Ibid.*, October 30, 1936.

100. *Ibid.*, November 1, 1936.

101. *Ibid.*, November 2, 1936.

102. *Ibid.*

103. *Ibid.*, November 1, 1936.

104. *Ibid.*, November 2, 1936.

105. *Ibid.*, November 3, 1936.

106. Elliot Roosevelt, ed., *F.D.R.—His Personal Letters* (New York, 1950), p. 602.

107. James Farley, *Jim Farley's Story* (New York, 1948), pp. 51ff.

108. *New York Times*, October 6, 1936.

109. *Ibid.*, July 19, 1936.

110. Arthur Schlesinger, Jr., *The Politics of Upheaval* (Boston, 1960), p. 627.

111. Hadley Cantril, *Public Opinion 1935-1946* (Princeton, 1951), pp. 598-99.

112. Schlesinger, *op. cit.*, pp. 552-53.

113. *New York Times*, July 21, 1936.

114. Herbert Harris, "That Third Party," *Current History*, October, 1936, pp. 77-92.

115. Edgar E. Robinson, *They Voted for Roosevelt* (Stanford, 1947), pp. 186-207.

116. Cantril, *op. cit.*, pp. 598-99.

117. *New York Times*, August 9, 1936; Norman Thomas, *After The New Deal What?* (New York, 1935), pp. 5-6.

118. Telegram of Governor Floyd B. Olson to Governor Philip LaFollette, August 19, 1936, cited in Schlesinger, *op. cit.*, p. 595.

119. Donald McCoy, *Angry Voices* (Lawrence, Kansas, 1958), p. 147 and pp. 16-17.

120. *New York Times*, July 2, 3, 1936; McCoy, *op. cit.*, p. 145.

121. McCoy, *op. cit.*, pp. 152-53.

122. *Social Justice*, July 13, 1936.

123. *New York Times*, August 24, 1936.

124. Harris, *loc. cit.*; Jonathan Mitchell, "Liberty Bill Lemke," *New Republic*, August 12, 1936, pp. 8-10.

125. *Social Justice*, November 2, 1936.

126. *Ibid.*, October 12, 1936.

127. *Ibid.*, September 21, 1936.

128. Lemke won reelection to Congress from North Dakota as a Republican.

129. *Social Justice*, November 16, 1936.

130. Samuel Lubell, *The Future of American Politics* (New York, 1956), pp. 152-53.

131. *Ibid.*

132. *Social Justice*, November 16, 1936.

VI. THE CHRISTIAN FRONT AND WORLD WAR II

1. *Social Justice*, January 11, 1937.

2. *Ibid.*, January 18, 1937.

3. *Ibid.*, February 1, 1937.

4. *Ibid.*, January 11, 18, 25, February 1, 8, 1937.

5. *Ibid.*, February 1, 22, 1937.

6. *Ibid.*, Feb. 15, 1937.

7. *Ibid.*, Feb. 22, 1937.

8. *New York Times*, March 8, 1937.

9. *Ibid.*, April 12, 1937.

10. *Social Justice*, April 5, 1937.

11. *Ibid.*, June 14, 1937.

12. *Ibid.*, June 21, 1937.

13. *Ibid.*, June 21, 1937.

14. *Ibid.*, June 21, 1937.
15. *Ibid.*, June 21, 1937.
16. *Ibid.*, June 28, 1937.
17. *Ibid.*, July 12, 1937.
18. *New York Times*, June 6, 1937.
19. *Ibid.*, October 8, 1937.
20. *Ibid.*, October 10, 1937.
21. *Ibid.*, October 17, 1937.
22. *Social Justice*, October 25, 1937.
23. *New York Times*, October 20, 1937.
24. *Ibid.*, October 26, 1937.
25. *Social Justice*, November 8, 1937.
26. *Ibid.*
27. *Ibid.*
28. *Ibid.*
29. *Ibid.*, November 15, 22; *New York Times*, November 8, 1937.
30. *New York Times*, November 21, 1937.
31. *Ibid.*, November 23, 1937.
32. *Ibid.*
33. *Social Justice*, November 29, 1937.
34. *Ibid.*
35. *New York Times*, December 7, 1937.
36. *Ibid.*, December 12, 1937.
37. *Social Justice*, December 13, 1937.
38. *Ibid.*, December 20, 1937.
39. *New York Times*, January 10, 1938.
40. *Social Justice*, April 4, 1938.
41. *New York Times*, April 2, 1938.
42. *Ibid.*, March 28, 1938.
43. *Ibid.*, April 1, 1938.
44. *Ibid.*, April 3, 1938.
45. *Social Justice*, April 25, 1938.
46. *Ibid.*, January 3, 1938.
47. *New York Times*, February 18, 1938; *Social Justice*, February 21, 1938.
48. *Social Justice*, May 23, 1938.
49. *Ibid.*, June 13, 1938.
50. *Ibid.*, July 25, 1938.
51. *Ibid.*, August 8, 1938.
52. *Ibid.*, January 10, 1938.
53. *Ibid.*, July 18, 1938.
54. *Ibid.*, July 11, 1938.
55. *Ibid.*, July 18, 1938.

56. *New York Times*, August 20, 1938; *Social Justice*, September 12, 1938.

57. *Social Justice*, February 7, 1938.

58. *Ibid.*, February 14, 1938.

59. *Ibid.*, April 4, May 23, 1938.

60. *Ibid.*, September 19, 26, October 24, 17, 1938.

61. *Ibid.*, July 18, 1938.

62. *Ibid.*, August 8, 1938.

63. *Ibid.*, August 8, 1938.

64. "Ben Marcin" was a pseudonym, as were most *Social Justice* bylines.

65. *Social Justice*, October 3, 1938.

66. *Ibid.*, November 21, 1938.

67. *Ibid.*, November 14, 1938.

68. *Ibid.*, November 28, 1938.

69. *New York Times*, November 21, 1938.

70. *Ibid.*, November 27, 1938.

71. *Ibid.*, November 28, 1938.

72. *Ibid.*, November 29, 1938.

73. *Ibid.*, November 28, 1938.

74. *Ibid.*, November 29, 1938.

75. *Ibid.*, November 26, 1938.

76. *America*, December 10, 1938.

77. *Commonweal*, December 9, 1938.

78. *New York Times*, December 9, 1938.

79. *Ibid.*, December 16, 1938.

80. *Ibid.*, December 19, 1938.

81. *Ibid.*, January 2, 9, 23, 1939.

82. *Ibid.*, December 12, 1938.

83. *Ibid.*

84. *Commonweal*, December 30, 1938.

85. *Social Justice*, November 28, 1938.

86. *Ibid.*, December 19, 1938.

87. *Ibid.*, December 26, 1938.

88. Samuel Rosenman (ed.), *The Public Papers and Addresses of Franklin D. Roosevelt* (13 vols., New York, 1938-50), VIII, 1-3.

89. *New York Times*, January 16, 17, 1939.

90. Robert A. Divine, *The Illusion of Neutrality* (Chicago, University of Chicago Press, 1962), pp. 236-38.

91. *New York Times*, January 30, 1939.

92. *Ibid.*, March 27, 1939.

93. *Social Justice*, March 27, April 3, 10, 1939.

94. *Ibid.*, April 24, 1939.

95. *New York Times*, April 9, 1939.

96. *Ibid.*, May 22, 29, 1939.

97. *Ibid.*, July 2, 1939.

98. James Wechsler, "The Coughlin Terror," *Nation*, July 22, 1939; *New York Times*, July 21, September 4, 1939.

99. *New York Times*, August 16, 18, 1939.

100. *Ibid.*, July 31, 1939.

101. *Social Justice*, May 22, 1939.

102. *Christian Century*, May 24, 1939.

103. *New York Times*, June 29, 1939.

104. *Ibid.*, July 17, 1939.

105. *Ibid.*

106. *Ibid.*, July 18, 20, 1939.

107. General Jewish Council, *Father Coughlin, His "Facts" and Arguments* (New York, 1939).

108. *Social Justice*, June 12, 1939.

109. *Ibid.*, July 10, 1939.

110. *New York Times*, August 17, 1939.

111. *Ibid.*, June 5, 1939.

112. Edward Doherty, "Is Father Coughlin Anti-Semitic?", *Liberty*, August 12, 1939.

113. *Ibid.*

114. *Social Justice*, July 31, 1939.

115. *Ibid.*, August 14, 1939.

116. *Ibid.*, December 11, 1939.

117. *Ibid.*, September 4, 1939.

118. *Congressional Record*, September 21, 1939, pp. 10-12.

119. *New York Times*, September 11, 1939.

120. "Peace Blizzard," *Newsweek*, XIV (October 2, 1939), 29.

121. *Social Justice*, October 9, 1939.

122. *Ibid.*

123. *New York Times*, October 16, 1939.

124. *Social Justice*, October 23, 1939; *New York Times*, October 23, 1939.

125. *Social Justice*, November 6, 1939.

126. *New York Times*, October 16, 1939.

127. *Ibid.*, November 6, 1939.

128. *Social Justice*, October 16, 30, 1939.

129. *New York Times*, October 29, 1939.

130. *Social Justice*, October 16, November 13, 1939.

131. *New York Times*, January 15, 1940.

132. *Ibid.*, January 17, 1940.

133. *Social Justice*, January 19, 1940.

134. *New York Times,* January 22, 1940; *Social Justice,* January 29, 1940.

135. "The Brooklyn Beer Hall Putsch," *New Republic,* January 22, 1940; George Brith, "Coughlin's Christian Front," *New Republic,* January 22, 1940.

136. *New York Times,* January 22, 1940.

137. *Nation,* January 20, 1940.

138. *Christian Century,* January 31, 1940.

139. *New York Times,* January 26, 1940.

140. *Ibid.,* January 30, 1940.

141. *Ibid.,* February 1, 1940.

142. *Ibid.,* January 21, 1940.

143. *Social Justice,* April 15, 1940.

144. *Ibid.,* May 20, 1940.

145. *Ibid.,* June 10, 1940.

146. *Ibid.,* June 17, 1940.

147. *Ibid.,* June 17, 1940.

148. *Ibid.,* June 24, 1940.

149. *New York Times,* June 25, 1940; *Social Justice,* July 8, 1940.

150. *Ibid.,* June 26, 1940.

151. *Ibid.,* June 26, 1940.

152. *Social Justice,* July 1, 1940.

153. *Ibid.,* July 22, 1940.

154. *Ibid.,* August 26, September 2, 1940.

155. *New York Times,* August 28, 1940.

156. *Social Justice,* September 11, 1939.

157. *New York Times,* August 28, 1940.

158. *Social Justice,* September 9, 1940.

159. *Ibid.,* August 12, 1940.

160. *Ibid.,* October 21, 1940.

161. *Washington Times-Herald,* March 11, 1942.

162. *Social Justice,* September 23, 1940.

163. *Ibid.,* November 4, 1940.

164. *Ibid.,* November 11, 1940.

165. *Ibid.,* February 3, 1941.

166. *Ibid.,* November 17, 1941.

167. *Ibid.,* August 25, 1941.

168. *Ibid.,* front cover, March 31, 1941.

169. *Ibid.,* April 28, 1941.

170. *Ibid.,* July 7, 1941.

171. *Ibid.,* September 29, 1941.

172. *Ibid.,* August 4, 1941.

173. *Ibid.,* September 22, 1941.

174. *Ibid.,* November 17, 1941.

175. *Ibid.,* December 8, 1941.
176. *New York Times,* December 9, 1941.
177. *Social Justice,* December 15, 1941.
178. *Ibid.,* December 22, 1941.
179. *Ibid.,* December 29, 1941.
180. *Ibid.,* December 22, 1941.
181. *Ibid.,* January 5, 1942.
182. *Ibid.,* January 19, 1942.
183. *Ibid.,* January 19, 1942.
184. *Ibid.,* February 23, 1942.
185. *Ibid.,* December 22, 1941; February 9, 23, March 9, 1942.
186. *Ibid.,* February 23, 1942.
187. *Ibid.,* March 16, 1942.
188. Francis Biddle, *In Brief Authority* (Garden City, N.Y., 1962), pp. 243-47. (Copyright © 1962 by Francis Biddle. Copyright © 1962 by American Heritage Publishing Co., Inc. Reprinted by permission of Doubleday & Company, Inc.)
189. *Ibid.*
190. *Ibid.*
191. *New York Times,* May 5, 1942.
192. *Ibid.*
193. Walker Papers, Francis Cardinal Spellman to Frank Walker, March 31, 1942.
194. *New York Times,* August 18, 1944.
195. *Detroit News,* December 15, 1962.
196. Bernard Eismann, "Reflections of a Radio Priest," *Focus Mid-West,* February, 1963, pp. 8-10.

INDEX